HOLLYWOOD BETWEEN THE STIRRUPS

Recollections of a Tinseltown OB/GYN

Boyd Cooper M.D.

ISBN: 1974338800
ISBN-13: 978-1974338801

CONTENTS

PREFACE   v

1   A HUMBLE BEGINNING   1

2   LIVING WITH NATURE   6

3   THE GAME OF WAR   13

4   BRINGING CALIFORNIA HOME   26

5   THE STORY OF IRENE   30

6   DOWN ON THE FUNNY FARM   39

7   THE BIG BOYS' CLUB   43

8   ROSIE THE RIVETER   52

9   STARGAZING   64

10 THE ABORTION CONTROVERSY   75

11 MY ILLEGAL ALIEN   84

12 MY FIFTEEN MINUTES OF FAME   90

13 THE CLOSET BABY   96

14 PARTIAL BIRTH ABORTIONS   103

15 HOLLYWOOD PARTIES   110

16 SEXUAL ORIENTATION   116

17 KITTY: MY UNFORGETTABLE PATIENT   125

18 ARE WE KIDDING OURSELVES ABOUT FREE SEX?   136

19 FIDELITY IS FOR EVERYONE   150

20 THE BLUEBIRD INN   158

21 HOOKERS   163

22 HOLLYWOOD: THE BIPOLAR CAPITAL OF THE WORLD   171

23 THE ESTROGEN CONTROVERSY   186

24 OBSTETRICIANS: A VANISHING SPECIES   194

25 STARDUST MEMORIES   201

PREFACE

From between Liza Minelli's thighs, I looked up at her frightened face. She looked ready to burst into tears, but instead she burst into song. Now when Liza sings, you have to stop and listen, even if you are temporally between her thighs. I've done pelvic exams under some strange circumstances in my life, but this was the only time I've been serenaded. While belting out her song at full throttle, I couldn't help but reflect on the irony. Here I am an ordinary guy, born on a run-down ranch near Oakley, Idaho, doing a pelvic exam on a Hollywood superstar.

From Liza's point of view, I must have looked equally bizarre with my astonished face staring back at her. She stopped singing, threw her arms into the air and yelped, "What?"

"Nothing!" I said and started to laugh. She let out that raucous Liza Minelli laugh. "I always sing when I'm nervous," she said. "It helps me relax."

Little did I know at the time of that mad moment between Liza's thighs that I would go on to enjoy a long career in Tinseltown. I would cherish as my friends some of the biggest Hollywood celebrities.

Boyd Cooper | Oakley, Idaho | 3 years old | 1926

1 A HUMBLE BEGINNING

I was born in a granary in the middle of a dust storm, the firstborn of a poor sharecropper in the small village of Oakley, Idaho. At the time of my birth, the wind was howling, and there was no heat, but at least the room was clean and free of dust. I spent the first years of my life on a leased farm, close to the land. I learned early on my dad's basic concept of life and death. He was a tough pioneering man whose childhood stopped at the age of nine. His father suddenly died and his mother, unable to feed him and all his brothers and sisters, gave him away to a neighboring farmer. They were kind to him, but worked him hard as there were no labor laws in those days. With a troubled life right from the beginning, my father was forced to be strong and independent.

One of my first memories was the horrible night my mother nearly lost her life. I was only three, but some of those terrifying moments still remain with me. There was no electricity on farms in those early days, but we had a Coleman lantern. One cloudy November evening, my mother went to light the lantern only to discover it was out of fuel. My father didn't own the farm, but did own a Ford Model T. My mother and I trooped out to the garage, pail in hand to drain some fuel from the car. It was getting dark and stormy as soft raindrops started touching the ground. When we stepped inside the garage it was much darker. My mother was getting the necessary gasoline when she accidentally dropped the petcock which is used to control the flow of the gas tank. The fuel continued to flow into the pail, and she was unable to find the petcock, so she called out for my father.

My father and my uncle were in the corral and they both came running. Mom screamed at me to go back into the house, but I didn't. I stepped out of the garage, and hesitated, which probably saved my life. I'm sure I had difficulty tearing myself away from the drama of the moment.

The pail was almost to overflowing and the petcock still not found. My mother went to get another container as my father held the pail catching the gasoline. At that moment, my uncle lit a match to aid in the search for the petcock.

Suddenly there was a big explosion and fire. The gasoline in the pail and on my father's hands immediately burst into flames. He was squatting down just inside the garage, behind the car. When the pail of gasoline burst into flames he jumped to his feet. Wheeling around, he threw the flaming gasoline out of the garage over his shoulder, only to have it completely engulf my mother who was moving toward the house with me.

Flames suddenly swallowed her as she started running like a human torch. I stood there like a stone unable to move or understand. Fortunately my father tackled her to the ground, where he extinguished the flames by packing her body in fresh cow dung. I remember kneeling down at the side of my mother wondering why my father was so mad at her that he packed her in wet cow shit. The whole event is still shockingly clear, forever implanted in my brain.

Even if this happened in modern times my mother may not have lived. There were second and third degree burns over fifty percent of her body, from the top of her head down to the calves of her legs. Because she was moving away, her face was spared. I was told later that the flames had come around one side of her body and burned her breast and her arm. I was later told that the damage was so severe that the muscles and tendons could be seen.

The only physician in the area was an old country doctor who really did travel by horse and buggy. Even though we were a poor family, he stayed at my mother's side day and night. She was delirious from the pain. Her burned body was oozing and draining with her life fluids leaving her on the verge of death. Though the doctor gave her many intravenous fluids, it was impossible to keep up. It was then that he came up with an ingenious idea to prevent fluids from draining from her burned body. He melted a large amount of paraffin wax and dipped rolls of gauze into the hot liquid and wrapped it around my mother's legs, arms, and torso. As the wax hardened, it kept the fluids from escaping. This was not a standard procedure at the time, nor is it today, but it was something that worked to save my mother's life.

I will never forget that kind old doctor any more than I can forget the odor of my mother's burned flesh, or her screams of agony during the changing of her dressings. It was an early lesson in both the preciousness and precariousness of life. My mother was almost taken from us in the time it took to light a match.

As a fitting postscript to this terrifying but life-affirming experience, my father said the doctor never sent a bill. For many years though, my father sent him money whenever he had it.

Following the accident, everyone dug in and helped -- the neighbors, the relatives, and especially my father. There was my mother, the three month-old twins, Miles and Marian, and I, all to be cared for. With help my father somehow managed to look after us, all the while continuing to work the farm.

When I was about five years of age, our old sow gave birth to a litter of piglets. It was a proverbial happy event because it meant food and income for our family. At the time, I didn't understand that particular facet, all I cared about was the sudden presence of tiny, pink piglets, darting about noisily and full of life. I was equally amazed and intrigued by the little piglet that lay motionless on the ground in the pen. With both the innocence and impatience of a child, I poked at it with a stick so that it too would delight me, but it failed to respond. Finally, my father came along and told me to leave it alone. It was dead. At my age, I could hardly know what that meant, but by his stern voice I knew it meant something ominous.

My biggest life and death lesson came later that year. There was a large circular watering trough in our barnyard, perhaps ten or twelve feet in diameter and about four feet deep. I was playing around this trough, with my latest playmate, a small kitten, who was another ubiquitous part of farm life.

In our play, I had the kitten in one hand while splashing the water with the other. Quite naturally, the kitten began to wiggle and extended its little claws into my hand. Not realizing the kitten was afraid of the water, I thought only of my pain and dropped the kitten. It immediately sank to the bottom of the tank. I stared in amazement as the little animal began to swim frantically back up to the surface. Fascinated by his performance I pushed the kitten down to the bottom of the tank again. I was unaware of the fact that while enjoying the game I was also drowning the tiny thing. Again my father happened upon the scene. When he saw what I was doing, he rescued the kitten from my unknowing clutches, and decided to teach me a lesson.

Throwing me into the tank, he began pushing me back down every time I struggled for the surface, just as I had been doing to the kitten. Just like the kitten, I experienced an instinctive reaction and attempted to swim to the surface even though I had not been taught how to swim. Thrashing about in the water I longed to breathe, and couldn't, but I kept fighting to get air. Ultimately, I did, of course, and was taken out of the tank, soaking wet and thoroughly chastised. It was an experience I never forgot and a rewarding, lifelong memory. As I grew up, I realized this incident was my first brush with the overwhelming will to live that resides somewhere inside all of us, ready to emerge like an angry watch dog when it becomes necessary.

When I was eleven years old, I still had yet to learn how to swim. By then we lived next to the Snake River, and I loved the water, but I was afraid to go into the deep parts. Again - my father taught me a quick lesson. He picked me up and threw me into the river where it was ten feet deep. I learned to swim.

My father wanted his first son to be tough like him. Unfortunately for him, I wasn't. I was more like my mother, a gentle artistic soul who supported me unquestioningly throughout my life. She was educated, too. She graduated from the eighth grade. My father only finished the fourth grade.

We were a close family in many respects during my childhood, but I often felt rejected. I was never rugged enough for my father. The last thing he wanted was for his first son to be a sissy. I don't recall my father ever giving me a hug. As I grew into my early teens, I wound up taller than my father. He wanted me to be big and strong, but I was only tall and skinny. His dream was for me to become the next heavy-weight-boxing champion of the world. I didn't stand a chance. My father was a physically strong man, and could whip any man in town, and frequently did. He was very proud of that. My father made several futile attempts to toughen me up without my knowing. He even paid tough kids to pick fights with me so that I'd learn to protect myself. His efforts were wasted.

As I made my way through my teenage years, I drew further and further away from him. I'd become a shy, sissy kid who found his gratification in the pages of books. When it came to school grades, I could whip any kid in town. My father's dismissal of my academic achievements, and his disappointment that I was not a chip off the old block helped my inward withdrawal gain momentum.

Boyd with Mother & Father | Brogan, Oregon | 1933

2 LIVING WITH NATURE

When I was in the fifth grade, a miracle happened that gladdened the heart of a child like me. I considered it a miracle, but for my family it was indeed a disaster. My father was already a successful businessman, and owned a service station with cabins for rent, but he wanted to become really rich. He was given the chance to buy a gold mine, so he sold his station, and we moved to the Blue Mountains of Oregon.

Our claim was in the mountains several miles above the little village of Brogan, which was only really a general store and post office. The nearest school was in a cluster of buildings in a long ago closed milling area. We were in the mountains miles away from everyone. It was there that my father proceeded to build a one-room log cabin with a dirt floor, into which he moved his wife and family of four. My youngest brother Ken was a baby at the time.

My father hired a man to help work the mine. I too, worked in the mine sometimes, but hated it. The hired man and I slept in a boarded up tent about a hundred feet away from the cabin. For one entire year and four summers, my family lived in that cabin. It had no modern conveniences whatsoever; even the water had to be carried up from the creek a long way below, and our toilet was in a cave. It was right out of *The Grapes of Wrath* I suppose, but for me it was paradise.

I was close to the natural beauty of the mountains with its many wild creatures. I actually became part of it. I spent my time wandering through the hills. Sometimes my brother, Miles, accompanied me. We hunted, had a garden, raised farm animals for food, and wild game was always welcome. I had always loved animals, but during the time I spent in the Blue Mountains, my collection grew to zoo-like proportions. I had every kind of pet you can imagine. First and foremost there was my dog, Old Demps, my best friend. She was with me wherever I went, and saved me many times by chasing away the range bulls that were set free to wander the mountains.

I had owls that I raised from babies. I would climb trees to rob birds' nests to feed them. When they were grown, they would fly away into their own world. All I had to do was whistle. If they were within hearing distance in the hills, they would come swooping down to find me. They knew I would have baby birds for them to eat. They apparently knew I slept in the tent because they would come around the tent at night and hoot. I would wake up and call back to them, feeling part of everything around me, and secure in being loved in return by the environment.

I enjoyed raising rabbits and Bantam chickens. Although, one of the great tragedies of my young life came to pass not long after I had trained a Bantam rooster to fight. Basically I would place him on a ledge and box with him. Bantams are not known for their sunny dispositions in the first place, and I merely helped his natural instincts along. He became quite a fighter, and frequently picked fights with anything or anyone. One day he picked the wrong fight and decided to take on my brother Miles until my father intervened. When supper reached the table that evening, my pet was the entrée. I was stunned more than my father will ever know. I refused to eat the meat and vomited repeatedly during that long night. I literally felt they had cooked and served one of my best friends.

I was really impressed with the fearlessness of these small chickens. Old Frozen Toes was a Bantam hen. Her toes had been frozen off one cold winter. Although she laid eggs, she would crow like a cock and she was unalterably brave. One early spring day she was out in the yard with her annual brood of baby chicks, when a hawk came out of nowhere and caught one of the little chicks in his talons. The tiny hen took off after the hawk with the speed of an eagle, pounced on his back and continued to claw and peck him until he released her baby and flew away. The chick was unharmed, and the hawk probably wishes he could say the same.

Flocks of sheep were herded in the lower mountain area. My brother and I would go with my dad when he went to the town of Brogan for supplies. We would occasionally find what is known as a "bum lamb," so called because it had been rejected by its mother, and left behind to die. These lambs must be bottle-fed every few hours to survive. The sheepherders didn't have time for that so they simply leave them behind. Seeing one I inevitably had dad pick him up to make him a pet. Just as inevitable, was my distress when he grew fat and my dad slaughtered him for us to eat -- same as with my friend, the rooster.

One of my most unusual pets was a large family of bats, which I kept near my tent. Bats are considered unsavory company as they sometimes carry rabies, but I didn't know that. They were really gentle, fascinating animals to me. Particularly when they suckled their young just like humans. It was incredible to watch and wonder as the baby bats suckled. I discovered the bats in a crevice in a big rock, caught them, and put the whole family in a cage where I had built a nest for them. I didn't know it at the time, but they were in hibernation. I left them alone expecting them to fly away. They didn't. When they did move about they would always fly right back into the nest I'd built for them. I got so close they would actually let me hold them in my hands.

The on winter I was there, I enjoyed an incredibly formative life experience. I attended classes in a country school where all the grades were taught in a one-room schoolhouse near the old gold mill. The mill was no longer functioning but a few families still lived there. A few others lived in cabins throughout the mountain. There were about a dozen students, with one or more at each level, giving me a great opportunity to learn. I can honestly say I picked up the fifth, sixth, seventh and eighth grades that year. When I later transferred to a regular school, I found I'd absorbed practically all of the information, and would probably have skipped a grade or two if that had been possible.

At this little one-room schoolhouse, I met the most encouraging person I was to encounter in my early life. My teacher was impressed by my scholastic achievements, and began to talk with me about becoming a doctor. It was the first time the thought passed through my conscious mind, although it had probably existed on another plane given my extended care for various pets and farm animals. She seemed to think I had the characteristics that would make a good doctor, and the academic ability to complete the studies.

In fact, Betty Lou Setters was responsible for several of my most pleasant recollections. One of them was the birthday celebration where I was given a "peanut shower", which is exactly what it sounds like. When the day arrived, Betty Lou called me to the front of the classroom. My fellow students took out small bags of peanuts (supplied by Ms. Setters) and began tossing them at me while singing "Happy Birthday". Then we all picked up the peanuts, ate them, and went home. I had never heard of such a custom, before or since, and I'm not positive she didn't make it up herself. Regardless, I was immensely pleased, and the year I spent as her student remains among one of my fondest.

By the following term, our family was back in Idaho. The gold mine never did pan out -- if you'll pardon the pun. Aside from my own meaningful experiences, the mine was nothing but a great deal of hard work and disappointment. My father went back to farming, broke. I continued my ways in school, still a loner and egghead, while desperately missing the mountains, the freedom and my pets.

I did, however, finally win my first and last fight. Never mind it was out of fear not courage. Three boys took a volleyball away from a group of girls who were happily playing their game. I wouldn't have dreamed of walking over to the culprits and demand the ball be returned, but I hung around and waited for my chance to catch it as they tossed it back and forth taunting the girls. When this finally happened, I gave the ball back to the girls. This didn't exactly cement my friendship with the boys. In fact, the three waited for me after school, and led me to believe they were going to kill me for my unforgivable sin. Scared out of my skin, I thought they were really going to do it, so I whipped all three of them out of fear. My father never knew about that. My newfound fame as a neighborhood pugilist was short-lived, mainly because I was truly non-violent. I did not like physical contact or hard physical work. Working out a difficult mathematical equation was as thrilling to me as I imagine scoring a touchdown was to the town football hero.

That being said - I still had to do my fair share of hard labor. During my teens school was let out for two weeks at harvest time. We were a farming community and the time for harvesting the crops was short and critical. The crops had to be left growing as long as possible, but harvested before the onset of a winter freeze. During that brief period there was much work to be done and all available hands were needed. We city kids loved it, not only because we were out of school, but we were able to make real money to buy our winter clothes. We were all poor. Not starving, but not able to have what we wanted. We all had gardens and some had cows, but new clothes were a luxury.

There were two basic things we city kids did, pick potatoes and top beets. The farmer would plow up the potatoes leaving them lying on the ground, row after row. We would come along afterwards and pick up the potatoes one at a time and put them in a sack hanging between our legs. We wore a belt with hooks on it to hold the sacks. We would fill the sacks with potatoes and then set them aside to be picked up. We were paid by the number of potatoes we picked up. Or the farmer would plow up the sugar beets while we followed and picked up the beets, chop off the green tops and lay them aside in a row. It was very hard manual work, but the pay was good.

That's where I first met a Mexican. In those early days seasonal workers came from Mexico during harvest time and then returned to Mexico and their families. A temporary visa was easy to get, and many didn't even bother getting them. They just came. A few brought their families with them and would stay. As young boys we worked in the fields right along with the Mexicans. Many spoke some English, and so we got to know one another. Most of the time we just worked quietly, because we were all paid by the amount of work we did.

Burley, Idaho at that time was all white and mostly Mormon. There was one black man that worked at the hotel, but I never met him. He was a curiosity to most of us. There were very few Hispanics that lived there permanently, but they lived on the other side of the railroad tracks with the poorer people. Gradually more and more Hispanics found permanent jobs and moved their families to the United States. In the beginning they would return to Mexico for a period of time to renew their visas. However, many of their children were born here and became American citizens. There were few good paying jobs in Mexico and many good jobs in America -- jobs that Americans didn't want to do. The border was easy to cross, and so the Hispanic migration began. Millions came illegally for a better life. Most were good citizens, even though they remained illegals. It is believed that eleven million illegal Hispanics now live in the United States, and there are those that want to send them all back to their place of origin, even if it breaks up families.

When I later opened my medical practice many of my patients were on "Medical". The state of California paid us at reduced fees to give care to indigent patients, many of which were illegals. I never refused them then, and didn't until the last day I practiced medicine.

When I was finally a senior in high school, another event occurred to help propel me toward becoming a physician. This was the first year of the batteries of a national testing program IQ, and psychological tests were given to try and help guide us toward higher education. Our class of around 100 students took these exams and my personal history was chosen as a classic example of what they were trying to accomplish. It proved, at least on paper, that I was suited for higher education, and medicine was an excellent choice for me. But at that time becoming a doctor was impossible, or even a physicist which was what I now wanted to be. My family didn't have the kind of money it would take to send me through college, let alone medical school.

When I entered my senior year at Burley High School my father said, "When you finish high school, I'm going to give you one-hundred dollars. If you want to live here after that it will cost you eight dollars a month." This was unexpected so I said, "Okay, let me think about it." I wanted to go to college badly, and I knew that I would have to find some way to get the money myself. I had heard about a telegraphy course that was being taught at night, and the railroad was hiring telegraphers. It sounded interesting, so I checked it out. The course cost exactly one hundred dollars for two nights a week throughout most of the winter. I told my dad, "Give me the hundred now."

The hundred dollars was the last money my father ever gave me. That following spring I applied for a job with the Union Pacific Railroad as a telegraph operator and got it. The night I graduated from high school I couldn't attend the graduation; I was too busy working for the railroad. My first paycheck was larger than my father's, and in a strange way I think that pleased him.

Later during Word War II, I received the only letter I ever received from my Dad. It was short and to the point with many grammatical and spelling errors, but it ended, "I love you, son." That's the only time in my life he ever said that to me. To write that letter took real humility. He was a very proud man. Five generations attended my dad's funeral. His many children were all there.

Officer Cooper with flight crew (bottom row, middle)
Bungay, England | WWII 1944

3 THE GAME OF WAR

On December 7th, 1941 the bombs of D-Day fell, and all our lives were changed forever. I was a senior in high school, more or less majoring in mathematics, as I was advised that the study of physics was just about finished. The atom and molecule had already been discovered, so if I continued as a math major I should consider being an engineer or a math teacher as physicists were supposedly on their way out. But I should have paid more attention to world politics than my adviser. When I entered my senior year I was informed along with two other classmates that we would be put on an accelerated program. I was to finish high school in two months, and then start college courses. My small town school superintendent was way ahead of the general population and knew war was imminent. As a student, we had heard about the war, but didn't think about it much. The three of us were told that we must rapidly prepare ourselves to become part of the war effort. We were only kids looking to our own individual futures.

Nevertheless, I was thrilled that I was leaving high school early to further advance my education quickly.

As I was already working for the Union Pacific Railroad, I was inadvertently made aware of the war. Trainloads of Japanese people came through my station on their way to a concentration camp in Jerome, Idaho. Honestly, at the time, they scared me to death. I'd never seen a Japanese person in my life, and the horror of what the Japanese did to Pearl Harbor was all over the news. I was the stationmaster, and they all stared at me. There were hundreds of them, and only one of me. I later learned that they were Americans like me, and more than likely just as frightened of me as I was of them.

The war turned out to be good for me in the beginning. Many of the senior telegraph operators were drafted into the Army Signal Corps leaving their civilian jobs open. Jobs on the railroad normally depended on seniority. As the newest recruit, I knew I'd be sent to a small station in the boondocks, but the war changed all that. Many of the railroad's senior telegraphers had been drafted into the war effort, so the railroad was short of operators. Seniority was gone, and if they thought I could do the job that's where they sent me. They advanced me rapidly to busier and busier stations, and I thankfully was never sent to the boondocks. I loved my job, but within a year I knew it wouldn't be long before I'd be drafted too.

The United States entered WWII late. There were two broad oceans between all the others and us. Their squabbles were none of our business. We Americans were for the most part content to be isolationists, but after the Japanese sneak attack on Pearl Harbor everything changed. Many of our ships and airplanes had been destroyed. The army needed millions of young men to fly and to repair a new air force.

The Canadian Royal Air Force had already been flying our B-17s and B-24s. Suddenly there was a massive drive to make more planes for the British and our own Army Air Corps. The methods of training the fliers and airplane mechanics had to be executed with whirlwind speed and because of the need to train dozens of men quickly, high levels of skill were not always obtainable. As a result, many eager young fliers were killed before they even met the enemy. Even flying domestically was risky. The hazard pay pilots obtained for flying nearly doubled the size of their paychecks.

In November 1942, I volunteered to join the Army Air Corps before being officially drafted. I wanted to become an aviation cadet and learn to fly. The recruiter told me all I had to do was get in the Air Corps unassigned, take the exam, and if I passed it with a score high enough, I'd be eligible to become an aviation cadet. Otherwise I had to be a college graduate to get into the cadet program.

I was disappointed when I found myself thrown right in with all the draftees. I thought I was different. After all, I'd volunteered. Thousands of us were herded from one exam to another: physical, mental, psychological, the whole routine. They were trying to find out the best way each of us could serve the Air Corps. I protested because I had only set out to become an aviation cadet. My protests landed on deaf ears. Oh, they did let me take the cadet exam, but that was the last I heard of that. I realized I'd been had, and they were going to send me wherever they wanted me.

First they sent me to Texas for gunnery training. After I completed that and was waiting to be assigned, they called me in for another interview. Apparently, they'd overlooked the fact that I was a telegrapher, and could serve the Signal Corps better. They too, were short of qualified good recruits, so they decided to send me to communications school. I was thrilled. The last thing I wanted to be was a gunner.

I was sent to the Stevens Hotel in Chicago on Michigan Avenue (now The Hilton and Towers). It was the largest hotel I'd ever seen, with three thousand rooms. I don't think there were even three thousand people back home in Cassia County, Idaho. Overlooking Grant Park and Lake Michigan, the Stevens Hotel was the largest hotel in the world and cost approximately $30 million to construct (more than ten times the cost of Yankee Stadium only few years earlier). The hotel boasted itself as a virtual "City Within a City". The Stevens housed its own bowling alley, barber shop, rooftop miniature golf course (the "High-Ho Club"), movie theater, ice cream shop, and drug store. In 1942, the U.S. Army purchased the Stevens Hotel for $6 million to use as barracks and classrooms for the Army Air Force during World War II. The Stevens housed over ten thousand air cadets during this period of time.

Suddenly I found myself selected to become a radio operator, and was again back in school. As I said earlier, I was a math and science major in high school, and at the top of my class. I even won the Bausch and Lomb Science Award for the most outstanding science student of that year. I was eager, bright, and I guess exceptional during my radio school training. So I was selected from thousands to be considered for officers training in the Signal Corps. It took a few days to get everything together before we were to be interviewed by the general and his staff.

The night before the interview I went downtown to the Loop to see a movie. The movie was about the Monroe Doctrine in which our 5th president, James Monroe, declared to all of Europe, "Any attempt to extend their system to any portion of our hemisphere would be considered dangerous to our peace and safety." The notion would ring all the more clear given my current circumstances.

There were thirty-two of us selected for interviews and four would be sent to officer's training. I was naïve, and not impressed by the general or his staff. To me they were just like teachers. The first question the general asked me was about the Monroe Doctrine. Obviously, I was brilliant. He then asked me what I thought about our obstacle-training course. I looked the general straight in the eye and said it wasn't that tough, and I thought even he could get over it easily. I'd spent my weekends hiking in the mountains my whole life, so it was easy for me.

In spite of my arrogance, or maybe because of it, I was one of four selected. I was twenty-eight days away from becoming a Second Lieutenant, (known as a "twenty-eight-day wonder"), but I had to wait until the next class started. While I was waiting, they advised me that I had been selected to join the Army Air Cadet Program. Since I was four weeks away from a commission, I told them I'd rather go to Officers Candidate School (OCS). They informed me the Air Corps had preference over Signal Corps, and I belonged to them. So I was now off to Ellington Field in Texas, and back to school, training one full year more before becoming an officer. Stupidly, I was disappointed. I wanted to get into the war.

After my classroom training as a navigator was completed it was off to flight training. Three students were assigned to each plane. The pilot would fly a predetermined flight-plan, which was unknown to us, and we would each individually keep a log of the trip. We were required to fly many trips in all kinds of weather. They gave each of us a vomit bag and told us, "Vomiting or not -- do your job, and do it right, or we'll wash you out of the program."

In the first week, one of our planes crashed killing three of my classmates and the pilot. They said it was mechanical failure. A senior official came to our barracks to pack up my three classmates' personal effects to send home to their folks. I looked at their empty bunk beds and had the weirdest feeling. They were simply gone. The next morning our training continued as if nothing had happened.

I eventually finished and received my wings. I was then sent to Westoverfield, Massachusetts to meet my crew and start bomber training together. We would learn formation flying and how to work together. Then that would be it. We were told that after bomber training, we would get a new B-24 and fly it to England. We were to fly together for the rest of the war.

Unfortunately, that's not the way it happened. While we were learning to fly formation, our B-24 bomber got tangled up with another plane. One of their propellers chopped into our tail assembly, and we fell into a tailspin. The pilots worked feverishly to pull the plane out of the spin. At the lower level in the nose of the aircraft, I'd been thrown from my desk against the side wall of the aircraft. I was held there by the centrifugal force of the spin. The plane trembled and violently shook my body. I had no idea what was happening and I couldn't move. I quickly realized that if I didn't get out of the plane I was going to die right there -- smashed into the side wall of the aircraft.

I was already wearing my backpack parachute. I'd always wondered if I'd have the guts to use it. That worry disappeared instantly. I wanted out of this death trap, but the force of the swirling plane had pinned me halfway up the wall. Looking below, I could see the closed doors for the nose wheel. This was my way out. I slowly crawled and pulled my body along the side wall down to the release latch. I pulled it. Thank God, the two doors flew open. Now all I had to do was get out, as the plane was spinning tighter and tighter. The force against my body was so strong I could hardly move. I used all the strength in my arms and legs to push my body down to the opening. Once at the opening, I grasped the door's edge and pulled myself free.

Suddenly, no longer under the pressure of the spin, I just quietly fell. The air rushed around me, but I was suspended in space. If it weren't for the air rushing around my body, I wouldn't have even known I was falling. I pulled the rip-chord, and my chute popped open jerking me to a sudden stop. As I slowly drifted through the air, there was such silence I could almost hear the Gods whispering to one another. What they had to say was unknown to me.

Below me I saw another parachute floating down. I felt good that at least one of the other guys made it out of our plane. Slowly I realized we were above a lake and were going to land in the water. We'd been trained to release our chutes just before hitting the water so the chute would drift away, and we'd not get tangled in the suspension lines attached to the canopy of the parachute. They'd warned us that it was hard to determine the distance to the water as we approached it. I soon learned it was even harder to wait with the water rushing rapidly toward you, but if released too soon the fall would be fatal. I waited and waited until I could wait no more. Even then I hit my release button too soon. I must have been thirty feet above the water. My chute drifted away, but I hit the water hard. While deep underwater, I released the air in my life preserver jacket and I popped up to the surface.

My crewmate was not so lucky. I was told he'd been killed. Perhaps he released too soon. Long before I landed in the lake, I watched our plane continue its spin until it crashed and burst into flames. The other plane was able to land, and they were all okay. I was the only survivor of our plane. At the time it didn't affect me that much. We young boys joined the Air Corps for the excitement, and we were doing what we were trained to do. I knew flying was dangerous when I joined the Army Air Corps. I think it was the danger that attracted young men with more guts than brains, anyhow. Even still, the real meaning of death and dying hadn't penetrated my soul. I was still naïve. I didn't realize that the angel of death had been with me from the minute I started flying. I just hadn't heard the flutter of its wings.

After a few weeks, I was placed on a new crew and we were again assigned to fly a B-24 over the Atlantic Ocean to England. A dozen of our planes took off one sunny October morning for Goose Bay, Labrador. We flew to Bangor, Maine for refueling, and then on up to Goose Bay in Northern Canada where we landed that night during a snowstorm. We were supposed to be taking off for Iceland the next morning, and then on to Scotland, but the snow kept coming down day after day. The whole squadron was grounded for thirty days in Goose Bay.

At first it was fun to have nothing to do. We hadn't had a vacation since our training started. It was a large base, but at this time it was almost empty. The permanent base staff was a small, friendly bunch and were glad to see us. They had great food and an unbelievable PX, where we could buy anything. They had loads of candy bars and cigarettes of all kinds. During the war those things were rationed, and rarely available in the states. Cigarettes cost 5 cents a pack with no tax at the PX. I didn't smoke, so I traded my cigarette ration for candy bars.

There had also been a group of WACS (Women's Army Corp) stationed in Goose Bay, and the PX still had silk stockings for sale. There were no silk stockings available in the states. In the big cities some women painted a line on the back of their legs to make it appear that they were wearing stockings. The young girls I knew in Idaho wore bobby socks. Being young and from a small town, I never understood the importance of silk stockings anyway.

A fellow navigator, Thomas, bought a whole bundle of them. I knew he was married, but I thought buying so many silk stockings was a little strange. Thomas was a very private guy, and the reason for his purchases was none of my business. However, I must have looked surprised because he looked at me and said, "Maybe I can trade them." In England they hadn't seen silk stockings in years, so I understood what he was saying.

Neither Thomas nor I wanted to spend our free nights hanging out in pubs, drinking and picking up barflies. We frequently rode our bicycles together into Norwich on the nights we weren't flying. After we got in town we both went our separate ways. I never asked Thomas what he did while in Norwich. Like I said, he was very private -- not even talking about his wife or his life before the war.

Near the end of hostilities in Europe, Thomas was waiting to return home. He'd finished his twenty-five missions and didn't have to fly, anymore but he took a domestic flight to secure his flight pay. Unfortunately, Thomas got his during takeoff. Life can be cruel that way.

The only thing about him that I knew was that he enjoyed photography and spent most of his free time alone on the base taking and developing pictures. He had all kinds of camera equipment. Frequently he obtained strike photos from the fighter planes' guns from the lab, put them together with our strike photos, and gave us all photo shows. He planned to be a cinema photographer after the war. After he was killed, I was assigned to prepare his personal belongings to send home to his wife. I got the shock of my life when I found a suitcase full of photographs of nude women in all kinds of exotic poses. Thomas had an unusual hobby. Now I understood the silk stockings.

After a while we got bored with Goose Bay, tired of doing nothing but wandering around the base, eating, playing cards, and watching the damn snow fall day after day. The snowplows would clear off the runways in anticipation of our leaving. We'd get out on the flight line in our planes ready for takeoff and wait and wait. But again the decision would be made not to fly. We'd taxi back off the line and return to our billets.

Those in charge of our mission were growing restless along with the rest of us. They really needed us and the planes in England. As time passed we became restless and willing to take greater risks. Probably more out of desperation than anything else, we tried to get our squadron into the air on two separate occasions, but a plane crashed each time. We should have waited. Two brand new planes and twenty men were lost during attempts to takeoff for Iceland. They simply disappeared into the icy North Atlantic. The humidity was high, and it was damn cold. Ice forming on the wings likely did it.

The English suffered massive plane losses during their daylight missions early in the war. Sometimes it was as high as fifty percent, so they changed to carpet-bombing at night. When we Americans entered the war we were assigned to daytime bombing with very specific targets. In all fairness to the English we were able to do it. We had aboard many fifty-caliber machine guns and the highly secret Norden bombsight, in addition to many support fighter planes, P-51's and P-47's. Ultimately, our plane losses were much less than the English.

Eventually my crew safely made our way to Iceland before being deployed to England. We landed in Northern England and it was off to the races. We were hit on my second mission. We were a bunch of greenhorns just learning to fly together. We flew in very tight formation over the target. Our plane was in the bucket position, behind the lead plane and between the four wingmen. Heavy flack was coming up but ultimately exploding far below us. They hadn't found our altitude. The first group was able to drop their bombs without a single plane being hit. It looked like we were going to do the same. All six of us dropped our bombs in unison. The lead bombardier automatically released all our bombs with his bombsight trigger. The officers in the lead crew got really excited when it looked like all our bombs landed within the thousand foot circle right in the center of the railroad junction. If it was confirmed on the strike photos, each officer crew would get a bottle of scotch. As we flew away from the target we were feeling fearless and elated. We'd hit out target.

But just as we were experiencing that joyous moment there was a big explosion under the nose of our aircraft -- right below my compartment. The aircraft lurched up as holes suddenly appeared in the sides of the plane. It felt strange looking at holes in an airplane. Our plane took several direct hits. The force of the exploding flack jostled our plane as chunks of metal burst around us. Air rushed into my compartment blowing everything, including the pages of my log, all over. Two engines were knocked out. Additional holes damaged the wings. We fell out of formation like a wounded duck. With only two remaining engines, we were unable to stay with the group. We were alone in the heart of enemy territory and no longer had the shared support of the dozens of sixty caliber machine guns from the rest of the squadron. It wasn't long before the Luftwaffe wolf pack spotted us and two Focke-Wulf 190's started attacking with their guns flashing. They were ruthless and hit us again and again with their wing guns as they dove at us. The rat-a-tat-tat of the bullets hitting our plane propelled our gunners to keep their guns blasting back until they were red hot, but we were no match for them. We were out gunned.

I thought we were goners and didn't have a chance. But then two P-51's showed up and drove them off. They escorted us out of Germany and most of the way across occupied France. Unfortunately, we were still losing altitude even though the pilot gave maximum power to the two remaining engines. The gunners threw everything loose out of the windows, including their guns, anything to reduce the weight. We were barely staying airborne. When we finally approached the English Channel a thousand feet off the deck. Since we were now no longer losing altitude, the pilot decided to risk taking the plane across the English Channel. It would be about a 45-minute flight. The Allies were in control of some of the areas along the coast of France. The pilot gave the crew the option of bailing out or staying aboard. The others bailed out over France. Holding our breath, we counted parachutes as they each opened. If the plane was unable to stay in the air we would be forced to land in the ocean where our chance of survival was not good. Ditching was not recommended in B-24's. Most of the time when a B-24 tried to land on water it broke up and sank immediately. The Atlantic was cold and rough. If we survived the crash we'd likely freeze to death in a few minutes. It was risky either way. To me the icy water looked very unfriendly, but I had confidence in the pilot. If staying with the plane was good enough for him it was good enough for me. Besides, I might be able to help.

There was an especially wide landing strip near the southeastern coast of England for crash landings, and we were directed to land there. Over the water one of the engines started running rough. When we finally approached the English coastline it was socked in with fog. We couldn't see a damn thing. We were told the fog was lifting about a hundred feet over the landing strip, and we should be able to see it if we were right on the deck. The disabled engine started smoking and losing power. Now we were right down near the water. I prepared to get wet. The pilot said, 'We've got one shot at the landing strip if we can find it, but I can't see a damn thing in this fog. These engines won't take us around for a second try. Do you think you can guide us to the landing strip with the G-box?"

I knew how to use it, I'd taken the course. I quickly put the landing strip quadrants in the G-box, and they came up clean and clear. Unfortunately my reading indicated we were headed off course. I'd never guided a plane with the G-box controls, but bombardiers guide planes over the target during bomb runs all the time. I'd been trained in the classroom, but this was no classroom. This was for real. I had one shot to save our lives. I assured the pilot I could do it. "Then do it, but hurry up," he said. I took over the guidance with the G-box and lined the plane up on the electronic path leading to the landing strip. I was able to guide the plane right on the line and we got lucky. The moment the fog thinned out, we could see the landing strip was right ahead of us. The pilot took over and dropped our wounded bird right on the landing strip with no problem. We rolled down the tarmac to a stop.

I didn't tell anyone about it, but after we stopped rolling I was unable to move. I was exhilarated but shaking inside. Finally I got out of the plane, went over to the edge of tarmac, picked up handfuls of it, and repeatedly squeezed fists full of dirt through my tight fingers. I had a strong compulsion to rub the dirt all over my naked body. I even wanted to fill my mouth with handfuls of dirt and eat it. I didn't do it. I don't know why I felt that way, but I guess I was frightened and at the same time, thrilled that we'd pulled it off. I know this for sure, when you're up in the sky and they're shooting at you, you can't dig a foxhole.

When we got back to our base the pilot and I were put on a little vacation. They called it flack-leave. After that I was sent to lead navigator training. So back to school I went and would emerge later with a new crew.

I spent the rest of the war as a lead navigator and loved it. It was 1945 when Hitler's war ended, and after about four years I was to be on my way home. I'd completed my missions in a B-24 Liberator as a lead navigator. I was in my element in that position, and wanted to stay in the Air Force. I felt very comfortable in the presence of fliers. They were not only my best friends but they appreciated what it was like to be in the war. Although I had finished my missions in Europe, I now wanted to fly the B-29 Super Fortress in the Pacific. The B-29's were much larger and faster than B-24s. Perhaps I would even become a career Air Force Officer. I was a credit to the Air Force, and reluctant to give it all up. I was just a kid and yet I was responsible for directing millions of dollars worth of aircraft. They trusted me and made a leader out of a country bumpkin. When I joined the Air Force I was an eighteen year old hayseed from a small town not even wet behind the ears. Now at twenty-one, I was an officer and gentleman in the Air Force, by no less than presidential decree.

On the trip home by way of the SS Île de France I was having reoccurring nightmares. Every night it was the same: first the deafening roar of the four Pratt & Whitney engines as the pilot pushed the throttles forward, then it was the heavy plane lurching forward slowly at first, and then increasing its speed until it was rushing down the bumpy runway. The plane trembled, creaked, and rattled louder and louder until it lifted from the earth. As it lifted into the air the wingtips bent upward higher and higher until they ripped off. Suddenly everything went silent and black. I was falling. My body was shaking violently. Each time I awoke gasping for breath, clenching my bed sheets all covered in sweat. Every night I was afraid to close my eyes and go to sleep. The nightmares continued a few months after I got home. Then they finally stopped. Being a lead navigator was exciting, but I was now fully aware of fear and death. Many boys were killed before even going on their first mission. I no longer felt young.

When the SS Île de France landed in New York, all I wanted was a big bowl of vanilla ice cream. Back home Mom made our ice cream from scratch. Later when she purchased store-bought ice cream, I'd eat it instead of her meals. She didn't much like that, but mom knew how I loved ice cream. I hadn't had a single scoop of ice cream since I'd left the states. And soon I'd be home to enjoy my mother's cooking. She was a great cook and made the best pies. On Thanksgiving, she'd bake a whole pumpkin pie and put whipped cream on it, a whole pie just for me.

It was exciting when we arrived in New York. Not to see New York City but to be back in the USA. There were thousands of people standing on the dock waving and screaming out to the soldiers coming home. It was thrilling to see all those people rushing into each other's arms. There were so many women, children, and babies. But it left me with an empty feeling. There was no one there for us. We were a small group of airman instructed to get on an Air Force bus to be transported to a nearby airbase. I didn't expect anyone to meet me. After all, Idaho is clear across the country. Anyway, it didn't make much difference. We got right on the bus, and took off for the airbase. I didn't even have a chance to get any ice cream.

We spent the night at the airbase, and the next morning we took off to another airbase in Santa Ana, California. When we arrived in

Santa Ana we were told that we were war heroes, and the general public wanted to show us the nation's appreciation. Everyone, even Hollywood movie stars, wanted to be with us and thank us for our war effort. We couldn't believe it, but it was delightful.

When we were taken into the mess hall for lunch, it was just amazing. It was like no mess hall I'd ever seen. There were small tables set with white tablecloths and silver table settings for four. When I saw all the food in the center of the room on a long table, I couldn't believe it. There were waitresses in shiny white outfits serving the food and what food it was! There was food we hadn't seen since we left the states. Some I'd never seen. We had all we could eat and then some. There was crab, shrimp, lobster, giant steaks, everything. It was unbelievable. Growing up in Idaho I ate all my meals at home or at a campsite. There was nothing fancy like this. And I finally got that big bowl of vanilla ice cream.

It was great to be back in the states. Restaurant food was expensive, and I never did learn how to enjoy all that fancy seafood caught in the sea. Though I did enjoy eating the trout and salmon caught while fishing on weekends in the mountain streams and lakes back home. It took joining the Air Force to enjoy my first restaurant meal.

When I heard that the bus was leaving for the movie studios to meet movie stars I was beside myself with joy. Before joining the service, I was very briefly a teacher in the Mormon Church and had never drank or smoked. It was against the health rules of the church. When on liberty in the service, I never went to bars like the other guys, instead I went to the movies. As a kid we couldn't afford to eat in restaurants, but I went to lots of movies and the movies were cheap. I could see three afternoon movies for the price of one milkshake. I remember sitting in dark theaters wondering what it would be like to meet a real movie star. I once met the Andrew Sisters back stage at the Chicago Theater downtown in the Loop. During the London blitz, Angela Landsbury came to our air base and sang to some of us under a group of tall trees. There was a blackout because of German bombings, and she couldn't use all her electronic devices for amplification. She belted out the songs to us anyway. She must have sung for over an hour. After she sang her songs, she insisted upon shaking hands of every one of us that wanted too. She was so cute and courageous.

I was in love with movie stars and had fantasies way beyond reality. Never in my fondest dreams did I ever think I would even meet one real movie star, and now I was about to meet several. I got all excited when I walked into the Hollywood USO, and there at the door stood Gary Cooper. As I walked in, he extended his hand to me and said, "Howdy! Welcome to Hollywood," with a big smile on his face. "What's your name, son? I want to introduce you to some of my friends." He led me into the room just like I was an old friend.

I was flabbergasted, and for a moment I couldn't remember my own name. He took me over to a table and introduced me to Angela Landsbury. There she was again - young, beautiful, and very friendly, just as I'd remembered her. I sat down, and we talked one on one. She treated me like I was the star. I reminded her of the time she shook my hand back in England. We laughed and joked like good pals. I met several other stars, went on studio tours, and watched them make movies. It was exciting, but I wanted to get back home and see my family. Shortly after that we dropped the atom bombs on Nagasaki and Hiroshima. The war was over, and I went home for good.

Many years later when I was practicing medicine my associate, Harry Lusk, introduced me to his patient, Angela Landsbury. She didn't remember me of course. Why should she? I said nothing about our previous meeting. It had been a long time ago.

Then just a couple of years ago, when I was ninety-two, my third wife, Susan, surprised me and took me to the Ahmanson Theater to see Ms. Lansbury in a production of *Blithe Spirit*. At the age of eighty-nine she was strutting across the stage with the energy of the seventeen year old I had met at the USO. What a delightful performance. After the standing ovation, Susan whispered, "I have a surprise. We're going backstage to meet her." Backstage was no easy terrain to manage in a wheel chair but somehow we got there. Ms Lansbury came out, fresh as a daisy after her big performance and graciously chatted with me. What a special memory!

Cooper's Drive-Inn | Rupert, Idaho | 1950

4 BRINGING CALIFORNIA HOME

My father was a strong, noble man and wanted us to go into business together when I came home. This was the first time he ever expressed such a desire, and he was a very smart businessman. But I had already made up my mind to find a way to go to college and do what my advisers said I should do from the beginning: become a doctor.

However, the death of close young friends day after day begins to change the thinking of even the naïve. Home and family took on a much greater importance after the war. During one of my lesser moments, I promised God that if he would get me through this terrible war alive, I would forget about becoming a doctor and join my father in business. Do it his way. With little education he had managed to make a good life for us. He could be right. Most of my colleagues in cadet school were college graduates, and I hadn't gone to college. Yet I was picked as a lead navigator. My dad said, "Going to college was the way lazy boys get out of going to work. Education only taught men how to get away with becoming lazy bums." In all fairness he had some right to feel that way. During the Great Depression he managed a pool hall bar and young college graduates came into his bar willing to work for food.

So after the war I did join my father in business for a time. He found a large service station on the main drag going through the resort town of McCall, Idaho. He made me put up my own money in our new venture. We bought the business to own together, but for me to run. When it came to business my father was tough.

Where could a kid fresh back from the war come up with that kind of money? Well, while I was growing up my dad taught me how to play stud poker; I put that knowledge to good use while overseas. At the end of the war I had already sent home the money I needed to put up my share.

The old guy that we bought it from was retiring, but had agreed to stay with me for six weeks to teach me the ropes. The old guy had three hired hands, two mechanics and a body man. The building was large with room to accommodate many cars for storage over night. It was very cold in McCall so many tourists left their cars with us, and either walked or took cabs to the resort. The back of our building extended into Payette Lake where we had a boat ramp. We did all kinds of auto and boat repairs. We even secured an Easel Auto Agency, however we never received any new cars.

The old man taught me well and the business made money. Less than a year later we were offered three times what we had paid for it. We sold it and I was a little richer, but now unemployed.

I moved back to Burley, Idaho and went into the candy manufacturing business. Life had yet to return back to normal. Many things were still rationed, including sugar. There hadn't been candy of any kind available for years, but over at the sugar mill they had plenty of sugar. I soon learned that as a returning vet I could buy all the sugar I could find. That Christmas I made sure the whole town had all the candies they wanted. I sold candies to grocery stores, confectioneries, everywhere. I didn't sell it cheap either. Soon thereafter sugar was no longer rationed and I knew the larger manufactures would be back selling candy a few cents above the price of sugar. I'd gone into the candy business primarily because I was one of the few enterprising men who could get sugar and had no competition. I knew it would be short lived. In 1949, four years after the end of the war, the economy had mostly changed from war to peace. So again, I was looking for something to do.

During the war everyone had learned to go without. No new automobiles were created during the war, and the old ones had been repaired over and over again, many were beyond repair. The government helped create jobs for men returning from war. Everyone was hopeful and excited about the future. People began to have money and wanted to buy everything.

During the time I'd spent in California waiting to be discharged from the army, I was able to spend a couple weeks with my cousin, Karalee. She took me to a drive-in restaurant on Sunset Boulevard. It was amazing. An artistic little building standing in the middle of a large open lot with many cars parked all around it. Several pretty young girls in sexy uniforms darted in and out of cars carrying food on trays to be attached to the opening of the window. Young people were eating, talking, and having a good time. Every young man wanted to show off his new car, and the girls wanted to be seen with them.

As I watched the action around me, I got excited about a new idea. I had a few bucks, was optimistic, and surprised to learn that no one in Burley had even seen a drive-in restaurant. I knew that young men in Idaho were the same as in California. French fries were all the rage in California, and even though Idaho was the potato state, there wasn't a single place in town that sold them. So I decided to exploit the drive-in idea and help the local boys fulfill the dreams they had yet to even have. I ran the idea by my dad.

"Hell yes, do it!" he said. I was glad he approved because I'd need his financial help again even though we'd already made money together up in McCall. This would be different. I'd have to buy a large piece of land in a good location and build the building with all its furnishings and supplies. I would need a lot of money. My dad said, "There's a large vacant lot at the corner of the city park over in Rupert. You should go take a look at it."

Rupert, Idaho was only nine miles away, but I didn't know that much about the place, so I checked it out. Located between the city park and the railway station, I couldn't understand how this big piece of land in the center of town was still vacant. I learned that it was owned by the railroad and was not for sale. I was disappointed, but decided to talk to the railroad people anyway. I learned it was on a 99-year lease to the city. So off I went to the city. They were very pleasant and said they'd love to lease it to the right party, but whatever business went in there would have to be an asset to the city. I made my drawings, met with the city counsel, and made my pitch. They accepted my proposal and I signed the lease. I built my little building, and we were in business.

"Go over to the high school and get the names of the most popular seniors and offer them a job," my dad said. I got very excited thinking about cute girls in sexy uniforms serving hamburgers and French fries to young people in hot new cars parked outside Cooper's Drive In. The letters I sent to the girl's homes said, "Experience not necessary."

With Cooper's Drive-in we got lucky. The drive-in was enormously successful. Rows of cars surrounded our place day in day out. Our pretty carhops delivered hamburgers, hot dogs, and French fries by the tons, along with all other kinds of fast food. Today, some sixty years later it's still a successful restaurant.

However, the first couple of years of the restaurant gave me my fair share of personal issues. During cadet training I fell in love with Avis, a young secretary from Houston, Texas. Though our affair was never consummated we kept in touch, and planned to marry after the war was over. When I started building the drive-in I sent for Avis and we were quickly married. It was a big mistake. Eighteen months after opening the drive-in we were divorced. It was simply a case of two decent young people not really knowing one another. She expected a nine to five'er, which I never was and never would be. I was very busy and crazy with ambition. She divorced me and rightly should have. Tragically, Avis died shortly thereafter in an auto accident.

Irene Mahler | Senior Portrait | 1948

5 THE STORY OF IRENE

Irene was desperate for a job. She was very pretty, only seventeen, and had no experience. She was referred to Cooper's Drive-in by one of my carhops. Irene's father had just died of cancer and her widowed mother suffered from the crippling paralysis of childhood polio. Somehow this woman was still managing to feed her young children. Irene wanted to bring in money to help her mother. At first Irene didn't stand out. She was shy, innocent, and had never even been in a restaurant. However, she impressed me with how exceptionally fast she learned and was very eager to please everyone. The hours were long and hard at Cooper's Drive-In. After the crowds went home at midnight we still had two hours of cleanup for the next day.

Irene lived a couple miles outside of town, and there was no transportation that time of the night, so I would drive her home. I soon learned that finding Irene was like finding an earthbound angel. She was honest, smart, and eager to learn about the world outside Rupert. She was different. Living among rednecks, she listened to classical music instead of country. On our way home during the wee hours we talked about everything. Not wanting to be separated, we frequently continued talking for a while after parking in her mother's driveway. One early morning after a totally exhausting day we fell asleep in each other's arms. Her mother's tapping on the window awakened us the next morning. Well, we were in love. Since she was only 17 we had to get her mother's permission, but soon after we got married. My Uncle George married us, in his capacity as a bishop in the Mormon Church. My father was a little upset with me and said sarcastically, "This is the last one of your damn weddings I'm going to."

The following year Irene got pregnant with our first son, Lonny. The first few months of her pregnancy she was hellishly ill with morning sickness, especially whenever she came near me. She continued to work her shift at the drive-in, even though I'd asked her to stay home. Her morning sickness was making me a little paranoid because every time I came near her she vomited. It was only after our son was born that she told me it was my after-shave lotion that made her sick.

We were happily married and we now had our first child. My father was my silent partner and stayed out of my hair. We were making loads of money. I had everything a man could want. But I was restless. I said nothing to Irene. After all, what else could a man wish for? A beautiful young wife whom I loved, a son, and all the money I could ever want. Still, I wasn't satisfied.

One night I couldn't fall asleep. Irene asked, "What's wrong?"

"Nothing," I lied.

"Are you unhappy with me?"

"No! I'm in love with you, and now you have given me a beautiful son."

"There is something wrong," she insisted. "You're not happy. It's plain as day."

A flame had been lit, and I couldn't get it out of my mind. I knew what was bothering me, but I thought it was silly to even think about it. The next morning it was still on my mind, so I had to tell her, "Before the war I wanted to try to become a doctor, but the war put a stop to that dream. And anyway I hadn't even gone to college. It's far too late to even think about that now."

"Boyd, it's never too late to follow your dreams." That night I lay awake thinking about what she had said. Was I really unhappy or just being selfish? A few days later I asked her if she realized what the consequences of my becoming a doctor would be. "Absolutely," she said.

"You have everything now. If I go to college it will take nine or maybe even twelve years before I'll be able to start practicing medicine. Right now we have everything. If I go back to school we'll be poor for a very long time. It'll be tough on Lonny, too. You'll have to work and we'll all have to go without."

"I know how to go without," she said. "I've always wanted to get out of this small town, and see the world. It sounds like a great adventure. Let's do it." So with my Angel's consent, we changed our life forever.

J.O., my brother-in-law, was already running the night shift. By making a very clever deal with him, I was able to earn money and go to school at the same time. Of course he benefited as well. I would give him with no money down and fifty percent of the business, which he would work to pay off over time. He still received a salary, but I received enough money through this arrangement to afford to go to school. I would start college, and Irene and I would see how it went. We could always return to Rupert later if it didn't work out.

I started college at a small pharmacy school in Pocatello, Idaho. There the three of us lived in a two-room basement apartment with a shared toilet down the hall. Despite our humble living arrangements, we were very happy. We went to the movies, college functions, and concerts. We did everything together, and always took Lonny with us. It was loads of fun going to college. Thank God we both had jobs and I had the GI bill. After my freshman year at Pocatello I transferred to the University of Washington in Seattle to finish my pre-recs. They were starting a new medical school there, and this would give me a better chance of getting in when the time came. At the end of my junior year I applied for admission to UW and to a couple of Ivy League medical schools. I really wanted to go to the University of Southern California in Los Angeles, but they required two foreign languages and preferred applicants from their own state. I was of course from out of state and only had one foreign language. I'd taken all the required courses for medical school, but didn't want to spend another year getting my bachelors degree. All I wanted was to get my M.D. as quickly as possible.

All my applications were turned down, and I was told to get my bachelors degree and reapply. However, I did get on the alternates list at UW. I was disappointed but not ready to give up. In my search for another medical school I learned that George Washington University in D.C. always accepted a few students from states that didn't have their own medical school. Since Idaho didn't have a medical school, I quickly applied and was accepted. I was ill-informed though and did not know it was every bit as highly respected as any of the Ivy League schools. So, again the three of us were off. I loved George Washington University and did well. We both got new jobs, bought a trailer house, and put Lonny in a private school.

Everything was great for a couple of years, but then I got sick. The doctor said I had nothing serious. I think I was just lonely and spending too much time alone. I worked all night at a clinic and went to school during the day. I was away from my family most of the time. The clinic where I worked had very little business, so I spent my nights sleeping and studying. I was able to remain in the top 10% of the class.

My extended family had moved to California, and I still dreamed of spending the rest of my life there, where the humidity wasn't so high. During the end of my sophomore year the humidity in D.C. was unbearable. I got quite sick even though I was taking medication. On a lark I called the dean at USC and asked if it would be possible to transfer to USC the following year. Unbelievably, I was accepted! I still had to fulfill a number of requirements, but I made it happen and also got well.

Thus I got my medical degree from the University of Southern California School of Medicine. It was a great adventure, and we had a lot of fun at USC. After I finished medical school, I had another four years before I could practice medicine. I was now making a little money and didn't have to get another job. Still it was very hard, especially for poor Irene. She worked day and night. We now had three children, Lonny and our two babies, Lynne and Doug. Irene took the two babies to her sister's house halfway across town early every morning, and then went to her job. After work she picked up the babies and went to the Laundromat to do our laundry. During my residency, I worked long hours and had little time off, so I was of little help to Irene. In spite of her heavy workload, she found time to be a great mother.

In 1960 I opened my practice in Hollywood, and soon after Irene reluctantly quit her job. She was much like "Rosy the Riveter," who learned during the war that it was more fun and satisfying to work outside the home, spending the days with other adults rather than being alone with the babies. Irene said, "It's hard to have an intelligent conversation with little idiots. They are my little idiots and I love them, but it's not much fun talking only about kaka, poopoo, and peepee."

But she stayed at home and did a great job as a mother. One Christmas she bought herself a little fox fur jacket, and put it in the trunk of my car. She then told me secretly to have our daughter get it out of the trunk, wrap it, and put it under the Christmas tree from me. I'm not sure my kids believed it -- they were not stupid. She did the same thing with my son's bicycle. She told them nothing, and in their eyes I became a better dad than I could ever have been on my own because of her.

My older son, Lonny, probably spent the most time with Irene and me. He attend a preschool at Hollywood Presbyterian Hospital and we would pick him up at the end of my day. Lonny was super smart and very verbal. He liked nothing more than engaging in an argument. As a teenager he called them discussions, but they were much more akin to arguments, sometimes heated. He went on to become a leader of many protests in school and college, and when it came time for the draft he became a conscientious objector. Our discussions about this issue were many and lasted for hours. Fighting for your country to me was a duty and a privilege. Lonny felt so strongly that the Vietnam War was wrong that he left the country with his friends and rented a small farm in Canada. Lonny always danced to his own tune and it has taken us many years to understand one another's point of view. I hate to admit it, but now I really do love our 'discussions'. Lonny has softened just as I have over the years.

During my residency I delivered many babies while working at the Florence Crittenton Home for unwed mothers. Their babies went out for adoption. I loved those girls and understood their broken hearts when they gave away their babies. Many became my private patients when I opened my practice. I continued to deliver unwed girls in my own private practice. Some were from out of town and they had no place to stay, so I brought them home. We had an extra room, and Irene agreed. They all loved Irene and many became her lifetime friends.

We lived in Sherman Oaks which at the time was a mostly Jewish suburb of Los Angeles. Our neighbors, Sol and Debby, became as good of friends of ours as friends can possibly be. We were Mormons, but not very devout. On the other hand, they took being Jewish very seriously, especially Sol. We never talked about it, but come Christmastime Irene innocently asked their children to help decorate the tree. The kids loved it, but I'm not sure Sol and Debby appreciated it. After that, they put up a Chanukah bush with blue lights, and we were invited to our first Shabbat dinner.

My daughter Lynne started riding horses when she was very young at Richard Widmark's cattle ranch. Irene would take her out to the ranch where Widmark's horse wrangler, Tom, taught her how to ride. Later he helped her get a registered American Quarter Horse, and he then trained her and her horse. With Tom's tutelage Lynne won many blue ribbons and trophies. Riding became very important to her.

Later, when our children were in school Irene started looking around for a new adventure. She was a health nut, exercised a lot, and didn't drink or smoke. She joined a bicycle group, and they cycled all over Southern California.

In the summer of 1972 her group made arrangements to cycle throughout Europe. Irene had always wanted to do that. With their summer railroad passes and their bicycles they were to travel throughout most of Europe for six weeks. I was thrilled for her. One month before they left she got a smallpox vaccination (it was required at that time, since she did not receive it as a child). She had a systemic reaction to the vaccination, and developed a fever, swollen glands and a severe cough. She was very sick for two weeks. Many tests were done, including a chest x-ray. But all were normal. She recovered, went on her tour and had a great time. Some days they cycled fifty miles. After she returned home she was a little tired, but basically felt good.

Upon her return from Europe, as ridiculous as it may sound, I had a weird psychic premonition that Irene was going to leave me. This thought kept coming into my mind. Rationally, the whole idea seemed crazy. Maybe I was working too much. Or maybe there was someone else in her life, though there was no indication of that, and anyway Irene just wasn't that way.

She was also breeding Kerry Blue Terriers, and one weekend she took the female to San Diego for breeding purposes. As usual I was very busy. She returned from San Diego on Sunday night a little tired. She thought maybe she had been doing too much.

One week later a strange thing happened while we were asleep. It was about four A.M. when I was partially awakened by her breathing. It was too fast. It was almost surreal, like part of a dream. Finally I woke up enough to check her respiratory rate. It was over forty breaths per minute. I was suddenly wide-awake. I took her pulse. It was one hundred and forty beats per minute, and she was sleeping. I was terrified knowing that something was seriously wrong. As I lay there beside her, I slowly recalled my premonition of her leaving me. I suddenly knew why she was leaving me, but not for another man. I didn't understand, but I knew.

Early that morning I took her to the hospital and had the best diagnostician see her. They told me that she had Hammond Rich Syndrome (interstitial fibrosis of the lung), which is to this day one hundred percent fatal. I was a doctor, and had never heard of Hammond Rich Syndrome. I'd heard of interstitial fibrosis, but knew little about it. It's a rare autoimmune disease and, her immune system decided that her own lungs were a foreign invader, and very rapidly she destroyed her own lungs by depositing fibrous tissue in the space between the lung air sacs and the blood vessels. It was a horrible death. She was forced to breath rapidly and deep just to stay alive. They put her on a respirator, which helped for a while. Finally her little body was totally exhausted, and she could breathe no more. Two days before her death I took the children into the hospital to see her. My twelve-year-old son said, "That's not my mother! That's an old woman!" He was right, she was. She was forty-three years of age, but she had become a gray-haired old lady in one week. Exactly one week after that night of my horrible premonition, Irene was dead.

After her sudden death, I was numb, utterly destroyed. I was in shock. I don't remember much about the funeral. I was told that it was enormous. Thousands came: our families, my friends, her friends, the children's friends, and many others. It was an unexpected death of a beloved lady, out of time and place. I have little memory of it all, but I do remember looking up and seeing tears running down the hardened faces of doctors who saw death every day.

Life after a loved one's death is never easy, and in more ways than just the obvious. I had always thought the maid was stealing from my wife, and when she told me that Irene had borrowed fifteen hundred dollars from her I knew she was lying. I wanted to fire her on the spot, but following the advice of the psychiatrist, I did not. I gave her the fifteen hundred dollars. I wanted to move closer to my office, and into the Hollywood Hills, but I managed to wait one year. Meanwhile, I asked Al, our close friend, to stay and help with the children.

After Irene died I had no way to take Lynne to the ranch to ride her horse. Irene was very friendly with everyone she met including an Italian stonemason named Frank Freni. He was a real artist when it came to setting tile. We became good friends and laid lots of beautiful tile together. He even inspired my sons to become great tile setters. Lonny creates beautiful murals out of tile. His artwork is on display in many churches and government buildings. Doug grew up to be a craftsman with tile. Doug took things to an all together higher level. His work is meticulous and artistically fine and has graced some of the finest homes in Los Angeles and Santa Barbara. During this time I turned the garage into a poolroom so Frank and I could play pool every chance we could get. Frank offered to take Lynne, and he did for a while. Years after Irene's death Frank came to my office and wanted to get paid thousands of dollars for the times he'd taken Lynne to the ranch. I was disappointed. It was then that I realized he was neither my daughter's nor my friend. I refused to pay him, and he threatened me. I think he thought because he was Italian, he saw himself as some kind of a Mafioso and that I'd be frightened. I was not. The next time he came to my office I had a friend "talk" to him. My friend, Claude, was at least six feet tall and weighed over two hundred and fifty pounds. He looked like he could swallow little Frank in one gulp. In reality Claude was a pussycat, but Frank didn't know that. Whatever he said to him, Frank left town and I never heard from him again.

I was unable to get Irene's untimely death out of my mind. I was an obstetrician not an internist. Nonetheless, I felt I should have known more about the auto-immune diseases than I did. It made me feel less than adequate having my own wife die of a disease that I hadn't even heard of. For a long time I wondered if it might have had something to do with her smallpox vaccination. It made her very ill, and it was a respiratory problem. Still, her chest x-ray was negative just before her trip. Why our immune system attacks our bodies and kills us is not fully understood even today. Auto-immune diseases remain mysterious to me.

One night I awoke from a sound sleep remembering that when Irene and I got married her serology test was positive for syphilis. As she was a virgin, this was highly unlikely. The doctor did another more specific test, which was negative. He said in addition to syphilis there were other rare conditions that could make her serology positive. At the time I thought little of it. I was not a physician then. Now I realized: the auto-immune diseases can give a false positive for syphilis. I suddenly knew that Irene had carried the seeds of Hammond Rich syndrome her whole adult life, and maybe even since birth.

I was married to Irene for one week short of twenty-five years. She was a wonderful woman and we shared a full life growing up together. Irene is the reason I am a doctor today. The tragedy is she died too young, and had precious little time to enjoy our success, or see our kids grow up. I am grateful she at least had that remarkable bicycle trip in Europe. It was a dream come true for her.

Mother, Boyd, & Father | USC School of Medicine | 1956

6 DOWN ON THE FUNNY FARM

One of the most pleasant years of my residency training was spent in Camarillo, California. At that time it was a mental institution with about 4,000 women in residence. During my senior year we started going there to give gynecological care to their patients. A doctor hadn't seen many of them in years, except in an emergency, and many needed surgery. As medical residents we needed training in women's surgery, so this was a great opportunity. Thus I found myself in an institution responsible for the female problems of 4,000 disturbed women.

I must say I was somewhat intimidated by the thought of spending a year taking care of mostly schizophrenics. I was a gynecologist, not a shrink. My only experience with mentally ill patients had been earlier in medical school in Washington D.C. at St. Elizabeth's Hospital. At that time, it was not only the largest mental institution in the world but the wildest. Bedlam USA. That was the extent of my psychiatric knowledge. No doubt they had shown us their most bizarre cases, but as a result, my memory of the experience rivaled movies like *The Three Faces Of Eve* and *One Flew Over the Cuckoo's Nest*.

When I entered my ward for the first time, I was prepared to be overwhelmed. The dayroom was clean, open and spacious and even smelled freshly scrubbed. There were large comfortable sofas and chairs and a television set with patients clustered around it. One thing was a bit novel, however, as there was a special fence around the TV set to protect it. I later learned that some patients would try to pick fights with the characters on television.

As I looked around me, I saw women sitting about in groups, talking quietly. Some were chatting with the nurses. It was all very civilized, much like the wards at Los Angeles County Hospital, and not the snake pit like I'd been led to expect by the movies and my own early experiences. As I overcame my concerns, I soon discovered that mentally ill patients are not deranged all the time. Most of the time, they are much like the rest of us. It's just that upon some occasions, they flip out.

Some were very bright, even brilliant, some were extremely creative and most were friendly and responded warmly to kindness and understanding. One of my most loving patients was a recovering mass murderess. She had come to understand that the voices in her head giving her orders were not real, even though she still heard them loud and clear.

When I first arrived they gave me a large key, which was important. Not only did it open all the doors, but it was also a way of differentiating the doctors and staff from the patients. I had three basic duties at the institution: examine all new females admitted, arrange to examine as many of the four thousand females in the outer wards as I possibly could, and perform surgery on those who needed it. At any given time, I kept about seventy patients on my ward whom were pregnant, postpartum, or surgical patients. My boss, Dr. Chuck Montague from Ventura, would come in twice a week and we would do surgery. My supervising gyno-surgeon came up from Hollywood periodically. The rest of the time I was on my own.

Three mornings a week I would gather six of my nurses, all our equipment, and head for one of the outer lock-up wards. Each ward contained about seventy female patients plus their nursing staff. When we arrived, the staff nurses would have the patients in their beds, all lined up and ready for their examinations. I then went from one patient to the next, doing pap smears, breast and pelvic/rectal exams. During these exams, I had to have the nurses hold the patient's arms, legs and head so my hands wouldn't get bitten. I soon learned to move quickly. I had to be swift and comprehensive. Even with nurses running interference, the women would only lie still for a few seconds. In three hours, I would examine all seventy of these ladies and be on my way. It was efficient -- not warm and fuzzy. They couldn't hit, kick, or bite but they could still nail me. I brought out their primitive instincts. I didn't blame them for their defensive reactions -- it must have been as bizarre an experience for them as it was for me.

Camarillo Hospital was a beautiful place with rolling grass lawns, widely separated white buildings and a gentle ocean breeze blowing across the campus. I visited it recently. It's now a college, and not as well kept as I remember. I was very disappointed when, the then Governor Ronald Reagan slashed the mental health budget in California, an act that resulted in the closing of Camarillo and other facilities that housed and treated the mentally ill. The patients at Camarillo were well taken care of, protected, and relatively happy. But they now became the first generation of the homeless, wandering the streets from Santa Monica to Los Angeles' skid row.

Our leaders said we just couldn't afford to keep the hospitals open, but some people were (and are) unable to take care of themselves. It seems strange that the richest nation in the world can't take proper care of its mentally ill. Currently, depression is at an all time high. I find that frightening, but on the other hand, what is mental illness anyway? Does it just mean we are different? They didn't ask to be the way they are and, believe me, there but for the grace of God go a lot of the rest of us.

Once I learned to understand my patients at Camarillo, I loved them. But that doesn't mean there weren't some strange moments. One of the nurses brought a patient to my office and said, "Annette says she's having severe rectal pain. She's one of our least complaining patients, and I thought you should see her as an emergency."

"Okay, take her to the examining room and get her ready for an exam," I said. When I came into the exam room I asked Annette to tell me about her pain.

"It's terrible, doctor. It just keeps going around and around, and it hurts."

"What keeps going around and around?" I asked.

"The Ferris wheel."

"There's a Ferris wheel in there going around and around?"

"Yes, doctor."

I did a quick pelvic and rectal exam on her, and everything was normal. "There! I turned it off," I said. She was one of my most grateful patients.

The nature of my work did get me in trouble at times. I'd done a vaginal hysterectomy on an older black woman, and every time I came near her she got a silly smile on her face. I finally asked the nurse what it was all about. She smiled, "She thinks you're having an affair."

There was a PX on the grounds where the patients could buy various personal items. The nurses would take them in groups under their supervision. One afternoon, I was walking across the campus when a platoon of patients came marching toward me. Suddenly they all began screaming hysterically. Breaking ranks, they started running in all directions. The nurses were frantic and unable to control them and strangely enough, they seemed mad as hell *at me*! I was baffled and when I asked the head nurse what was going on she said, "The patients are frightened to death of you."

Shocked, I asked, "Why me? What did I do?"

The head nurse glared at me and retorted angrily, "They think you raped them all one afternoon."

All I could do was shake my head. Of course it wasn't true. Despite that ridiculous claim on my reputation, I learned a lot at Camarillo. I received very good surgical training under Dr. Montague, and what's more, I learned a lot about life. The patients, even the nutty ones, taught me how to appreciate and respect being sane and alive. We are all valuable, even the crazies among us. But Lincoln was wrong about one thing: All men are not *created* equal. We may have equal rights but we have different potentials and abilities. Some human beings need custodial care for a time, some forever. To protect them and also to protect us from them. But they still deserve to live like human beings.

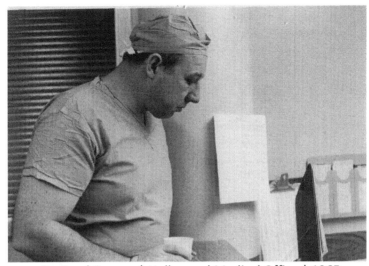
Dr. Boyd Cooper | Hollywood Medical Office | 1965

7 THE BIG BOYS CLUB

I was scared, not of the plane I was flying in that November afternoon, but of where it was taking me: to Chicago and the Board of Certification. And if you don't think that's reason for fear, just ask any certified physician. I was about to confront three complete strangers, the examiners of the American Board of Obstetrics and Gynecology. I had been a doctor for twelve years, the last nine in private practice. I was busy. My practice had grown rapidly and I had a large caseload of patients. But now the members of this board, within the course of about one hour, would evaluate me to determine if I was good enough to join the "Big Boys Club". This was important and would seriously impact my medical future. It made me even tenser to know it was questionable as to how much of the decision would be based on my competency, and how much would be based on what my competitors, the local certified doctors, thought of me.

Every category of medical practice has a board similar to the American Board of Obstetrics and Gynecology. As knowledge expanded, doctors found themselves unable to cope with the ever-increasing volume of medical information. They were unable to learn everything, so they started limiting themselves to special areas of academic pursuit and calling themselves specialists. Before long the medical academicians banded together and called for a mandatory certificate to prove that doctors calling themselves specialists had received additional training and were indeed qualified in their specialties. It seemed like a good idea at the time, and it probably was. Unfortunately, as time went on politics became another part of the equation, and the process became less academic and more competitive.

Today a doctor cannot get on the staff of most first class hospitals without being certified in his or her specialty. At the time I took the boards, certification was not mandatory. But this was changing rapidly. Soon doctors certified in other specialties would not refer patients to non-certified doctors. To be known as the best you had to be a member of the "club." Without it you lacked power, integrity and prestige.

There were two facets to the certification examination, written and oral. After finishing one year of internship most doctors start their residency training, for an OB-GYN this takes three to four years. After residency training, the written exams are given. After a doctor passes the written exam, he or she is considered board eligible. However to become certified, one must wait two or three years before taking the oral exam.

I passed the written exam upon completion of my residency at Hollywood Presbyterian Hospital. Three years later, I submitted my application to take the oral examination. My application was refused with a correspondence explaining that they had not received enough "blue letters". I was instructed to get to know the local certified specialists in my field and reapply next year. I was disappointed to say the least. I had never even heard of "blue letters". Apparently, when a doctor submitted his application to take the oral examination, blue-colored letters were sent to the certified OB-GYN specialists in the area. If enough of those doctors responded favorably, the applicant would be allowed to take the final examination. I knew only the OB-GYN specialist in Hollywood and none of the powerful ivory tower doctors from UCLA or USC. University teaching professors did not approve of private hospital teaching programs such as Hollywood Presbyterian's. Their attitude was probably right because there were no private hospital teaching programs left that don't have a medical school affiliation.

Frankly I was pissed off by this rejection, and I have to admit it hurt as well. I made the excuse to myself that I was too busy to play this game and didn't need certification, but deep inside I really wanted it. For the time being, I decided that I would remain an uncertified specialist.

One of the senior members of my department had been re-elected several years in a row as chairman. He did everything in his power to prevent young doctors from progressing into leadership passions. He was losing patients, and in return I was accepting them. In those days this was a political no-no. I was asked to run for chairman of the department against him. We had several elections that always ended up in a tie. Six months passed and we still didn't have a chairman. Ultimately, the president of the staff declared I wasn't able to run because I was not certified, and he won unopposed. I was humiliated. Finally, I realized I was not a fully accepted specialist without certification. Period.

A few months later, I received a letter from the board suggesting that I should reactivate my application. By this time the infamous "blue letters" had been eliminated from the process. On November 13, 1969, I was on my way to the oral exams, feeling uncertain and ill-prepared. It had been years since I'd had a chance to hit the books. I kept up with all the latest advances in my field, but otherwise all my time was spent taking care of patients.

As I sat there in my aisle seat, feeling sorry for myself, I happened to notice a colleague seated several rows in front of me. I remember thinking that Paul must be feeling even more unnerved than I. He had already failed the oral exam twice.

I knew Paul and his story quite well. He was a non-certified specialist at my hospital, trained at an Ivy League medical school hospital complex back east. During his internship, Paul started dating his professor's secretary, Melissa. The professor was not only the head of the department at the hospital and chairman of the department at the university but a member of the certification board.

Paul, attractive and charming, and Melissa who was young, beautiful, and naïve made a striking couple. Melissa had the power to make any young doctor's dreams come true. In addition to being the professor's secretary, she was the daughter of one of his closest friends who was also a fellow physician and teacher at the university.

Many of us knew Paul was quite capable of not only enjoying Melissa as a woman, but of using her to ensure himself a position in the residency program. At least that was the gossip. Anyhow, whatever his motives, by escorting Melissa to various medical functions and becoming acquainted with her family and their powerful friends, Paul had ingratiated himself strategically.

Paul's connections weren't the only laurels he had going for him. He was as gifted as he was handsome and confident. Paul had graduated in the top ten percent of his medical school class. He was also rated as one of the better interns. He did equally well during his four-year residency program. He conducted himself in an admirable manner, both in his doctor-patient and doctor-doctor relationships.

Surprisingly, after he completed his training program to everyone's satisfaction, he decided to leave the hospital facility. Instead of accepting the promising post he had been offered, he entered private practice. While this was somewhat of a disappointment to the professor, who had hoped Paul would join the medical teaching staff at the university, Paul was anxious to get on with his life and private practice. He was given their blessings and he said goodbye.

Those blessings went sour when he abruptly ended his long-time relationship with Melissa and moved to California. After eight years of waiting, perhaps foolishly, Melissa was deeply hurt. Paul had been secretly dating the daughter of a well-positioned actor who had arranged an association with a successful medical group in Beverly Hills. Melissa was furious, humiliated and bitter. She vowed to get even with him for wasting her life with empty promises. She swore that if it were within her power, Paul would never receive certification.

As I said earlier, Paul had already been before the board twice and failed. I have no way of determining if this was politically motivated or not, but it was rumored that he would never get certified. It was a long time ago, and I wasn't there. Now here he was trying again. I quietly hoped he would make it this time.

I had never been involved in situations comparable to Paul's but as I looked up the aisle, I wondered if I could have inadvertently offended some of my senior colleagues at some point. After all, my practice had grown very rapidly. Maybe I was too aggressive. What if some of them thought I had stolen patients from them? Maybe from some I did. I was worried. Here I was, a qualified doctor at forty-six years of age, sweating like a schoolboy. And if I didn't make it this time, would I, like Paul, have the courage to try again?

At that moment Paul suddenly turned toward me. Seemingly glad to see a familiar face, he got up and walked over to my seat.

"Well, good luck, Coop," he said, smiling.

"You too," I replied. After that we exchanged a few pleasantries, mostly to cover our anxieties. Then a stewardess cautioned about seatbelts, and Paul went back to his seat. "Damn", I thought, watching him. Maybe he was selfish and a cad, but he should be given full recognition on his qualifications alone.

Stepping off the plane a few minutes later, I was welcomed by a chilling blast of air. The day was gray. Damp flakes of snow were falling. It was just as I had remembered Chicago twenty-eight years ago during the war. Shivering, I took a taxi into the city to the Conrad Hilton Hotel, the same place I had attended radio school during WWII. The name of the hotel had since changed, and now there was not a uniform in sight among the throngs of guests and visitors in the busy lobby. A lot of years had gone by, and now the tall, skinny GI loner was an overweight doctor who had treated over five thousand women. I'd seen practically every variety of female ailment and had spanked at least a thousand babies into the world with nary a mishap.

Alone in my hotel room, I watched television for a while, thinking of Irene and our three children back home in California rooting for me. Then hoping to fend off anxiety and loneliness, I went to bed early. But it was quite late before I was able to fall asleep. When I did, for some incomprehensible reason, I dreamt of the old country doctor who had saved my mother's life some forty years before. Perhaps this was because he still remained my mentor, an ideal symbol of what a doctor ought to be. He was a man who had lived his life as a true physician and never had bothered with the politics of it all.

The following morning, I was one of two hundred doctors who were ushered into one of the hotel's huge banquet rooms. We ranged in age from twenty-five to fifty-five. Some of us sat, some stood, and others milled about. Some were stone quiet, others were smoking and chatting nervously, but the overall tone was subdued and depressing. We were all under extreme tension. One middle-aged man was so nervous he became nauseous and had to rush out of the room. I saw several colleagues from California, including Paul, and we nodded, speaking a word or two across the space.

As I took a chair in this tense congregation, I knew that approximately twenty-five percent of us would fail. I looked around asking myself, "After eight years of college and four or five years of post-graduate training, what are we all doing here, taking another exam? They should have determined a long time ago whether or not we belonged."

When a senior examiner and his younger assistant entered the room, a hush fell over the two hundred applicants. The senior examiner called two names and the designated applicants came forward. They shook hands and then disappeared through the door. When another applicant and I were called, we came forward and were greeted. The other applicant was led down the while I accompanied Dr. J. D. Rose and a younger examiner into another hotel room where the twin beds had been thrust to one side. I was encouraged to sit in a comfortable chair while Dr. Rose took a straight chair at the desk. He turned to face me. He was a small man in his fifties with a warm smile and a Southern drawl. The other examiner, who sat on the edge of one of the beds, I scarcely remember.

Dr. Rose's initial questions were not difficult and I began to feel a bit at ease. One question dealt with the cancer smears I took daily in my office. At that time the Pap smear had just became available. This led in turn to a general discussion of the routine management of the Pap smear and cancer in females. The other doctor joined in and the three of us discussed the therapeutic use of radiation therapy for cancer. In those days I did my own radiation therapy. Today radiologists with a special license do it. When I was asked what dosage of radiation would be given to a malignant growth at point A and B, I answered immediately and I was sure I was correct. But then I was asked a question about the dosage at point D. I hesitated, frowning. As far as I knew, there was no point D.

A choice lay before me. I could attempt to hide my ignorance and make an educated guess or admit that, within the scope of my medical education, I knew of no point D. Uncertain, I stated that I knew of no point D; later I learned that they were testing my integrity, and my response had been correct.

There were other questions, some of which, like point D, I was not certain, but I did my best. About forty minutes later I was escorted into another examining room where my third examiner was introduced. Almost immediately the hotel room went dark and slides began flashing on a screen. I was then expected to make swift responses to a series of tissue slides and pictures of cancer and other abnormalities. Some of them were inquiries that harkened back to my medical school days, the answers to which had to come from my subconscious. I knew I was correct more than sixty or seventy percent of the time, but once again, I took my best shot. Finally the lights switched on, the examiner shook my hand and uttered a polite, "Thank you very much. You'll be hearing from us."

I left with one thought uppermost in my mind in both examining rooms. The exam had been fair and there had been every chance to give my answers. Only forty minutes? How could they possibly judge men after only forty minutes? But I knew full well that they had the power to flunk or pass me no matter how long the exams were. They had the option irrespective of my answers. Maybe that was the whole point; they just wanted to evaluate me as a person.

I couldn't get out of there fast enough. I returned home to California on the next plane. I tried to put the entire matter out of my mind, telling myself it was over and done, regardless of the results. But as I went about my work and enjoyed my Los Angeles life I could not forget Chicago. For thirty-four days I had to sweat it out before I received a "yes" or "no" from the Board of Examiners.

During this time I found myself giving some additional and very serious thought to the entire concept of certification. Was I a better doctor now if I got certified? Were the questions I had been asked truly important or were some of them only to assess my integrity? Were my responses the true deciding factor or was this a childish game? How about the other applicants, probably all fine doctors, but some were destined to fail. If they did fail, was it because they were too freethinking and had possibly irritated their powerful competitors? Were they offensive in some other way, and not what the powers might consider of good appearance? If I didn't make it, would it be because of any medical or academic reason?

I also began to think about the subject of competition, in particular the medical fraternity's fear of competition from bright young doctors. I was a well-established doctor before I retired, so I can say it as I see it: Doctors are competitive and many are also fearful of competition, especially in Hollywood. Here they strive to keep the VIPs for themselves. It's as simple and as cruel as that. I suspect it's not much different in the legal profession. They have the bar, and they make it just as difficult to pass as possible, too. Or just like in a brothel, the old keep the young away from their favorite clients. Forget ability; forget skill. Fix it so the young are stuck with the unimportant work; keep them on the outside looking in, so the important, moneymaking cases come to the established physicians. Do not allow too many similar specialists to practice in your area. Let them be damned. The academic institutions share some of the responsibility. Some of them want to control us and keep us as students for as long as they can. Did gender and ethnicity play and part in it? I may be wrong, but it wouldn't surprise me. I'm sure the powers that be thought they are protecting the public.

This is a horrendous practice, and a waste of good doctors, who are so badly needed. To restrict youth, including the non-conformist, women and minorities from the upper echelon of medical practice is flagrantly unjustified. These young people are fresh from years of study, full of dedication and vigor. They have peak surgical skills, attained as the result of operating every day as a resident. Instead of being allowed to practice their trade, they are relegated for far too many years to submissive roles.

This is wrong! Medicine should not be an arena for charades and competing physicians. A doctor's effort and energy should be spent dealing with patients who are in great need of quality care. Doctors should not be dueling with colleagues nor tiptoeing around them and their hallowed grounds. The practice of medicine is very close to my heart. It is my life's work. In many ways it is my life. What goes on behind the scenes: the in-fighting, the competition, and the doctor vs. doctor politics, has troubled me deeply for years.

Once a doctor has finished training and passed the written board exams, he or she should be accepted as a qualified doctor. We don't need a Kangaroo Court making that decision years later. If training programs turned out inadequate physicians, then intensive investigation should be undertaken and the necessary changes of the program made. While there are bound to be a few immoral doctors who perform unnecessary surgeries and practice dishonest medicine, they can later be controlled by the hospital boards. The same effort should be spent to keep a doctor from becoming incompetent, and I'm happy to say a system of medical checks and balances does exist.

At the time I finished my board exam the heat was off. Once a doctor received certification, educational requirements were finished for the rest of his or her life. However, that was also problematic. Eventually re-certification became a requirement. That's a big step forward. But it would also be nice if professors were required to demonstrate clinical competence by doing the work by which they judge others. Many answers to the questions that present themselves in the practice of medicine are not in the books. The practice of medicine is more than academic. It is without question an art.

Thirty-four days after my return to California, the letter arrived from the board in the morning mail. I opened the letter. There it was, the certificate, all signed and sealed. I let it lay on the desk for several moments, gazing at it. Then I handed it to my nurse so that she could have a look at the document. "That's just fine doctor," and handed it back to me. There was no particular exultation in her voice.

I remember a thought coursing through my brain at that moment: "Certification is only important when you don't have it," just as it was still important to Paul, who had failed to pass *again*.

I've been retired for over fifteen years now, and much has changed for the better. A lot of the politics have been removed. Gender and skin color are no longer of primary importance, in fact more women practice OB/GYN than men today. Senior physicians don't have the power they used to have. But many things in life don't change that much. Our preference of our own kind clandestinely persists.

Westinghouse Manufacturing & Electric Co. Poster | 1943

8 ROSIE THE RIVETER

During World War II American women entered the workforce in remarkable numbers as men enlisting in the army left holes in the industrial labor force. Women became the workers for the munitions industry, thus creating a most iconic image in "Rosie the Riveter". During the forties the women's workforce soared, and by 1945 nearly one out of every four married women worked outside the home. They soon learned life was more exciting than being a housewife. Many didn't want to return. Their new lives were more rewarding, and they didn't want to return to their old boring ways. Some wanted a life more like men and less like housewives. They loved their new sense of freedom. They made their own money and no longer needed a husband. However, they soon found themselves searching for love just like men.

Love. What is love? Poets describe love best. Men of science such as myself attempting to describe love find their words cryptic, clinical, and lacking sensuality. If love makes the world go around - it makes mine spin. Without love and lovemaking, I wouldn't of had a career. That being said, passion and love are not the same, though they are frequently linked. To many, love is analogous to sex. Most sex books even interlock the word love with sexual pleasure. If the sex is great it's only ten percent of the marriage, but if it's poor, it's ninety percent of the marriage. There are few happy marriages without a good sex life. However, if we are to make a serious attempt at establishing a more enjoyable sex life, we first have to recognize that lovemaking encompasses far more than the act of coition.

The basic purpose of sex in all living organisms is procreation. Among lower animals, courtship displays serve to attract the desired member of the opposite sex. This promotes propagation and at the same time assures species' specificity. Color displays and movement patterns are unique and attractive only to their own-kind. In that way we human beings are the same, although our courtship displays are a lot more complicated. The males in most species, including human males, are almost always ready. They are just waiting for the right female to give them the signal. These displays set up a chain reaction of stimuli in which a signal from the female triggers a reaction in the male. Unfortunately, she often sends a broad signal. Unintended males may receive it as well. They all in turn make their moves. She must pick the right male and he must win over the rival males. Having won he must now make his own right moves in order to trigger the female to make the next successive step. Human courtship displays are varied and mysterious. Some men don't get it right. If anything interrupts the flow of this chain reaction from one step to the other, successful lovemaking may not occur. This can be the end of the affair.

It's not much different for the modern female. The male black widow spider must do it right and do it quick and then run like hell or he will be lunch. They don't call her a widow for nothing. It's not much different for the tarantula spider. He also has a good chance of being his mate's lunch. The male porcupine only has one day per month to make his attempt and he better do it very carefully! All a young lion (the king of beasts) has to do is kill or drive out the current king, and the pride is his and all the females in it. The females even tolerate the killing and eating of their young so they will come into estrus. Thank God it's not that way for us humans.

Humans are much more complex than lower animals. Each woman has her own needs and wants and most of the time she doesn't even know or understand what it is she needs and wants. These feelings swirl around in her brain and become a sensuous response called love. These needs and wants come from her DNA as well as her early childhood experiences. Her young adult interaction with her father, mother, and others as she grows up also has an influence but to a far lesser degree. By contrast, the male is simple. All most want is to have a good meal and sex. Getting him to sign a long-term contract, however, is against his basic nature as his long term needs and wants are often unknown to him.

Not to mention, we are molded by the culture of the society in which we are raised. Distinct courtship displays for both men and women have been utilized by different societies at varying times. At the turn of the century, it was the turn of a woman's ankle that turned a man on. The early Polynesian women were amused by the foreign sailor's sexual interest in their bare breasts. In their society, breasts were not involved in sexual display. With the same disregard, Polynesian women would masturbate their children (both girls and boys) to sooth and quiet them. During and after WWII, the topless bar became a very popular place for men to view breasts, large or small. Now many young women have their breasts augmented at great expense and discomfort just to have breasts they feel will appeal to others. Even high fashion models that were once required to have a flat chest are now lining up to get theirs done.

Remember, among humans the first step is for the female to attract the male. Men are often more stimulated by what they see, while women are more stimulated by what they hear. Some women like "dirty talk". They like to hear all about the nasty things he's going to do to her. For others, this same talk turns them totally off. They would rather attend poetry readings. Human sexual attractions vary from Chaucer's long-suffering Griselda to the wives of Henry VII of England and his murdering ways. What does it all mean? There are all types of human beings and as many human courtship displays as there are people.

DORA

Dora first came to me shortly after graduating from UCLA cum-lade -- still a virgin at twenty-one, she was ready to start her sex life. She was a tall, stately and beautiful, Vargas-type woman. She planned to join the corporate world and be the next president of a major corporation - I thought, "a bit unrealistic even in today's times." But I said nothing. Her father was a successful self-made man. Her mother was artistic and very supportive.

She had just met Vic, a pit-boss gambler in Las Vegas with a tall, dark and handsome appearance. Dora said, "Victor C. Mobius is a man of the real world. I was raised as a protected snob. Vic said I was sent to him for my 'karmic experience'." She laughed and I thought, *that's different*. I wanted to hear more. She continued, "I'm still a virgin and I want to get rid of it. It's time. I want to learn the real aspects of life. But I want to do it right. I don't want to get pregnant."

"It's none of my business, but are you in love with Victor?"

"Vic is older and so virile and he loves me. He's good for me." I examined her, gave her a prescription for the pill and wished her good luck. A few months later Dora came in pregnant. "What happened to your pills, didn't you take them?" I asked.

"I stopped taking them. They made me fat." This didn't make too much sense to me. She was a sophisticated mature woman talking absolute nonsense. "What are you going to do?" I asked.

"Get an abortion. Vic is married, you know."

"No I didn't know."

"It's not his fault. His wife won't give him a divorce. He wants to marry me." I just looked at her. "He's going to divorce her and marry me, but he can't do it right now." I didn't argue the point. In the end I did an abortion for Dora and she went back on the pills. This time she took them.

I didn't hear from Dora for over a year, and then one-day she called to tell me that she was getting married to Vic. I was really surprised. I didn't think Vic would ever marry her. It wasn't very long thereafter that she came in pregnant and was very happy. On one of her prenatal visits she asked, "Are women supposed to have orgasms like men?" I just looked at her and said nothing. "Men seem to have more fun than women. It's not fair." There was a long pause then she continued, "I was talking to my girlfriend. We agree it's better to be a man. They get all the breaks. In the company where I work they promote those stupid assholes just because they are males." She looked at me, "Vic says it's not necessary for a woman to have an orgasm." She looked down at the floor, then continued, "He likes me to go down on him most of the time."

"How do you feel about that?"

"It's one-sided. It's not fair."

"Then why do you do it?"

She looked up at me and said, "I love him and he likes it so much." I agreed that it didn't seem fair but unfortunately it's not that unusual. Some women never achieve a full orgasmic response, yet they say they are happy. It's been my experience that many women are not orgasmic with every man all the time. On the other hand, some women are just as orgasmic as their male counterparts.

I delivered Dora's son and later a little girl. We never discussed her sex life again. When her two children were in their teens Vic left Dora for a younger woman. Dora became the CEO of a multimillion-dollar corporation. She is now menopausal and seems reasonable happy. There have been affairs through the years, but as time has gone on she has become more and more angry and bitter toward men. Many of us live our lives in what appears to be unsatisfactory relationships, yet we stay the course just like Dora. Maybe she is happy in her own way. I'm not one to judge that. One thing I know for sure, with all his faults, Vic is the only man that Dora ever loved.

GEORGETTE

Georgette Mosbacher, a prominent socialite and businesswoman, was not just one of my patients but also the wife of my longtime friend and business partner, Robert Muir. I helped Bob early in his real estate career to create and design the twin high-rise office buildings on La Brea at the entrance to the Hollywood Walk of Fame. I became a junior partner and partial owner of those buildings. My offices were in the penthouse of 7080 Hollywood Boulevard and I spent about 15 years practicing there. I went on to deliver two of Bob's children (with his second wife, Robin) and became their godfather.

But back to Georgette, a fiery redhead who's father died when she was only seven. Her mother was forced to work outside of the home, leaving Georgette to look after her three young siblings. I'm assuming that tough beginning left Georgette with one goal -- become rich and powerful so as to never relive her upbringing again. Beautiful and charming, Georgette set her sights on Bob Muir at a nautical auction where he bid on nearly everything. She told him she was a journalist for a magazine and wanted to do a story on him. They met for lunch at the Hungry Tiger, the restaurant in our office building, and they got along swimmingly. Halfway through the interview, Georgette confessed that she wasn't a journalist but had merely found Bob fascinating.

Shortly thereafter they were married and they went on to throw wonderful parties in their Bel Air home. They would hire the likes of Kenny Rogers to play the piano at such events. Their hallway was lined with framed photos of them with countless celebrities. One time, Georgette moved my wife, Susan, out of the photo she was posing for with me. This was long before PhotoShop where she could have just nixed her in one click. Only high profile people would be framed in those photos. I'm not sure what she saw in me.

Georgette divorced Bob Muir, taking one of the Rolls Royce with her and moved on to George Barrie. Given he was the head of Faberge, she was given a prominent position on the board which gave her access into the cosmetics world. Two years later she divorced George Barrie and moved onto another man of prominence. She married Robert A. Mosbacher who went on to become Secretary of Commerce and confidant for George H.W. Bush. Georgette became the hostess with the mostest in D.C. holding fundraisers for the Republican Party.

She also maintained her business associations with cosmetics, buying upscale La Prairie Cosmetics beating out Revlon in her bid. She later sold La Prairie and is now a consultant for the cosmetics company Borghese. Though Georgette's book titles certainly give perspective to her life, *Feminine Force* and *It Takes Money, Honey* -- she has spent a lot of time as a philanthropist. She founded The New York Center for Children which provides free, comprehensive evaluation and therapy services to victims of child abuse. I certainly have to admire her, Georgette achieved her goal and then some!

KAREN

In the nineteen-seventies the sexual revolution created many strong independent, young, intelligent women trying to cope with their newfound sexual freedom. Karen was just such a case. Tall, proud, with elbow length strawberry blonde hair, Karen was a student at UCLA. She sat before me dressed in blue jeans, a sweatshirt and sneakers with rolled up white socks. Her artistic face was immobile. Only in the nervous play of her long fingers, toying with the curl of her hair was there any external sign of her inner tensions and anxieties. She was twenty years of age. My pelvic examination confirmed that she was indeed pregnant. Though her coltish body had not yet given any outward indications to the casual eye that she was already four months along. I did notice that she had stretch marks on her lower abdomen and presumed that this was not her first pregnancy.

I looked intently into her eyes, "Yes, you are pregnant." I paused, then added, "Again."

"How do you know?" She was shaken from her studied pose, her voice scarcely audible, "About the first one, I mean?" Before I could answer she asked in an unbelieving tone, "Are you sure? That is, am I really pregnant?"

I assured her that there was no doubt about my diagnosis. This young woman of strength stood up, went to the window and gazed at the nearby Hollywood Hills. She was stony silent.

"What are you going to do?" I asked.

She stumbled into her chair with her face drawn. She had the face of a woman fully-grown before her time. She slumped in her chair looked me straight in the eye and said, "I - I don't know." She turned, looked out the window and continued, "Have an abortion, I suppose."

"What about the father? What is preventing you from getting married?"

Her lips tightened, "It wouldn't be right. He's a medical student living at home and he's too poor to study medicine without his parent's help. Besides, I wouldn't let him make that sacrifice for me. I wouldn't impose myself on him. He'd never really love me. He'd hate me and the baby." She stood up challenging me to dispute her claim.

I changed the subject, "What happened the last time you were pregnant?"

"I was seventeen, I had my baby and gave it up for adoption."

"How did you feel about that?"

"I didn't feel very much of anything. It was the only right thing to do."

"Why?"

"Because of the way it happened, I mean, my getting pregnant. You see, we live in a community of very nice people. They're bright, even intellectual. My dad is a research chemist. He and mom's friends are all college graduates some of them with two or three degrees like dad. I spent my childhood and adolescence trying to escape these learned bores. When I went to the State University, I thought it would be heaven. It wasn't, I hated it. I felt more lost than I did at home. The courses in college were dull, duller than they were in high school. My freshman companions seemed like children. Although I was one of the

58

youngest in the class, they were all immature. Just as everyone my age has always been to me." She paused, lit a cigarette, and with a smile on her face continued, "I was a drop-out from kindergarten you know. They wanted us to paint with our fingers, and I didn't like finger paints. The teacher made us take a nap on hard Japanese mats. I couldn't curl up and be comfortable. They wouldn't teach us to read. I wanted to read and draw with a pencil, and paint with a brush. I guess I've always been different."

"A maverick?"

"I guess so, the boy I was going with was alright. We started having sex, not so much because we wanted to, but because everyone else our age was doing it. When I came home for the Christmas holidays I didn't want to go back to college, but I knew I had to because mom and dad expected me to. I got pregnant the last night I was home. My boyfriend and I had been at a dance. We weren't getting along very well because he had started drinking since he'd gone to college. That night he was quite drunk. When we got home, he wanted to have sex. I didn't want to, but he was insistent. He was determined and I was afraid of him. I lay down on the floor in the library and just kept hoping he'd finish before my folks came home. We didn't use contraceptives. We never did. He always withdrew, but he was drunk and couldn't stop before he came. I rushed him out of the house and went to bed and cried and thought how silly everything in my life had become. Secretly, I think I really wanted to get pregnant so I wouldn't have to go back to school with those dull kids, those dull teachers, and those dull classes where I couldn't even concentrate. When I returned to college, I withdrew more and more into myself. In no time at all I knew that I was pregnant. I'd run down the corridor early in the morning and vomit before the other girls in the dorm would even get up. I knew I was pregnant and didn't care. I didn't know what to do though. I'd sleep and sleep and when I was asleep I'd dream that it was all in my imagination. When I'd wake up, I'd think maybe it had all gone away. Then I'd be sick again, and my breasts had started swelling and I hadn't had my period for nearly three months. When spring vacation came, I went home."

"Did you tell the boy?"

"No, because I knew our parents would want us to get married and I didn't want to marry him. I knew it would be an awful marriage. He'd eventually go to work in his dad's factory, and I'd be trapped in the same old world, with the same standards I'd always hated. I knew it would be a living death for me, but I can't explain it. My mother got suspicious because I was terribly nauseated and losing weight. She said she thought I was anemic and dragged me to see her doctor, that's when I told her that I was pregnant. She was shocked, but she and dad were really groovy about the whole thing. Especially when I consider how much older they are, and how they're so conservative. When they asked me what I wanted to do, I said I wanted to come to Los Angeles and stay with my older sister who was going to UCLA, have the baby, and give it up for adoption. This worried my mom, because you see she has four kids and she was able to keep and love her children. She couldn't imagine giving up a baby!"

"Do you think it would have been different if she were seventeen instead of forty-seven?"

"No, I don't think so, I don't think it was a generation gap in thinking. She just couldn't understand. We were talking to each other but we weren't communicating."

She paused, smiled and a slight flush rose on her high cheekbones. "My sister and her friends were really groovy. I stayed with them right up to the last few weeks, and then I went to a home where my folks had arranged for me to have my baby. It was a strange experience. I mean, the whole physiological change. I was really interested in what was happening to my body, but I wasn't interested in the baby. I didn't even see it. I asked if it was alright. They told me it had red hair like mine. I felt like I had created the baby all by myself. I forgot all about the guy, or what part he had played. I just knew I never wanted to see him again. Not that I'd deliberately avoid him, but I wouldn't seek his company. It was when I went home that all the confusion set in. I couldn't understand my parents' attitude. My mother didn't think I should talk about my experience. Not out of shame or disgrace to her and dad, but because it would set me apart, make me different. She and dad just didn't realize that I was already set apart. They refused to face the fact that I had given birth to a child, that I was really changed inside and out, and despite the difficulties. It had been a wonderful experience. Finally I told them I couldn't live at home any longer. I didn't want to go back to school and room in a dormitory with all those silly do-wells who were different from me. I was just too bored. So, dad gave me an allowance and I came back to LA and enrolled at UCLA. I began to meet some real people. I had to study hard to catch up. I met Robert and we started having sex almost a year ago. I had my sister's contraceptive pills. They worked fine, but one weekend I forgot to take them."

"Why did you take the chance?"

She was quite tense, but thoughtfully looking hard at me she asked, "Do you really want to know?"

"Yes."

"I think I felt unsatisfied. I wanted to be pregnant again. Even though I knew everything was wrong, I wanted to have a baby."

"Do you want to have this baby and keep it?" Her face answered for her. "Yes, I can't possibly give up another one. I'd rather have an abortion and take a chance with my own life than give up my baby."

"Do you know that you can go on welfare, which would make it possible for you to keep your child?"

"No, tell me." The eagerness in her voice rang out through the room.

We made arrangements for her to go on welfare. I knew, psychologically it was important for Karen to have this baby and keep it. Again, during this pregnancy, she came to dismiss the father as being any part of her pregnancy. She later confessed to me that when she finished her first visit, she walked out of my office onto the street and had a desire to run up to strangers and shout. "Look at me! I'm going to have a baby!" Her reactions then naturally went from stages of euphoria to hard-core questioning of how she was going to accomplish the project of having her child, keeping it and raising it. She continued her studies, dropped out of school for one semester to have her baby and then returned to finish her education. Among her "groovy" new friends, she found acceptance of her chosen role. The times had changed especially in Los Angeles. She admired herself for her determination to have a child and keep it.

In actuality, she was acting out her innate antisocial personality, which had been a part of her being since she was born. She was by nature a "loner" and her behavior pattern was in accord with the rules she had laid down for herself. By being a "loser" (a two time loser, actually, by her parents standard) Karen was determined to prove that by losing in the eyes of society she was in truth winning in her own eyes. She was a strong-willed, strong-minded young woman. Her inner hostility toward her parents' way of life, whom she professed to love and respect was evident in her tendency to berate the men with whom she had become pregnant. Unconsciously, Karen was hitting back at her father (who was an all A student, top athlete and graduated magna cum laude). Being the third child, she possibly resented the social activities of her older sisters who were a carbon copy of her parents. Since little Karen was different she wasn't treated like her sisters. The birth of a fourth child (a much-desired son) robbed her of being the "apple of her father's eye". Almost in defiance she deliberately selected "weak" men. Though there is no logical reason why any young man would not be proud to marry a girl like Karen, with her family background, financial independence, good looks, and above average intelligence. Perhaps that's why Karen selected men who were willing to let her do it her way.

Now alone, she had an unconscious thought, "Oh, I wish I could go home and get all my maternity clothes that I had from my last time. That would be one expense I wouldn't have." She carried on through the pregnancy, refusing to face the fact that, in time her parents would have to know. I asked, "Why don't you want to tell your parents?" She said, "I reckon they'd think I ought to be sterilized doing the same foolish thing again, or at least have my head examined!"

Karen was constantly torn between her rational thought and her different behavior. She was a profound individualist thriving on the words of her favorite philosopher, Friedrich Nietzsche, a German philosopher moralist who rejected Western bourgeois civilization. In her fantasy, she was the super-woman initiating a new heroic feminine morality. Lacking the creativity of Nietzsche she linked her procreative forces to her passion for motherhood and hoped to live a level of experience beyond the conventional standards of good and evil. Karen would never be the traditional incubator to grow the male's sperm into a child.

Only time would tell if the results of her convictions were correct. Karen gave birth to her baby and she went on to raise it, maybe alone. I knew though that when she first came to my office, she knew full well she was pregnant. The fact she let three months go by before coming to my office for an examination proved that. She'd been there before. She *pretended* to be seriously considering an abortion, but the medical student who impregnated her in the first place could have easily arranged this if she had that desire. Subconsciously, Karen got pregnant purposely, as a result of her metamorphosis following the first pregnancy in which she gave up her child. The entire experience may have been therapeutic for Karen in that she was forced to realistically act out her idealistic fantasies. Frequently the maternal instinct is much stronger than any love a woman may have for the father of the child. It certainly was the case with Karen.

So-again - what is love? It's a unique mysterious feeling, different but distinct for each living being. In the end, the purpose is the continuation of our own mankind. The problems that have to be faced today and tomorrow require a reaffirmation of love and spiritual feeling, which leads to sex. In order to gain this understanding one must know that love is the supreme act of communion between two people, but it it's only the beginning. Out of this act there can come commitment, responsibilities, and maybe children. Sex is most likely to be gratifying if there is regard, trust and expectation of further experiences without the feeling of exploitation. Passion is short lived. Love is forever. And although Rosie the Riveter may be an outdated reference point, her independent streak is more alive than ever in today's women. From the boardroom to the bedroom, men cannot look to sex as a way to manipulate women into getting what they want.

Marlon Brando

9 STARGAZING

After I finished my internship at Harbor General Hospital in Torrance, California I wanted to continue my residency there, but I wasn't accepted. Irene was pregnant with Lynne, our second child. I needed to secure an obstetrician to deliver the baby, and he would have to be connected with the hospital where I'd be working. I decided to go to Hollywood Presbyterian on the recommendation of my professor at USC. It's a decision I'll never regret. Hollywood Presbyterian turned out to be the very best place for me. All I wanted was to learn how to be a woman's doctor, and deliver babies. Some of my teachers at USC delivered their private patients there. There were many prominent doctors in private practice to teach me as well. I felt good about that, but their patients -- wow! Some were movie stars!

My first brush with celebrity from a medical perspective occurred there in 1959. I was in my mid-thirties and had just been accepted into the residency program. At the time a movie called *The Misfits* was very much in the news. Although it turned out to be a brilliant film, the shoot was fraught with many problems for its three major stars. It was the final film for all of them: Marilyn Monroe, Montgomery Cliff and Clark Gable. At that time Clark Gable was the true "King of Hollywood."

I was told that his role was physically taxing and that he was also under a great deal of stress working with the more and more unpredictable Marilyn. When he suffered a massive heart attack, shortly after filming was completed, he was admitted to Hollywood Presbyterian Hospital -- not by a cardiologist, but by his wife's obstetrician, Richard Clark M.D., under whom I was a resident. Of course the best cardiologist available treated Gable, but it's a little known fact that he was sequestered in a big corner room of the gynecology floor. In spite of all heroic attempts, the King died.

As news of Gable's death circulated, friends and fans all over the world went into mourning. A few months later his widow, the lovely actress Kay Spreckles, had his son. The whole of Hollywood was electrified, awaiting the birth of Clark Gable's son. Guards were posted all around the hospital to keep the press out. The pressure was intense, and I still remember vividly the awesome responsibility Dr. Clark (and all of us in attendance) felt during this delivery. My introduction to Tinseltown was on its way.

The 1930's started the Golden Age of Hollywood. In the beginning most of the movie moguls were from New York. We had five major Hollywood movie studios. The studios had many of the stars under contracts, and owned large theaters throughout the country. So there were many good paying jobs for many.

In 1948 the Supreme Court ruled that movie studios could not own it all, and the era of the powerful Hollywood studio had unofficially ended. When that monopoly law went into affect and movie moguls were done. At the same time other states and countries offered the movie industry better and better deals, so the movie stars followed their jobs. Slowly the movie industry began to collapse in Hollywood. But for most of us it was no problem. Hollywood is a wonderful place to live, so millions flocked here from all around the world. The days were warm, and the sun light was long and bright. In the early days artificial light was not strong enough for shooting many films.

So it was no surprise that near the end of my residential training I obtained the unusual job of providing doctors to go on location for Paramount Studio movie shoots. When a film went on location, the studio sent a doctor along with the cast and crew, and it was my job to supply doctors. I supplied the doctors from my fellow residents around the city, and went on several shoots myself.

Most of the shoots were for one day, so it was easy to free up one of us to go. We would just cover for one another. If a week or two were needed I would find someone that had vacation time coming and wanted to spend that time working for the movies.

This may sound glamorous, but believe me, it wasn't. We were far "below the line", essentially an unsanctimonious member of the crew. We would get on the bus with the crew at the crack of dawn, and work until the day wrapped, whenever that might be. The important people would arrive much later and leave much earlier. The fact that we were highly-skilled doctors meant very little.

I went on one quite abnormal shoot with Anthony Quinn and Sophia Loren. It was a Western and was filming in the mountains of Arizona. One morning I got a frantic call from the production office. Instead of going through us for the shoot, they had obtained the aid of a local doctor and many members on the crew were sick. The stars were fine, spending most of their time playing chess, but many of the crew and other cast members were a mess.

They had hired two crews and were shooting at two different locations. Many of their people were too sick to work, and it was costing the studio big bucks. So at their request I personally went there to see if I could sort things out. Fortunately it was an offer I didn't refuse. It all began with a huge limo pulling up in front of my humble abode (and believe me, it was very humble). From then on, it was first class all the way. I had a driver all the time I was there, ate at the stars' table and was made an honorary member of this and that. I was elevated to near star status. I had the best of everything. Fortunately I even healed the sick.

The local doctor had been giving them only throat lozenges, which doesn't do much for pneumonia! And the young woman who was complaining that her arm hurt had something to really complain about - it was broken! With a lot of antibiotics for the crew and B12 shots for the executives, I got things going again.

Another unforgettable moment from my time as a studio doctor came when I received a call to send a different doctor to a set in northern California. The doctor I had already sent to the shoot was too "uptight" for them. When Marlon Brando sent a girl around to keep the doctor company, the doctor apparently was not amused and refused. He didn't understand Hollywood and their liberal ways. Who needs a working girl while they're working? He was fired on the spot and the production wanted me to send up another more *easygoing* medical man. I must say I rather enjoyed telling them to forget it.

The 1960's were a time of radical social change especially in California. We now had hippies, druggies, and back to nature-ies -- multitudes of young adventurers came to sunny California seeking a new way to live. Young people who wanted to break with the "establishment", and live outside the structured society of their parents. They wanted to have their babies delivered by a midwife at home in a more natural setting with all their friends sharing in the experience. This was all very romantic, but had been abandoned many years earlier by doctors because it wasn't safe for either the baby or the mother. Midwives were ill-equipped to get some babies to start breathing after delivery. When the babies were rushed to Children's Hospital it was often too late. Some young mothers were rushed into our emergency room all bled out from uncontrollable postpartum hemorrhage. This foolishness had become serious. Lives were being lost, but it didn't deter the hippies. They were willing to take the risks. Most of the time having a baby is a beautiful natural experience, but when it doesn't precede normally it can be disastrous. Nature doesn't always get it right.

A group of OB and pediatric nurses at Hollywood Presbyterian and Children's Hospitals were complaining and wanted to stop home deliveries. I was chairman of the department at that time, and I'd heard of a hospital in San Francisco where they were delivering babies in an ABC (alternative birth center), so I sent a couple nurses to investigate. As a result we opened the first ABC in Southern California hoping we could get these ill-informed young people out of their homes and into the hospital for their deliveries.

We set aside a large room just outside the delivery area. The patients would labor, deliver, and recover in that room. They could invite their family and a few friends, play their music, and make a big event of it, if they wished. The doctors and nurses would come and go, as the patient desired. They frequently stayed for just one day after delivery, so it was also cheaper.

The ABC way of having babies had become of interest to the Los Angeles Times, so they sent a reporter to interview me to learn all about our new birthing center. She spent a couple days, took pictures, and wrote a two-page article in the *View* section of the Times. I ended up back in the news, thankfully this time with praise.

Ultimately, young couples were looking for a better way to deliver their babies with less medical interference and drugs. This was even true for the rich and famous. Loni Hall-Alpert was one of my pregnant ladies, and she wanted me to attend a lecture on a different type delivery. Apparently French author and obstetrician, Frederick Leboyer, was giving a lecture on a new Russian way of delivering babies under water. It sounded crazy to me, but Herb, Lonny's husband, wanted me to attend so I did. I even discussed the method with Leboyer, but I told them I didn't think it was a good idea. It would be difficult for me to assist properly during delivery, there would be an increased risk of infection, and the baby may inhale the water. Just because Igor Charkovsky, a male midwife, had done extensive research in the Soviet Union didn't mean I was ready to be the first one to do it here. I still think it's risky, but midwives continue to perform water births.

I knew I had to do something very special for this couple. Loni was a star in her own right. I first met her when she was a star singer with Sergio Mendes & Brazil '66. They'd already had many smash hits. Herb was a musical legend, writer, producer, singer, and creator of A&M records along with Gerry Moss. At the time A&M was one of the most successful recording labels in the world. He also created The Tijuana Brass. In 1966 his TJB albums outsold the Beatles.

Herb said, "When I make a record I hire all the people involved personally. I want to control all the elements. That's the way I get the best results. I don't want you to do anything less for the delivery of my baby." So, I assured him I'd be on top of everything. I went to the administration of a small hospital and worked out a deal where I would be totally in charge of everything. Herb agreed to pay for it all. I'd pick the nurses, the anesthesiologist, an assistant surgeon on stand-by, in addition to all the other elements. We did a very special delivery for Aria although it turned out to be routine. Everyone was happy.

By the 1970's, this little boy from Idaho was sitting pretty in a well-appointed penthouse suite at the corner of Hollywood Boulevard and La Brea Avenue. I had a view stretching from the Hollywood Sign to the Pacific Ocean. On a clear day I really could see forever, even to Catalina Island. But inside my office I was getting a much different kind of view. I was seeing a privileged side of Hollywood that very few were privy to. I was to share with many stars their excitements, pleasures, and all too often, their tragedies.

Patsy Sullivan walked into my consultation room with the confidence of a top dog and handed me a note from her father and famous actor, Barry Sullivan. It read: "This will introduce my daughter. I want you to be her gynecologist and this note gives you my permission to prescribe and care for her." I looked up from the note. What a beauty! She was only fourteen, but she had all the anatomical attributes of a Hollywood superstar. I later learned that she had been on the cover of *Teen* magazine. I'm very happy to say this was the beginning of a lifelong friendship.

While still a teenager, Patsy would marry the talented young composer, Jimmy Webb. Their wedding in Ojai at the ranch of Jimmy Messina (of Loggins & Messina fame) was a sight to behold. Half of Hollywood was there, including The Beatles' John Lennon. Patsy arrived in high style, riding in the car that James Dean had driven in the film *East of Eden*. At this time I was remarried and I remember my third wife and I sitting among the throngs of guests when Barry Sullivan put his hand on my shoulder. "You're on the wrong side, you're a Sullivan -- not a Webb."

Patsy and Jimmy went on to live in a wonderful home on six-acres in Encino. Their family room, with its incredible twenty-foot stained glass window of the four Beatles, was a friendly gathering place for the likes of Cher, Glen Campbell and Michael Douglas.

On Jimmy's thirty-eighth birthday, they went all out with a full orchestra and dinner for two hundred. Since Jimmy was an avid glider pilot, Susan, my second wife, had found him an antique altimeter. When we entered the house, there was so much going on that Susan tucked the gift behind a vase of lilies in the living room. Hours later when Jimmy finally got around to opening his presents, surprise, surprise; they were all gone! A truck, driven by thieves, had pulled up during the celebration, loaded up all the gifts, and had taken off. The only present Jimmy got that night was the altimeter hidden behind the vase of lilies.

Through the Webbs, I got to know Michael Douglas who sent his first wife, Diandra, to me. I delivered their son, Cameron. After my own daughter, Samantha, was born (two weeks later) -- a group of us were all spending another evening at the Webbs. While we sipped cocktails, several of our children were bedded down in their beautiful nursery, which was complete with antique cribs lined with European lace. When Anne Douglas went into the nursery to check on her grandson, Cameron, he was screaming away at the top of his lungs. So were most of the other babies. After getting them quieted down, Anne came back to report that through it all, my baby, Samantha, laid there angelically, fast asleep. "Hah," said Anne. "Trust the obstetrician to keep the best one for himself."

Susan and I were later invited to Michael's own elegant Spanish hacienda near Santa Barbara for a Cinco de Mayo party. Upon our arrival a big Mariachi band welcomed us along with lots of people in colorful costumes. After sipping a few margaritas we learned that we were at the wrong party, Michael Douglas lived a few doors away. We left and went to Michael's, but his party was a lot tamer with a much smaller band and no costumes.

One of my very good friends was Eddie Kafafian who started out as an actor and then went into Public Relations with Fox Studios. I treated Eddie's aging parents and I delivered his son, Lee Newman. Later on, when Lee was singing on stage at the legendary Troubadour night club, Lee would introduce me as his gynecologist. Lee had two famous grandfathers on his mother's side, Eddie Cantor, and the songwriter Jimmy McHugh who wrote classics like "On the Sunny Side of the Street". Eddie Kafafian and his wife Leah were wonderful at socializing and would befriend many of the great stars with whom Eddie worked, Steve McQueen and Anthony Hopkins among them.

Eddie would arrange large screenings of the latest films at Fox and would always allow me to invite as many friends as I wanted. For the film, *The Man with Bogart's Face*, about twenty-five of my friends attended and what a lovely surprise awaited us. The star of the film, Robert Sacchi, was there of course and we got to sit close to him in the VIP section. But then suddenly there was a small commotion accompanied with some quiet "oohs" and a reverent silence. I looked up and there was Grace Kelly, at that point known as Princess Grace of Monaco, looking as elegant and lovely as she ever had on screen. She laughed when Eddie introduced me to her as his gynecologist and then quickly explained that I was his whole family's doctor. Sadly, Grace passed away just two years later at the young age of fifty-two from a stoke resulting in a fatal car accident.

Meanwhile, back at the office, the pace continued. One day my secretary Eunice was typing away and looked out into the waiting room. She became catatonic. She rushed in and grabbed me by the arm. When I went out for a look, there sat the Godfather himself, Marlon Brando, amidst a number of very pregnant women!

Unbeknownst to me, he was there with a female friend. When I asked him if he wouldn't rather wait in a private sitting room, he politely declined. "Nah, I belong out here with the other big bellies." I was glad he didn't remember that I'd been the doctor who'd refused to recruit a new doctor for his earlier film.

Lynn Carlin was a patient of mine. Among all the starlets and Miss Universes on my books, Lynn could have initially been considered unremarkable. Well, apparently I was wrong. Lynn was working as a secretary for noted director, Robert Altman, at a division of Columbia Pictures known as Screen Gems. At the same time the renowned actor and avant garde director, John Cassavetes, was also working at Screen Gems. Cassavetes would often borrow Lynn to read lines with him while he was writing the script for his movie *Faces* which starred his wife Gena Rowlands. When Altman fired Lynn it was the best thing that happened to her. Cassavetes hired her to act in his film and wouldn't you know! Lynn was nominated as Supporting Actress for an Academy Award. She lost out to Cassavetes own co-star in *Rosemary's Baby*, Ruth Gordon. All the same, I was so excited for her!!

When I first started private practice I was called to see a patient in the emergency room that the regular on-call doctor refused to see. I had very few patients at that time so I was glad to see any patient. As I looked down at Betty (her skin was whiter than her blonde hair), she was desperately ill. Her temperature was 105° and she was still bleeding heavily. She'd had a criminal abortion a few days before (abortions were illegal at that time), and she had a very good chance of dying. If she did, there would be a criminal investigation and the doctor would become part of it. No doctor wants to be involved in a criminal case even if it's only as a witness.

I was no hero, I had just opened my practice and had very little else to do -- so I took the case. I put Betty on IV antibiotics, gave her blood transfusions and did a D&C (dilatation and curettage) to remove the infected tissue. I did my best, knowing if she died I'd be in court. We must have gotten some help from above that day because this desperately ill lady recovered in spite of the fact that she had gas gangrene and was in the hospital severely infected for several weeks.

At some point I met the young man that had gotten her pregnant. I was prepared not to like this guy, even if he was a big star. As a child he was a well-known western singer, and at the time I met him he was a well-known music arranger and guitarist.

Betty recovered and they eventually got married. When they decided to have a baby I thought that would be a real miracle, as severely infected as Betty had been. I didn't think she had a chance of getting pregnant, but I was wrong. Betty was soon pregnant with a little girl. While Betty was in labor I was invited to join the star and his friends in the hospital dining room for lunch. I did and he introduced me to his four friends, Mr. And Mrs. Lambert and a Mr. And Mrs. Somebody-else. Well, as the luncheon progressed I slowly realized that I was having lunch with Nancy Sinatra and Marlo Thomas and their lesser-known husbands. A perfect example why women shouldn't be introduced by only their husband's name.

At that time Betty's husband had just completed the arrangement for Nancy Sinatra's TV special. The song and the special were big hits. When Betty's husband became Frank Sinatra's conductor, he invited my wife and I to Las Vegas for one of Frank's concerts. Wow! He knew a lot of famous people and would share his friends with me. One such friend was Roger Miller, a wild composer and singer. Roger wrote crazy songs like "You Can't Roller Skate in a Buffalo Herd". He also had a big hit with "King of the Road". Roger's wife Barbara became my patient.

Some days my office seemed like a Hollywood menagerie. One morning I was to meet two hippies who would change musical history. Separately, he was a short Italian, she a skinny Armenian. Together they were Sonny and Cher. Later, when their daughter, Chastity was born, I was there helping my associate, Dr. Harry Lusk.

One of my long time dearest friends was Carrie Snodgress, the mother of Neil Young's son. I loved her until the day she died, which was far too young. Another patient of mine was one of the women from the still-rocking Fleetwood Mac, as was Johnny Cash's daughter, Roseanne Cash. I love all kinds of music, but really liked the country western musical people as they always seemed more real. Even my son Lonny wrote country music, playing and singing beautifully in many bands -- often hanging out with the likes of Jackson Browne.

My Hollywood moments weren't all wonderful though. When I saw two of my patients the day after Sharon Tate's gruesome murder by cult leader Charles Manson and his "family", they were terribly shaken. One was a famous director's wife the other was Mama Cass's sister of the Mamas and the Papas. There was talk about a drug deal gone bad or getting revenge on the previous renter of the house - but none of it added up to the murder of six innocent people, including Sharon's unborn baby with Roman Polanski. Mama Cass and the director's wife had visited Sharon's home a few days prior to the tragedy. Thank God they were not there on that awful day.

A few days after the Tate murders, the LaBiancas were murdered in their home just down the hill from my house. For the next few weeks, fear and speculation ran rampant and many of us were frightened to death. Hollywood in a lot of ways was like a small town then; everybody knows everyone else's business. My telephone went crazy until they caught Charles Manson and his "family".

On another day, Karen Black, the Academy Award nominated actress for *Five Easy Pieces*, came to me after seeing several other physicians. I had been warned that she was a Scientologist and did not think too highly of doctors. She had been diagnosed with cancer of the cervix by other gynecologists but had refused treatment. She was a tough cookie, but somehow I managed to talk her into treatment. So I did a regular cervical biopsy in the office the results of which were inconclusive. I advised Karen that we would have to admit her to the hospital to do a more extensive cervical cone biopsy, but she was in the middle of shooting a studio film. I believe it was *Day of the Locusts* and the studio would not allow her the time off. Fortunately, it was very early cancer and I was able to eventually treat it easily.

Karen and I became "Hollywood" friends. When I invited her to one of my birthday parties, she came and we danced and had a great time. Later, when she became pregnant by the screenwriter, L.M. 'Kit' Carson. she would come into my office with her entourage, tear off all of her clothes and jump on the weight scale. She came in after-hours when none of my other patients were there, so no one was shocked, except maybe me, just a little.

When Karen was about six months pregnant, she married Kit. We received an invitation to attend their nuptials 'by dawn's early light' — somewhere around 5 AM, I believe. A wedding at that time in the morning made sense to no one, but it did for whatever reason to Karen. It was held in an unspectacular part of what is the otherwise lovely, Franklin Canyon and she must have spent many thousands of dollars clearing the grounds as poisoned ivy had been rampant in that area. Huddled around large coffee urns, the guests gathered, some in elegant evening gowns, some in jeans and parkas. Charlton Heston covered all sartorial bases by wearing a turtle neck sweater, an off-white dinner jacket and just to be cool, a pair of jeans! Karen and Kit said their vows standing in front of an unceremonious leaking lead pipe. Their vows were personal and sweet and at the end a flock of gray doves were released into the sky. In the end, it was a fun wedding with great music, revelry and lots of fascinating celebrities.

Sometime during the reception I cautioned Karen that she was getting too fat. I might have said it in a cruder manner, but it was said out of concern. Either way, it turned out to be a big mistake. Without a word, Karen abruptly left me for another obstetrician. Ah, Hollywood. Stars get rid of spouses, directors, and agents with the greatest of ease - -- apparently doctors are dispensable too.

Doctor Who Performed Over 4,000 Legal Abortions Claims They Leave Fewer Heartaches Than Adoption

By IAIN CALDER

Abortions leave fewer heartaches than adoptions, according to a California gynecologist.

Dr. Boyd Cooper, who has performed more than 4,000 legal abortions, told The ENQUIRER that all solutions to the problem of unwanted pregnancy, including abortion, are bad ones. But he sees abortions as being less damaging physically, psychologically and socially than the others.

"It comes down to a very simple fact," says the author of "Sex Without Tears." "There are and always will be unwanted pregnancies.

"For many years, abortions were not legal in the U.S. and there were only three solutions available to the girl: Giving birth and handing the child to another woman to raise through adop-

tion; forcing a man to marry her, a bad situation; and raising the child alone — which is unhealthy for the child.

"Knowing these three solutions were bad, when the opportunity came along for a new solution (legal abortion), I had to explore it, even though I was not fond of it."

Dr. Cooper, chairman of the Dept. of Obstetrics and Gynecology at Hollywood Presbyterian Hospital, says abortions are "distasteful to all, including myself," but he also sees grave problems for an unwed mother who gives her baby out for adoption.

"Adoption is a solution to a bad problem," says Dr. Cooper. "But you can't forget carrying a baby for nine months, having it and giving it away as easily as you can the much

lighter experience of an early abortion.

"If a girl goes through pregnancy, and her baby is adopted out, she spends a year in punishment for an accident or a careless moment. She suffers.

"Her family rejects her.

"Often the boy rejects her, and society punishes and rejects her," said Dr. Cooper.

"When a woman has an abortion, all these people and society don't get involved.

"She solves her problem and carries on with her life.

"There's very little psychological or anatomical damage done to a woman having an abortion."

Dr. Cooper concedes that some women may be psychologically damaged by an abortion.

"But," he said, "this kind is the kind of woman who'll feel bad no matter what she does."

Dr. Boyd Cooper

The National Inquirer | 1970's

10 THE ABORTION CONTROVERSY

Doctors are dedicated to saving the lives of their patients, and one of our missions was to put an early end to unwanted or dangerous pregnancies. For almost any doctor the appeal of a patient in need of his unique services is an irresistible attraction. We are vulnerable to the searching need, and the desire to be helpful. Some are seduced by the sense of power, and are too readily trapped in a God-like role. When the patient is a young woman desperately in need, the situation is doubly charged. Her need is poignant and highly personal. Frequently what she asks of her doctor is loaded with overtones of intimacy. Few men are unmoved by this situation, but some have been so moved that they said yes for the wrong reasons.

I performed abortions legally and responsibly, and I believe that everyone concerned benefited from what I did. I feel that a life was saved, the mothers, and more than likely two of them were spared an unhappy future life. I also brought thousands of healthy babies into the world, and shared the joy of happy women who were delighted to become mothers. An abortion is a woman's choice -- no one else's. It is

HER body, HER future, and HER life. It is not the rightful concern of the government or the church or her neighbors or even the reputed father. It is her decision and hers alone. I simply helped her act on that decision. The group of cells growing in her body is a potential human being, no more no less. It is not unlike the frequent miscarriage that occurs, many times before the period is even missed. It is little more than the many unfertilized eggs that are washed away every month or the sperm that are squirted away. Our bodies don't always work perfectly and neither do our minds. Today having babies has become a definitive choice. Mistakes can now be corrected, and should be if that's the woman's desire.

I did not come to this position suddenly or easily. To reach it, I had to free myself from the teachings of the Mormon Church in which I was raised and the powerful traditions of the conservative medical profession in which I was trained. During my residency training, I delivered many babies at the Florence Critendon Home for Unwed Mothers. Most of these babies went out for adoption. I soon learned that this was not the answer for the unwed mothers.

So I had a dilemma. What was the best way to help this young unwed woman? A woman, who in the eyes of society had made an unforgivable mistake. A mistake she must pay for, for the rest of her life. A sin both she and her baby (the "bastard" child) must face social condemnation for through eternity. It just didn't seem fair. When I was a little boy my very religious mother would not let me play with the little boy next door. He was the bastard child of the single girl that lived with her parents. The punishment didn't fit the crime.

When I opened my office in Hollywood in 1960, abortion was still illegal. Most illegitimate babies were delivered, not aborted, and most of them were placed with adoption agencies. In those days, it would bring disgrace to the whole family for a young, unmarried girl to keep her baby. It was even a disgrace for a young girl to have a baby too soon after marriage. Friends and neighbors counted the months, weeks and days. This was the prevailing attitude of most people then and still is today for some.

At this point, I had never done an abortion and had never been trained to perform one. However, I had seen many post-abortal infections and hemorrhages, and I knew that unskilled, unsafe abortions were not the answer. It was the time of the bra-burning feminist vs. the Bible-thumping religious zealots, and nearly five years still way from Roe v. Wade. The solution to my dilemma came shortly after I opened my office when I was coerced into doing my first abortion.

LISA

Lisa was a vibrant 22 year old Israeli. She was very much in love with a young man, and somewhere in their future were plans for marriage. But Lisa's problem at that moment was that she was already pregnant.

For this woman, pregnancy was more than just an inconvenience. It was a death sentence. Lisa had heart disease as a result of a childhood illness, and her heart was too weak to carry her through a pregnancy or the delivery. By the time her cardiologist knew she was pregnant, she was in the fourth month of her pregnancy and already in early cardiac failure. The physical strain of the pregnancy was over-taxing her defective heart, and the cardiologist said that she probably would not live another month unless the pregnancy was terminated.

At that time in California, a doctor could perform a legal abortion in a reputable hospital only if the life of the mother was in uncompromising danger and only if a committee of doctors had approved her for the procedure. In Lisa's case, the hospital committee had no choice but to agree that her life was at stake. In those years, our hospital approved no more than two or three abortions a year. Nevertheless, I was granted permission to perform the abortion.

At four months gestation I could not do the simple D & C (dilatation and curettage) type of termination. Lisa would require a mini-Cesarean section. This procedure calls for an incision in the lower abdomen, and in those early days was the only known safe way. I had previously performed many Cesarean deliveries, so I approached the operation in a rather matter-of-fact manner. Then, as I slipped my gloved hand into Lisa's uterus and cupped it around the unborn fetus, everything changed. I brought the baby, encased in its sac, out of Lisa's unconscious body, and as I stood there looking at it. I trembled and broke into a cold sweat. Within its glistening sac, the fetus struggled to stay alive. By separating it from its mother, I had ended its life.

For weeks I was haunted by the memory of that awful moment. What I had done was contrary to everything I had been taught in my home, my church and my professional training. The ethics of my profession were strongly imprinted on me, and they still are. But after months of soul-searching, I found a new meaning. I came to understand that the value of life is more than its mere existence. The quality of an individual's life is an important factor, too.

I had put an end to a life, technically, but that life could not have been. What's more, the fetus and Lisa would not have survived. Both lives would have been ended. The baby had a potential life, but Lisa was a full-grown live human being. That's the reality. It had not been a mere trade-off of one life for another.

Eventually, I made peace with myself. But then began to ask myself -- why shouldn't every woman have the choice I had been able to give to Lisa? Why must the life of any woman be on the line before a pregnancy can be terminated? I recalled my experience while on the staff of the home for unwed mothers. I agonized over the feeling of shame and bewilderment those girls experienced, trapped in a situation they were unable to cope with. I remembered the times when girls were brought into the hospital emergency room after crude attempts to abort the fetus themselves, bleeding so profusely we were unable to save them. I thought of my shock at examining a girl devastatingly infected while in severe pain and emotional distress after having an illegal abortion by some untrained and unscrupulous person.

And, what about the pregnant teenage girl pressured by her parents to get married, even though she was too young to even understand what marriage was all about and too often didn't really love the father of the child anyway? What became of the unwed mother who was told she had no choice but to give her child up for adoption and who, even though she later married and had other children, was torn by longing for the child she gave away? Was this agony what they deserved? Few men worry about the consequences or their sexual behavior. I didn't think they did then and they certainly don't today.

In those early years following Lisa's case, there was appallingly little I could do. Abortion was still illegal, and I wasn't about to break the law. At the same time, others were attempting to cope with the problem. Dr. Louis Belous, a well-known Los Angeles obstetrician, was convicted of having supplied a patient with a telephone number through which she could arrange a safe, but illegal abortion. The American Civil Liberties Union petitioned the U.S. Supreme Court on his behalf, arguing that the intrusion into the patient's privacy was "drastic and oppressive". Partly because of this case, in 1968, a Clergy Consultation Service was established. A group of young rebellious clergymen banded together to provide referral services for abortions in Mexico where the procedures would be done with reasonable safety and at a fair price. They personally checked the doctors and hospital to make sure that everything was clean and safe.

The guru of these young clerics was Reverend High Anwyl. We became associates and started working together. During those next few years, thousands of girls, single or married, with unwanted pregnancies, made the pilgrimage to Mexico to obtain illegal abortions preformed by doctors cooperating with the Clergy Consultation Service. In spite of their efforts, thousands of abortions were still being done illegally and dangerously by unqualified opportunists here in California.

Pressure was building to change this, but the conservative minority (commonly referred to as the Religious Right) was in control in California. California was almost one-fourth Roman Catholic and together with a large percentage of the other religious groups influenced by Roman Catholic theology they largely held legislative change back. The senior citizen population was against abortion, too. All of these forces prevented any legislative attempt of getting legislation off the ground.

Then in 1964 to 1965, a rubella (German measles) epidemic swept the country. Approximately fifteen thousand defective babies were born to women exposed to this disease during the first three months of pregnancy. Many of these infants were born blind, deaf, and/or mentally retarded. Seizing on this opportunity, many doctors were able to use rubella to justify the abortions they wanted to do. The hospital abortion committees knew that the procedure was still against the law, and the mother's life was not actually in danger, but they also knew that no court had ever punished physicians for doing abortions in hospital-approved settings. Some major hospital committees began to relax their rules. Nevertheless abortion was still a hot issue for most major hospitals. Some limited the number of abortions a doctor could do in their hospital at any one time. They didn't want to be labeled an "abortion mill."

As the controversy grew, there was a barrage of statewide and national publicity that played up the paradox, emphasizing the rising demand for abortion reform among the young. The publicity enraged Dr. James V. McNulty, an eminent Beverly Hills Catholic obstetrician, husband of former actress, Ann Blyth, and brother of singer Dennis Day of the *Jack Benny Show*. Dr. McNulty had testified against the 1962 reform bill, submitted by a group of doctors and lawyers. At a 1966 meeting of the Medical Association he demanded the floor again. He announced that he intended to stop all doctors who were performing abortions. His threat was not to be taken lightly as he was an associate clinical professor at the University of California as well as a member of the Board of Medical Examiners, which is part of the State Department of Professional and Vocational Standards. His words to his colleagues were: "We took an oath to uphold the law. These doctors who admit doing abortions for rubella are saying they are above the law. If we don't punish them, we are guilty of malfeasance."

Dr. McNulty's proclamation resulted in the Standards Department dispatching investigators to certain hospitals in the San Francisco area. Arriving on a Saturday when the hospital administrators were not present, the investigators procured from nine doctors, tape-recorded accounts of abortions done for exposure to rubella. The nine doctors were then ordered to appear before the Board on charges of unprofessional conduct. Rumors ran rampant of a statewide crackdown on hospital abortions. The result: most obstetricians stopped doing therapeutic abortions, at least in the case of rubella.

However, physicians throughout the state rallied to help the nine accused doctors, and raised a large legal defense fund for their support. In the meantime, additional medical and legal support was developing for a new bill that had just been introduced into the state legislature by Anthony C. Bielenson of Beverly Hills. They had the votes to get it passed, but Ronald Reagan, the newly elected governor of California, threatened to veto the bill if the section permitting abortion to prevent the birth of a defective baby was included. The governor said, "A crippled child has a right to live." Ironically, the section Reagan opposed was the one, which originally had inspired most doctors to seek reform. Bielensen struck out the objectionable part in order to get the bill passed.

The California Therapeutic Abortion Act went into effect November 8, 1967. It was actually an amendment to the Criminal code of 1872, which originally permitted a doctor to legally perform a therapeutic abortion only to save the life of the mother. During the next year, nearly five thousand legal abortions were reported, a seven-fold increase above the estimate. The new law was still very restrictive; therefore many abortions continued on illegally. Behind the statistics the alarming truth was that the total effect of the Act was far removed from what its original supporters envisioned.

With the passage of the Bielensen Bill, I started doing abortions myself. We were required to present proof to the Abortion Committee that the mother's life would be endangered if the pregnancy were not terminated. At that time, ninety percent of abortions were approved on psychological grounds: contending the pregnancy would be a danger to the mother's mental health.

I was also concerned about the other side of that coin, the psychological consequence of having an abortion. My review of available literature indicated to me that having an abortion would generate psychological problems for the mother for the rest of her life. With that thought in mind, I brought a psychologist into my office to do evaluations on all our patients -- before and *after* an abortion. Much to my surprise, the only patients who had psychological problems associated with an abortion were the very few who already had impaired mental health issues before the procedure.

In retrospect, it all seems ridiculous. As one of my patients said, "You have to be crazy or be raped in order to get a legal abortion in California." This mindset continues to be nothing new. I believe that it was the illegality and perceived immorality of abortion that has created mental problems for women throughout history. That stigma unfortunately still remains at large.

I wish I could say, with any assurance, that the presence of the criminal abortionist is now a matter of historical interest. But that day has not yet come. I do think that the criminal abortionist is on his way out, but he is making a slow exit. It has been said that morality is a matter of geography, and where abortion is concerned, this could not be truer. As long as there are places that do not permit legal abortions, the pressing need of unwanted pregnancies will be dealt with by a criminal abortionist. There are states in which abortion is in the gray area of legality, legal only for certain women under certain conditions, so criminal practitioners will still be found. In short, as long as there are legal restrictions on an issue that ought to be entirely between a woman and her doctor, we will have law-breakers.

I'm happy to say that such intrusions into a woman's private life have for the most part been greatly reduced in the United States. But it was not always that way and it may not always be. There are continual attempts to rescind abortion rights. Early in the twentieth century, we created the lethal subculture of the bootlegger by legislating against drinking. The only way we could extricate ourselves from that irrational disaster was by repealing the Prohibition Amendment. Much in the same way we passed Roe vs. Wade in order to eliminate the abortion rings, the abortion mills, and hole-in-the-wall solo operators. The more we restrict abortions the greater the likelihood women will seek drastic measures. We mostly got rid of those criminals by changing the law, but I worry there are still very strong anti-abortion forces out there doing their best to impose their will.

JENNIFER & ANNETTE

Jennifer, a beautiful well-known actress who would ultimately become my patient, found herself victimized by an unscrupulous doctor. Jennifer had been a young showgirl in the heyday of Hollywood at its most glamorous. In the "good old days", and even up until recently, a girl who "put out" had a better chance at success; she might even end up marrying a studio executive. I'm happy to say this "social contract" is becoming less acceptable. However, that is how it went when Jennifer bedded down with a famous man at age sixteen, married him at seventeen and presented him with an enchanting little girl at eighteen.

The marriage broke up while the daughter, Annette, was very young. Unfortunately, Jennifer raised Annette quite permissively and it didn't disturb her that Annette was sexually active by fourteen years old. Nor did Annette's experimentation with drugs trouble her. In her youth, Jennifer had made her own decisions and was willing to let Annette do the same. I remember Annette saying to me in front of her mother, "My mom says that the guy ought to take you out to dinner first, but that's old-fashioned. We just smoke a joint and get it on."

When Annette reported to her mother that she was pregnant, Jennifer said, "No problem, we'll get it taken care of." Abortions were still illegal at the time, but Jennifer was confident that her daughter's problem could easily be solved. A doctor, who was courting her at the time, was performing illegal abortions.

She didn't care that much for the doctor. In fact, she was a little put off by the ardent love he professed for her, and considered him a bit too eccentric to be an acceptable suitor. She had been keeping him at arm's length, but all that changed when she asked him to perform an abortion for Annette. He met her request and she met his. My only comment on that: any sex act between a doctor and a patient seeking gynecological services is "illegal" at best.

A few months later, Annette was far from being a healthy girl. Something was wrong and Jennifer could not quite understand why. When she brought her to me, it took little time to determine that

Annette was still pregnant. In fact, she was over four months. In a word, you might say, that both Jennifer and Annette had been had. I don't know exactly what that Beverly Hills doctor had done under the pretense of performing an abortion, but he certainly had not removed the products of gestation.

I was quite uneasy about the course of that pregnancy. Annette had continued to do drugs, and was totally irresponsible about her own health. I didn't know what kind of a baby I was going to deliver. As it happened, the baby was premature yet normal, and was promptly put up for adoption.

A number of years later, I got a phone call from a little girl who said she found my name on her birth certificate. She wanted to meet her birth mother. Fortunately Annette was still my patient, and in time I introduced her to Annette. I'm sorry for both of them that the meeting didn't work out. They met a few times, and then discontinued their relationship. The curiosity of one another was overwhelming, but the reality is, it's frequently disappointing.

Susan & Boyd Cooper | Las Vegas

11 MY ILLEGAL ALIEN

After the sudden death of Irene, I was devastated. It was so unexpected. I wasn't remotely prepared. She was only forty-three. At first I didn't know what it really meant, but slowly the real meaning of sorrow settled in. I'd spent many a night in the hospital waiting for an expected baby, and tolerated sleeping in a room with snoring doctors instead of being with my wife. It was okay, I knew Irene's welcoming arms were home waiting for me. More importantly, the kids always had their mother right there when they needed her. Now we all had no one. We intensely needed Irene, but she was gone forever. I began to think life without a soul mate wasn't worth living.

No one knew the depths of my sorrow, and I was unable to share it. I'd been trained to comfort others, but not trained to reach out to others with my own pain. I had built a shell around myself and no one was allowed to enter. I had to be strong and not let this tragedy destroy me. I had two young kids who had just lost their mother, who was everything to all of us. I'd never had the time to be the kind of a father I should have been, and now I had to try to fulfill her role, all while being a doctor, too. I missed her so badly.

The only thing that saved me was that I could do my job almost automatically. It helped me escape from myself. Eventually I consulted a psychiatrist, who advised me that this was much more of a tragedy for the children than for me, and that it would be best not to make any other changes in their lives for at least two years. The truth is I tried to take his advice, but I was unsuccessful.

As a woman's doctor I was around thousands of lovely women, but none of them could measure up to Irene. I loved being married, it was all I knew. My kids needed a mom, but I could not imagine any of my patients being my wife or a mother to my children. Many well-meaning friends tried to help me, but I did not want to be sociable. I was a solo obstetrician, and had to be free to take care of my patients.

I had a dilemma, and didn't know what to do. I didn't want to date. It took away what little free time I had to be with my kids, and I certainly could not bring a strange woman into the our home to replace their mother. It was a tough time and I needed help. Sure the maid came in twice a week to clean, and Al took care of errands and arranging dental appointments for the kids. He would even prepare simple meals for us every night, but having our physical needs met didn't fill the hole in our lives. The children needed nurturing. My parents lived in an apartment about an hour away, so they were willing to stay with us to be there for the kids. Since I had to go to work every day and throughout many nights I thought my parents might be a lasting solution. However having them move in with us turned out to be a mistake. My dad, God bless him, saw this as an opportunity to make new rules and start correcting all the mistakes Irene and I had made while raising our little ones. As I experienced as a child, he was too tough a disciplinarian. As much as I needed help and loved my parents, I soon learned they had to go.

Then out of the blue came Susan. She was a young girl from Wales who came to my office with a minor problem. I was used to seeing beautiful young women every day, but she was absolutely stunning. At the time, I didn't remember her specifically, but she wrote a poem and sent it to me along with a single red rose after her appointment. I had never received flowers from a woman, much less a poem. I wasn't a reader of poetry, so I couldn't believe the deep feeling the poem gave me. I read it over and over again. Somehow she had penetrated my protective shell and shared in my grief. I had said nothing to her about my wife's recent death. I wondered, how did she know of my pain? Was I that transparent?

That poem haunted me for days. I had to know the poetess. I asked Karen, my secretary, if she remembered the new patient from Wales I'd seen the week before. She did and gave me her name and number. I called her. Susan had a unique voice with a cultured British accent. She sounded warm, interesting, and gave me the same deep feeling of her poem. She invited me to her friend's house for dinner, but I felt a little insecure about that arrangement. Instead I asked her and the friend she was staying with in Beverly Hills to join us on my friend Jimmy's small yacht. Jimmy was dating my niece, Eunice, who worked for me in my office.

Susan agreed to come and arrived alone. What a surprise awaited me! The voice that had charmed me on the telephone was attached to a voluptuous, spirited, intelligent girl who simply mesmerized me. Susan and Eunice got along like two peas in a pod. Susan looked at Eunice that first night and said, "I don't think your name suits you. If you don't mind I'll call you 'Tuesday', " Susan said.

As it was a Tuesday night, it seemed fitting and charming. Then of course I had to add my two cents. Tuesday loved to eat and had no problem finishing up whatever food was left after dinner so I suggested, "Let's make it 'Tuesday Garbage'." We gave it a little special flair and pronounced "Garbage" as if it rhymed with "garage." Funny enough, Eunice liked the nickname so much, that to this day she is known to the world as Tuesday. Needless to say, my snarky contribution didn't make the cut.

I barbecued steaks, and we spent a beautiful evening cruising the inland bay. Sitting together at the bow of the boat with the cool ocean breeze gently blowing her beautiful blond hair is a picture that is engraved on my soul forever.

Shortly after that first date Susan called me at home. I was not there, but my 11-year-old son, Douglas, answered the telephone. They talked a long time and were fascinated with one another from that first moment. I was thrilled because Douglas had been very closed up since his mother's death. He never showed pain like my daughter, Lynne, but I knew he was hurting like the rest of us. After the funeral Lynne and I were huddled together crying, and he said with dry eyes, "Why are you crying? My mother's gone!" His pain was so intense, he couldn't even cry. Somehow over the phone, Susan made him feel comfortable and at ease. I knew he had more of a need for his mother than any of us.

Doug is a love. He is the definition of a decent person and to my knowledge has never said a bad word about anyone. As a boy he was painfully shy and kept very much to himself. Irene avoided cleaning his room as much as she could because it was a teenage boy's mess and Susan eventually adopted the same tactics. She tried to give Doug all the privacy a teenage boy needs. But, one day, Doug announced he was bringing a girl home. He spent hours in his room cleaning up and banging on walls with a hammer. Apparently the posters needed to be a little more mature for a date with a girl. He told me, "Dad, one of the girls is gorgeous and the other one, not so cute and I'm going to try and snag the pretty one." When the two girls walked down the steps, to my puzzlement, I could not for the life of me figure out the "stunner" from the plain girl. They were both cute, but neither was gorgeous or plain: But then again, I wasn't a teenager.

As I spoke about before, my young friend and patient Patsy, was the daughter of well-respected actor, Barry Sullivan. Patsy invited me to a semiformal dinner party at her father's house. Early on in our relationship, I thought this might impress and be fun for Susan, since she was an actress. Patsy's father had appeared in more than eighty American films and was a big star in England, too. When I told her we were going to Barry's home for dinner she was excited.

At his beautiful home up on a hill, Barry was casual, warm, and friendly. Everyone there was over forty except for Susan and Patsy. Patsy lived with and looked after her father. This fourteen-year-old cooked and hosted a delicious formal dinner for a dozen movie executives and actors in a manner I couldn't believe. She was the woman of the house and simply took over. I was amazed at how well these two young girls held up their end of the conversation. Susan really knew film and impressed everyone, forcing me to take a serious look at her. They say a man is lucky if he finds one great love in his life. I wondered if I might be finding my God given second.

A few days later Susan Crosby, another of my special friends and patients, invited us to her home. Susan Crosby was married to Bing Crosby's son, Lindsey. In addition, she was the recent former Miss Alaska, and a beauty just like my own Susan.

It was serendipity. The two Susans got along splendidly, soon becoming fast friends. Shortly thereafter - I asked Susan to marry me. Even though I was many years older than her, much to my surprise, she said 'yes'. Later she told me that when she was ushered into my office the first time, and saw my nameplate she instantly knew she would be my wife. This had to be our destiny. She must have been sent to me from afar. She could have married anyone, but she fell in love with an old guy like me.

Initially, Susan had needed to be in Los Angeles for only a few weeks and had come to America to help design the interior of her friend's new restaurant. From what she had hear, she was not at all impressed with LA. She was told it was a smoggy city with lots of vacuous people. She anticipated returning to London where her acting career was just taking off. So she only intended to secure a short travel visa. She lived in the elegant neighborhood of Mayfair in London and walked a short block to the American Embassy where she was asked two simple questions. Do you have a permanent job in England? Her answer was 'no'. There's nothing permanent about a fledgling acting career. Are you married or engaged in England? Again her answer was 'no'. Without missing a beat, the gray-haired bespectacled interviewer put a red line through her visa. When questioned, she told Susan, "I believe you intend to emigrate to the US." Nothing was further from Susan's mind at that time, but she called her friends and simply told them she was unable to come. Undeterred, her friends asked her to fly into Mexico and they would drive there to pick her up. Fearlessly she took off for Mexico and after touring around with her well-traveled friends she walked across the border in Juarez to Brownsville, Texas. Being blonde with only a giant red paper flower in her hands, the border patrol was not suspicious. Much later when the press got a hold of the story, they had exaggerated and claimed she had swam across the Rio Grande to enter the US. Susan loves to swim, but that was a bit much.

By asking her to marry me I had drastically changed Susan's original plans and this green-eyed, Welsh goddess became an illegal alien. Before we could get married though, we would have to clear all this up. Through the help of a lawyer we had to straighten out the paperwork with a flight to Vancouver to reenter the country legally. After which it would take Susan two years to become legal. In those two years Susan could not see her parents as she could not leave the country -- a very hard time for her, I'm sure. After our wedding she would eventually be eligible for full American citizenship - which she went on to finalize several years later.

So, at the Little Church of the West Wedding Chapel in Las Vegas we both presented certified copies of our birth certificates to get the marriage license. Yet another hiccup awaited us. There, in clear handwriting on my certificate, was the word "female". It seems that the old doctor that delivered me at my father's farm had made quite a mistake. Susan was cool though and didn't mind marrying a girl. I'm still a girl legally, but what the hell? We're in Hollywood!

Soon afterwards Susan, she was able to become a member of the Screen Actors Guild by getting a small part in a Clint Eastwood film, *The Eiger Sanction*. Later we got to know Clint Eastwood and his wife Maggie. Maggie and Susan became friends. Even though Clint is an intensely private person who goes to great lengths to protect that privacy. When Maggie invited us to a party at their estate on the 17-Mile Drive in Monterey, California we were at first unable to find our way onto his compound. When we finally found the property, there was a high fence all along the front with no visible means of entry. We walked the length of the property, and never did find a gate. We had to get back in the car and drive to the nearest phone (this was before cell phones) and call for help. Only by following the meticulous directions (something like "find the 15th piece of wood after the pine tree") were we able to locate the magic square. When it opened, we groped inside it in the dark and came up with the house phone.

The party turned out to be worth the trouble. I remember in particular the director Michael Cimino discussing architectural problems with Clint who does a lot more than make films. Clint had designed his house with the help of Michael Cimino who had been an architect before becoming a film director. To this day, Susan still receives an occasional residual check from her role in *The Eiger Sanction*. When she does, she always takes me out to breakfast and says, "Breakfast is on Clint."

Dad reading *Sex Without Tears* (1972)

12 MY FIFTEEN MINUTES OF FAME

After the legalization of abortion in California, most doctors were still against it. They are basically conservative and resisted change. I felt so strongly about a woman's right to choose that I wrote the book *Sex Without Tears*. I did an official book tour around the United States. Over the next year, I spent over one hundred hours on radio and television. I got very comfortable with it and did a lot of appearances in Hollywood and New York. I even did a pilot for my own television show, but I was terrible. Johnny Carson I am not, and the show went nowhere. I was an instant celebrity and was asked to make media appearances. I had never done that sort of thing and was scared out of my skin, but if I wanted to sell my book I had to accept. My first appearance was on radio where three of us debated the pros and cons of abortion. It seemed easy enough and I felt very little tension during that show. I was then asked to appear on Charlie Rose's radio show - we spent an entire hour talking about abortion. Next I was asked to be a guest on Regis Philbin's show *People* on KHJ-TV, a local Hollywood station. This would be my first appearance on TV. I was excited, but at the same time uptight. The show opened with Regis discussing my book's content. Then with my face filling the TV screen, Regis continued his monologue: "I've read your book. It says that you have done 3,500 abortions. I think that is murder!"

My immediate retort was, "You are entitled to your opinion, but you're wrong. Murder is a legal term. Murder has nothing to do with abortion. Abortions are legal." I was amazed and felt good about my quick response. I must admit I drew some strength from knowing that Regis, a Catholic with two children, was in court at the time fighting with his ex-wife over child support. I never used that information, but it did give me more confidence just knowing it.

When the calls began coming in with the public disagreeing with Regis's position, I felt vindicated. Several women revealed that their hearts still ached over babies they had given away years ago. I'd had many patients with those same painful memories. It's one thing to go to a doctor, be told that you are pregnant and have an abortion early in the pregnancy. That experience can soon pass from your memory. It's quite another matter to feel a baby grow inside your body, then go through labor and delivery only to give the baby to someone else to raise. Ask any woman who has done it.

I also remember participating in a debate at Pasadena City College. My position was to support the right to choose abortion, euthanasia, and genetic engineering. All were against the teachings of almost all religions. I was supported by a group of bright young women who were searching for new and less intrusive rules to live by. They prepared me well, but when I looked out and saw the first five rows stacked with nuns, I figured I was in real trouble. I silently asked myself, "What the hell are you doing here?"

Nevertheless, the debate began. They made some good points and I made a few good points. After it was over, the nuns treated me kindly. They were ladies, not vindictive, and although they didn't agree, they thanked me for illustrating a different point of view.

One afternoon I received the weirdest telephone call from a network producer out of New York. She wanted to know if I was willing to partake in a televised interview, while performing a normal pelvic exam in my office. I was surprised to say the least. It turned out that they were going to do a show about a group of liberated women, a band of real do-it-yourselfers. The producer wanted to demonstrate the difference between what they were doing and a normal examination.

Without knowing what I was getting into, I agreed. Apparently, these women were getting together and examining one another. They wanted to start a movement to establish self-help clinics where women would examine women without doctors and nurses, in part to reduce the establishment's influence over their lives. These women were especially against males dominating the field of gynecology. For some reason these DIY'ers cited me as the enemy, and gave my name to the New York producer. Maybe it was because I was already on television, but I don't think they really knew I was different. When I opened my office I'd decided not to be paternalistic like most doctors. On the contrary, I wanted to be my patient's colleague, not a father figure.

One of my patients, Dada, came to my rescue and volunteered to be examined on television. The show went well and was done very discreetly. I thought that was the end of it, but I was wrong. Two things happened: first, the cameraman sent his wife to me and later I delivered her two daughters. Second, I got very angry and aggressive with these ill-informed know-it-alls when they started performing what is called *menstrual-extractions.* This practice was not only stupid, but down right dangerous. They had decided to not use any type of contraceptive during sex, but instead would stick a little tube up inside their sterile-uterus, and extract the uterine lining once a month, pregnant or not. They would never know their pregnancy status and didn't care. What they didn't seem to know was, if they infected their uterus they may die of Sepsis, or at the very least make themselves sterile. I don't know if I was of any influence, but thank God they stopped performing these dangerous procedures on themselves or others.

The National Organization of Women (NOW) then asked me if I would serve on a panel to discuss female problems. I was to support a male doctor's point of view. I agreed, but I was concerned. At that time, NOW had no love for male gynecologists.

As I entered the hall, I saw there were about two hundred women present, but no men. I was asked to come up on the stage while my now friend, Dada, and her friend, Bob Linkletter (TV Host Art Linkletter's son), were given seats. I looked around for the other members of the panel, but there were none. I was the panel. I thought there must be a misunderstanding, and I became a little concerned. I began wondering what was up. Then following a bit of organizational business I was introduced as the principle speaker with questions to follow. That's when I learned what was up – Me! They weren't just having me for lunch and some conversation.

Now I knew I was in real trouble. I had no prepared speech, but as I walked to the podium, I made a quick mental outline. I'd studied speech in college and knew how to do an impromptu presentation. I certainly knew my subject matter. I managed to give a 45-minute address and then opened the floor for questions.

Those women were tough and they let me have it, but I held my own. I remember one beautiful young woman in particular. She stood up with her fists clenched at her side, with hair bristling from her armpits, and asked, "What kind of man makes a living looking up inside of a woman?"

My retort was simple: "What kind of woman?" It didn't make a whole lot of sense, but it got a big grudging laugh from the crowd. At least they had a sense of humor.

When I finished, Bob Linkletter was the first to applaud. He stood up and clapped vigorously. The others finally joined in and as we left an elderly lady came up to me. "Thank you very much," she said. "I really admire your courage for coming here in the first place."

As the seventies raged on, the religious fanatics and militant feminists were in their respective corners ready to fight. In Los Angeles, I was one of the few doctors at the center of the abortion controversy. Most young women supported my pro-abortion position, but older women and men wanted to crucify me. I was the godless monster that opposed "God's will" and their religious beliefs. They sent me threatening letters and pictures of mutilated fetuses.

A future Republican Congressman named Bob Dornan hosted the Robert K. Dornan syndicated talk show on KTLA. Dornan an Irish Catholic with political ambitions definitely fit into the "Crucify Cooper" camp. Through my literary agent, he set up a thirty minute abortion debate. I would be debating a pro-lifer and Dornan would be the moderator. I was to bring along a patient who'd had an abortion and the pro-lifer was to bring a girl who had given her baby up for adoption. The ladies would be seen only in silhouette, heard but not identified. It all sounded very fair and honorable, but I was no fool. I knew I wouldn't stand a chance, not with Bob Dornan as the moderator. He was a war hero from the Air Force. He'd been forced to crash land and bail out several times. I knew I had to find a very smart, articulate woman with proverbial bigger balls than me to help me with the debate.

That's when Dada once again came to mind. She had now recently graduated cum-laude from UCLA. When I first met Dada in 1969, a surgical nurse I worked with referred her to me. After the examination, when I started to leave the room, her voice stopped me. "I'm amazed," she said. "You made what I thought would be an embarrassing situation into a natural, non-stressful experience. Thank you for that," she smiled. "You're a keeper." I was a bit embarrassed but flattered. The next time I saw Dada, it was nearly two years later. She came straight into my consultation room and announced that she was pregnant and unprepared for motherhood. I suggested we sit down and talk about it and when we did, she decided to have an abortion. She was only six weeks along, so the procedure was simple, over in five minutes, and her recovery uneventful.

When I called Dada to asked if she would go on the Dornan show with me, she immediately said yes, and we agreed to meet at KTLA for the taping. When she walked into the studio, my agent and I stared in amazement as all heads turned toward her, followed by whispers passing through the crew. No wonder! Not only was Dada a tall beautiful woman, but she was also wearing a floor-length white monk's robe with a large black jade cross hanging from a long gold chain.

The cameraman came over to me. "Is this young woman from some religious order?" he asked. I just smiled and said nothing. Bob Dornan looked uncertain as well. The pro-life team consisted of a frightened seventeen year old accompanied by a woman from a home for unwed mothers. The teenager was in a very delicate psychological state. She had just given her baby up for adoption. The pro-life spokesperson was a man with more hate than compassion, and with little respect for classical debate. He was ill-prepared for intellectual confrontation.

Dornan's show opened with a picture of a church and religious music playing in the background. This was followed by a close-up shot on a statue of the U.S. Marines raising the flag on Iwo Jima sitting atop the Bible. He closed each segment with a picture of the Virgin Mary holding the Baby Jesus. Just before they opened the second segment, my agents slipped *Sex Without Tears* between the Bible and the statue, giving a little attention to my book and trying to offset Dornan's attempt to make the debate a religious issue.

The debate actually went very well. Dada and I were both well-prepared, educated people while the other team was not. Dornan kept coming at us from a religious angle, but we kept coming back at him with hardcore science. No one ever mentioned Dada's costume, or questioned her possible religious connections. They didn't ask, and we didn't tell, but her outfit definitely had an effect on the proceedings.

The debate was much too interesting and long to cram into thirty minutes, so we ended up taping two one-hour shows. I have to give Dornan credit as he did serve our country. Although he is a very religious man, he allowed me to have my point of view and gave me a chance to participate in the debate.

After the show, Dada and I were both elated. We'd had the deck stacked against us, but we still came out on top. We left the studio on a high note, and to celebrate we stopped to have dinner. We talked for hours. At that point our relationship changed, we had become best friends and our homes have been open to each other ever since. I later delivered her two daughters and introduced her to my wife. Today Dada is my wife Susan's best friend in addition to still being one of mine.

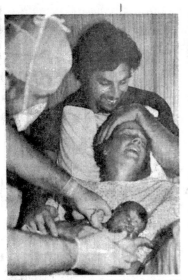

First Alternative Birthing Center in Southern California

13 THE CLOSET BABY

Actors, Maggie and Mark Damon were my friends. I had delivered their first son two years earlier, but now Maggie was about four months pregnant with their second child when she started bleeding. This happens sometimes in the mid-trimester of pregnancies and is usually no big problem. After I ruled out all the serious causes of her bleeding, I treated her very conservatively: bed rest, vitamins, etc. She continued to bleed, not heavily, but enough to be worrisome.

One Sunday, when Maggie was about 22 weeks pregnant, she invited my wife and me to their exquisite home for Sunday brunch. At this point, Mark was a big film producer, and I was flattered to be their guest. While we were there, it became obvious to me that Mark was extremely worried about Maggie and the baby. I tried to comfort him with assurances that bleeding during pregnancy was common and usually not that serious. Mark was not satisfied. He was rightly concerned about the possibility of having a premature and damaged baby. Walking over to the edge of his patio, Mark looked down at his neighbor's house. "Their baby was born very prematurely," he said quietly. "It's been such a strain on their lives. I don't want that to happen to us."

Going over to Mark, I put my hand on his shoulder and let him know that we were a long way from that scenario. He pointed again to his neighbors, "Their baby was in intensive care for over a month. The little boy is now three years old and can't hold his head up." He shook his head. "Their hospital bill was unbelievable, and the baby's still costing them a fortune."

Before we left their home that day, Mark made it clear that if their baby was delivered prematurely, they didn't want heroic measures used to keep a potentially retarded baby alive. They wanted to help their baby with oxygen and general support, but they didn't want all the tubes and IV's. I understood, and I assured him that was not likely to happen. Privately though, I was worried, too.

One week later, in the afternoon, Maggie called to tell me she thought she was in labor. I told her to meet me at Cedars-Sinai Hospital. I was an outsider there, because it was not my primary hospital. I was Chairman of the Obstetrics Department at Hollywood Presbyterian, the hospital where I delivered most of my patients, but Maggie wanted to be delivered at Cedars. When Maggie arrived at the hospital, she was indeed in labor with membranes ruptured. This usually means the pregnancy is going to terminate, and at this point in gestation, the baby probably wouldn't make it. Ruptured membranes also meant there was the serious risk of maternal infection.

Mark was out of town on business, but when we reached him, he said he would get on a plane immediately. During the next twenty-two hours I stayed with Maggie, administering antibiotics and tocolytic drugs to try and save her baby. It didn't work; the labor continued unabated. I did everything I could do to prevent Maggie from delivering her baby. Jeffrey Pomerance was Cedars' chief of Neonatology, which was a fairly new sub-specialty dealing with at-risk newborns. I explained to Jeff that the Damon family did not want heroic measures. Also that it was my personal feeling that their baby had little chance of survival, let alone a meaningful life. Even if the baby did live, it had a very strong chance of being severely mentally retarded. Jeff was aggressive in his response, and told me flat out, "You deliver the baby, then I'll decide what care should be given." That ended that discussion, because he was right. The premature baby is the responsibility of the neonatologist once the baby is delivered.

Some time during the night, Mark arrived and that was comforting to Maggie, but labor continued resolutely. About an hour later we took Maggie to the delivery room. A few minutes after Maggie was prepared for delivery, she began hemorrhaging. I rushed over to assess the problem. The baby, placenta, and all were suddenly gushing into my hands, along with a frightening amount of blood.

This was horrible! An Abruptio Placentae, meaning the placenta had separated from the uterus and the baby was getting no oxygen. There was no way to know how long the baby had been deprived of oxygen. With Maggie bleeding profusely I quickly placed the tiny, motionless baby, along with the placenta, in the warmer and turned my attention back to Maggie. I stopped her bleeding, and then I went back to the baby.

The anesthesiologist, Doctor William Wright, was looking at the baby. I looked at the nurse, Laura Van Arsdale, who stared back at me with an ashen face and shook her head. The anesthesiologist carefully checked the baby and left the room. The baby was very small, 475 grams. In delivering him to the warmer, I was able to easily cup him and the placenta within my hands. He was purple, flaccid and had no signs of life. The baby was a stillborn. Nothing could be done.

Mark approached the baby and put his fingers on the infant's tiny chest. The chest didn't move. Tears came to Mark's eyes. He said nothing. It was an extremely sorrowful moment for me, too. Here stood this restrained executive with tears running down his checks while his wife lay on the delivery table quietly sobbing. It was enough to make me cry with them. I was extremely upset. I said to nurse, Laura, "Please remove the baby from the room. He's stillborn." Later this would come back to haunt me.

After we took Maggie to her room and made her comfortable, I signed a stillborn certificate and went home feeling very sad. When I got home, I shared the bad news with Susan. It made her just as upset. We talked a while, and then I fell into an exhausted sleep.

Early the next morning my phone rang. Nurse Laura Van Arsdale said, "The baby is still moving!"

"What do you mean?" I asked, not quite awake.

"Baby Damon," she replied. "We left him in the closet for the people from the morgue to pick up in the morning. When I came in the room to wrap him, he had little jerky movements. I don't know what to do."

"Take him to neonatology immediately," I ordered. "I'll be there as soon as I can."

The baby was moved to the neonatal unit as I sped across the city to the hospital straight to Maggie's room. Mark was there, having spent the night with Maggie. I now had to tell them that the baby we thought was a stillborn was still alive and in intensive care. Maggie was exhausted and confused, sad yet delighted. Despite hearing what he had feared the most, Mark, too, was optimistic. No baby at such a low birth weight had ever survived, but the doctors were trying.

Mark and I took Maggie to Neonatal in a wheelchair. As we rounded the corner coming into the unit, we could see the sick babies strapped to machines, and we could hear the sounds of the machines breathing for them. We saw the white-coated personnel rushing around the room, going through their routine. We approached Maggie's tiny baby, strapped down in a big machine with tubes and IV's running everywhere. He had tubes in his nose, bladder, scalp and umbilicus, and a respirator breathing for him. This was not a pretty sight, particularly for the mother. She began to cry and Mark took her out of the room.

That night there was a small article in the Los Angeles Times about the Damon baby. It was at the bottom of page one. I thought little about it. The next morning there were banner headlines: BABY LEFT IN CLOSET TO DIE.

That afternoon I was called to the hospital administrator's office at Cedars-Sinai and suspended, on the spot. I protested, "What about my patient?"

"Get another doctor to assume the care of your patient," he ordered. "At this moment you no longer have privileges at this hospital."

At Hollywood Presbyterian the reaction was entirely different. Jerry Chamberlain, the hospital administrator, informed me that they were behind me one hundred percent.

But this made no difference to the press. "The Closet Baby" was in the headlines and the lead story in all the Los Angeles media for the next four days. I don't know what was said elsewhere, but The Los Angeles Times assassinated me. Paul Conrad drew a cartoon of a gloved hand giving thumbs down to a little baby reaching up to God for help. Just a few months before, the same newspaper had featured a two-page article glorifying me. Now the same newspaper painted me as the butcher of the innocent. I didn't get much rest that night or many nights thereafter.

Two days later, Maggie and Mark's baby died. In reality, he was dead from the moment of his birth. Both his kidneys and liver were unfinished in their development and never functioned. The baby never developed a drop of urine. The only organs that were alive were his heart and lungs and his lungs only worked with the assistance of a machine. Every cook knows that if you make a cake using all the right ingredients, but take it out of the oven too soon, it will never be a cake. That is just how it is. Although the baby's heart continued to beat sporadically for two days, the baby was dead. In order to stay alive ALL vital organs must function. The heart can function for a while outside the body. Any biology student has seen a frog's heart beat while floating in a nutrient solution. The whole body does not live or die in the same moment. In reality dying is a slow process. Each organ dies at its own rate. Just recently, new research on cell death indicates that some cell may still be alive for over a month after death.

The only reason the little baby's heart survived at all was because it was placed in a cool room; premature babies take on the temperature of their environment. In this cool area, the metabolic demand for his heart muscle was very low and simply prolonged the dying process.

That night my friend Paul Levinson called. As my attorney, he warned me that I was in a lot of trouble. District Attorney John Van De Kamp was running for re-election. He had the support of the pro-lifers and they all wanted my scalp for my position on abortion. The following day, I was summoned to appear at a coroner's inquest to be presided over by Frederick S. Lacy, Chief of the Inquest Division. This was to be no ordinary inquest. Normally, the coroner calls in a group of witnesses and interviews them before a jury. The jury then finds one of four things: death at the hands of another, accidental death, suicide, or natural causes. I knew I'd not be charged with a crime at a coroner's inquest, but the information from the inquest could be used against me if there was to be a trial.

This case had enormous publicity and was not handled in a routine manner. Usually attorneys are not involved in a routine coroner's inquest, but this time was different. There was a television camera right in the courtroom with us. The deputy district attorney, George Oaks, and two assistants made up the prosecution. The coroner acted as the judge and he loved the camera. I had four attorneys, including my lead attorney, Marvin Rowen. My malpractice company wanted someone there to protect against any possible malpractice charges. Mark hired his own attorney to help me, and also to protect him against any possible conspiracy charges. Cedars-Sinai also changed its position upon realizing they were as much involved as I was. They lifted my suspension and called in their attorney to become part of my defense team. They were also protecting themselves and their employees in case some action was started.

Routine inquests usually last less than a day, but this inquest lasted three and a half days. Three and a half days from hell. My wife and I sat there in that courtroom day after day, with me feeling like a convicted child murder, and I was in the eyes of some. Everyone else seemed to enjoy the media attention, the witnesses, and the attorneys. My wife and I just wanted to be out of there.

I was unable to speak to the press or anyone else to explain my side of the story. I had been advised by my attorneys to take the Fifth when my time came. In a coroner's inquest, they are allowed to ask questions that are not permitted in a regular court trial. For example, the district attorney asked one of the nurses, "What do you think Dr. Cooper was thinking when he told you to remove the baby from the room?" She answered, "That the baby was dead, a stillborn." This kind of information could be used against me if the matter came to a trial later. Regardless of the outcome of the inquest, it would be at the discretion of the District Attorney whether or not to proceed with further investigation and possible prosecution.

During this awful period of time, my wife persuaded me to go to a friend's party to take my mind off my problems. At the party, I overheard several women discussing "the closet baby." I worked my way into the group. The women didn't recognize me, so I asked, "How big was the baby?"

One of the women spoke up very authoritatively: "Five pounds, twelve ounces."

The weight had been published in the newspaper at five hundred and seventy-five grams. I don't know why she exaggerated the facts to such an extent. Maybe she simply read or heard wrong, but her version certainly made a more sensational story. Sensationalism sells, even socially. Needless to say, this was a very tough period, not only for Maggie and Mark's family, but for our family as well. Misleading claims can hurt, severely. Celebrities have perhaps learned how to cope with lies or embellishments of the truth. But doctors are not in the public eye for the most part, and they normally don't want to be. They have not learned how to deal with dishonest melodramatics.

This coroner's inquest should never have been held. When it was over, the jury's decision was split. Two found that the baby died of accidental causes and three of natural causes. There was no further action taken. I spent thousands of dollars and put my family through absolute hell, all to further someone's political agenda. Freedom of speech is one of the things that makes America the greatest nation on earth. The problem is, when the press exaggerates a story or gives misleading information, it can destroy lives. There's never an apology. They simply move on to the next story.

Later I had to go before the Medical Licensing Board for their disposition. The chairman informed me that they had investigated my case and that I had been cleared of all charges. He then asked if I had any questions of the board. "Yes," I said. "What did I do wrong?"

He replied, "You got in the newspapers."

It's now many years later, and the law still has not changed. Doctors still have no guidelines to follow when they deliver severely premature babies who are too small to live. Pro-lifers want us to save all life at all costs. But if the pre-viable baby survives, what kind of quality of life will it have? Who will pay its survival costs for as long as it lives? If one can even call that living. I believe it's the quality of life that counts, not it's mere existence.

Two weeks later, the district attorney admitted that the baby could never have survived. The Los Angeles Times printed this at the bottom of page sixteen. On a happier note two years later, Maggie and Mark had a healthy little girl. I delivered her.

Ten sponsoring legislators with President Bush as he signs the
Partial-Birth Abortion Ban Act in November 2003.

14 PARTIAL BIRTH ABORTION

In the fall of 1996, Congress passed a law outlawing partial birth abortion. President Clinton vetoed it, I feel, for good reason. Congress apparently didn't fully understand partial birth abortion, and its effect on the lives of living people. They seemed to envision some drug-crazed mother demanding that we get rid of "the little bastard" or a "money-hungry doctor" destroying an innocent baby for a buck. It's possible there are a few like that, but perhaps the congressmen were just blindly following some religious ethic. They certainly didn't worry about the effect an undeveloped child can have on an otherwise normal family.

Much of the public doesn't understand what partial birth abortion actually is, and the term we use to refer to it makes it sound even more heinous. In many minds, its name alone has been enough to cause an emotional reaction without considering the facts. It is this kind of ignorance and insufficient knowledge that paints an ugly and grotesque picture for us all to see. It is time for the adults of this great nation to grow up and stop blindly following outdated dogma. What was good fifty years ago is not necessarily good now. In the 21st century, our choices have become complicated. Even our ethics cannot be set in stone for our global community.

The medical profession is an ethical organization, which means medical situations are dictated by ethics, not religious dogma. This is not acceptable to some religious ethicists. Religious ethics are fixed and then passed down from generation to generation. Medical ethics must be flexible and deal with real, modern people. Doctors need to be able to help their patients solve today's situations which can arise out of today's technical society. The world is changing very rapidly and so are its ethics, morals, and ways of living.

SONJA

At one point my career, I had to deal with a partial birth abortion. It came into my life unexpectedly one busy afternoon. I had met Sonja many years before, when she was only twenty-one years old. She worked for a large cosmetics firm and at that time her only passion in life was to meet Mr. Right, get married and have a family.

Well, life didn't go that way for her. It was many years before she met Mr. Right. Instead, her career blossomed and she advanced very rapidly until she was soon a senior vice president of the company. Some years later she came to my office deliriously happy. She had at last met the man she had been hoping to find. They were soon to be married and wanted to have a large family. I reminded her she better get busy. She was now 38, and her biological clock was about to stop ticking. Much to my surprise she came back to see me a few months later, pregnant.

I advised Sonja and her new husband, David, about the risks of having a baby so late in the mother's reproductive life, and advised amniocentesis. I explained that we would need to insert a small but long needle through her abdominal wall into the uterus and withdraw some of the fluid from around the baby. Amniotic fluid contains the baby's chromosomes, which we could analyze. I continued to explain that the procedure is done under ultrasonographic guidance. This made it very safe for both the mother and the baby because it's possible to see exactly where the needle was going inside the uterus. As frightening as this might sound, it's no more painful than drawing blood from a vein.

When they questioned the necessity of the test, I explained to them that it was important to study the chromosomes to understand the genetic status of the baby. With this information, we would be able to determine the baby's DNA. If we found the fetus to be abnormal, we would be able to give them the option of an abortion.

Sonja did not want to hear this. "I don't want an abortion. I don't even want to know if the baby is abnormal. This is my baby and I wouldn't kill it, no matter what." David agreed and that ended that conversation.

When Sonja was twenty-four weeks pregnant, she and David came in together and wanted to know if they could have a sonograph to see the baby. I agreed and the sonographer, Sue, ushered her to a bed. A few minutes later, Sue entered my office with a drawn white face.

"What's the problem?" I asked.

"The baby has no head," she gasped.

"What do you mean the baby has no head?" I asked in disbelief.

Sue told me to come and see for myself. When I viewed the sonograph, I saw the proof of her statement. The baby was an anencephalic, (today called micro-encepholy) with no head above the eyebrows. Its ears were abnormally low, and there were no skull bones over the top of the head. The only thing that covered the top of the baby's head and its brain was a layer of skin and hair. These babies have little neurological function and usually die before they are born. Unfortunately, some of them live several difficult years. Would it have been ethical to force Sonja to nurture this poor little thing until its death? This would have been an even worse disaster if there were other children.

Members of Congress do not have to live with nature's mistakes; few of us do. Thank God anencephaly is very rare, but severely handicapped babies are born frequently to normal healthy people. Technology gives the information in advance, and the parents should be given the choice to have a late abortion.

This dilemma was tragic for Sonja and David, and for me, too. After many tears and a consultation with their clergyman, they asked me to arrange for a partial birth abortion, which I did. Sonja was twenty-four weeks pregnant and an abortion done that late is difficult for everyone involved, but I managed to find someone to do it for her.

There have been no babies. They never tried again. Sonja left me as a patient shortly thereafter, in spite of many years of positive experiences with me. When things go wrong and a patient shares a grievous episode with a doctor, they frequently leave because they don't want to be reminded, even when the doctor did nothing wrong.

Recently this problem has been reintroduced to Brazil and other South American Catholic countries due to the emergence of the Zika virus. It appears the Zika virus can be passed from a pregnant woman to her fetus. Infection during pregnancy can cause micro-encephala (anencephaly) as was the case with Sonja's baby. The Zika virus is primarily spread by infected mosquitoes, but the Zika can also be spread through sex with infected males. Catholic clergy will have to revisit their stance on partial birth abortions in the case of Zika-infected pregnant women.

These late abortions are always sad, not only for the patient but for the doctor and his assistants as well. They usually involve a severely malformed baby, which is in itself a disaster for all family members. Although there should be no fault attached, blame is often aimed at the parents, especially the mother. They have failed to produce a "normal" offspring. Is there something "wrong" with them? What about the next time? Each side of the family worries that the other side may have bad genes.

Sonja and David condemned their first born to death. Some will call them murderers, which only brings more disgrace. Thank God the religious zealots never got a hold of this story. They might easily have distorted the facts to make everyone believe that this was a full-term, normal baby. Some politicians would have had a field day, condemning the parents and perhaps the abortionist. They certainly would have blamed him. They expect doctors to explain how this could happened, and why wasn't it discovered earlier. The trouble is, most of the time no one has all the answers, including the doctor.

Obstetricians select their specialty because they want to assist in giving life, not taking it. Even the obstetricians who do abortions shy away from partial birth abortions for the most part. I certainly do. It's vile, and no one wants to pull parts of a living baby out of the mother's body, even if the baby is grossly malformed.

I personally strongly discouraged patients from having abortions after three months of gestation, unless it's a case like the one just discussed. Doctors know that late-term abortions engender physical and psychological risk for the mother, and they can be emotionally devastating to everyone. Too many people still believe in fairy tales:

marriage, the baby carriage, and happiness forever after. Few believe that a horrendous genetic mutation like anencephaly could ever happen to their baby. Partial birth abortions are done to save the mother's life. There are many conditions that would endanger the mother's life should the pregnancy continue. Too many feel the White Knight will always be there to save them. I wish it were true…

MARIA

Maria, a twenty-two year old Latina, was rushed to our hospital in severe heart failure. Maria was here from Mexico, cleaning people's homes and sending money back home for her two-year-old daughter who lived with her grandmother. I first met Maria when she was about 20 weeks pregnant. At that time, she was already in early cardiac failure. She had severe pulmonary hypertension with a leaky heart valve and with this condition she would surely die before reaching full term. After consultation with a cardiologist I advised her to get a partial birth abortion to save her own life.

Maria left my office, but never went to the hospital. We tried to locate her, checking with everyone who knew her, but she was nowhere to be found. When she returned to our emergency room, she had reached the point in her pregnancy where her heart was at its maximum stress load, and unable to support her and the baby any further. Maria was dying. Fortunately for her baby, she was now thirty weeks pregnant and at the suggestion of the cardiologist, the baby was delivered immediately. The baby was two months early and small, but he made it. Unfortunately, Maria died nine days later. The only way we could have saved Maria would have been for her to of had a partial birth abortion followed by proper cardiac surgery. Maria died leaving two orphans, a premature son, and her two-year-old daughter in Mexico.

Partial birth abortions are rarely done today. Doctors doing late abortions on normal mothers with normal babies are not real doctors. They are businessmen. There should be a law against it, and there is in most states. Today's woman usually knows very early on when she's pregnant. A simple pregnancy test is as close as the nearest drug store, and an ultrasound is as close as one's health plan. Today, most women who want an abortion get it in the first six to eight weeks of pregnancy.

In the early 70's, partial birth abortions were actually more common. In those days, a pregnancy test necessitated a visit to the obstetrician and maybe even a pained confession to parents. As previously discussed, pregnancy out of wedlock was considered sinful. Abortion was frightening and even more sinful. Many of today's women don't depend on the man of her dreams as her forbears did.

In an idyllic world, these cases do not exist. In the real world, nature makes mistakes, and so do men. Elderly religious men believe all life is precious, and created dogma for all of us to live by many generations ago. They believed that God never makes a mistake and some still believe it. No allowances are made in their doctrine for nature's errors, errors that commonly affect women and rarely affect elderly men. Generations ago, women were considered to be less than equal to men. Today, women have more rights, although total equality is still an ongoing struggle. There is a new morality, a new ethics. As information travels around the world at the speed of light, morality can no longer be manipulated as easily as it was by local religious zealots. Morality as a function of time and place is weakening. Even the mud huts of darkest Africa have television sets. Life moves on; our society must change, too. Our Congress, consisting of predominately elderly men, must change. Only then will our government represent the people in today's world.

SARA

All things considered, some questionable partial birth abortions can still have a positive effect on the lives of some. Sara was pregnant with her first child when I first met her. She was forty-one years of age and over four months pregnant. When I asked her why she had waited so long, she explained that she and her husband, both attorneys, had been busy with their careers. Now they were ready to start their family.

Once again I advised amniocentesis, but I didn't have to explain it to her. "I know all about that," she said. "I'm sorry I got here so late in the pregnancy." I ordered an amniocentesis that day. A few days later we got the report. It was very bad news. The baby had Down syndrome, a condition that results in varying degrees of mental retardation.

"I don't want a retarded baby, even if it's just a little bit retarded. Life is tough enough even if you have all your faculties," she said. I arranged for her to have a partial birth abortion. Happily, this is not the end of the story. Shortly thereafter, Sara became pregnant again. This time she had a healthy little girl and one year later she had her boy.

The last time I saw Sara was at the mall. I was shopping with Susan when in the distance we saw a beautiful woman with two children, a boy and a girl about five. They were having fun, laughing, talking and enjoying one another. Susan said, "What a lovely family." As they came closer, we recognized each other. It was a happy reunion. I later asked myself this question: What would this family be like if they had had to deal with a Down syndrome child? Probably they would have been okay. Now there are so many more resources for dealing with Down syndrome. We ended a life that could have survived at some quality. Most now want to give a Down syndrome baby a chance and I would agree. But for Sara and her husband back then the abortion short-circuited years of family grief. It was a matter of choice.

Boyd's 50th Birthday Party
(Ellen & Mickey Hargitay [left], Kitty Lee [glasses] in background)

15 HOLLYWOOD PARTIES

When I started my medical practice doctors in specialties did a lot of entertaining. Specialists got all their patients by referrals from other doctors. If a new doctor was lucky enough to be invited to the senior hospital staff's parties that meant you'd been accepted, and your future practice appeared to be secure. Fortunately, they had given me a chance to join the club. That also meant I'd have to reciprocate the favor, even if I couldn't afford it. We threw many big parties and thank God for Susan. She was a perfect hostess.

Our home in the Valley had become too far from my medical practice. The traffic was becoming too much, and what used to be a fifteen minute drive was now forty-five. Besides I had always wanted to live in the Hollywood Hills. Living in the Valley was originally Irene's choice. She said it would be better for kids with many young families nearby, and that was okay with me. It was my job to provide for my family and our home was a woman's sanctuary. I understood our Valley home had been another woman's, and I wanted Susan to have a home of her own. We got lucky and were able to buy a Hollywood Hills estate from a guy who needed the cash immediately. The creator of the Forest Lawn Memorial Parks was the original owner of the property and had built the beautiful, spacious home. Many Hollywood celebrities had spent time in our house. Guitar God, Jimi Hendrix once lived there. Myrna Loy had carved her initials on one of the old oak trees. It had always been a place with a vibe of its own.

Because of Susan's theatrical experience, my Hollywood medical practice, and our new home -- we were able to give our share of elegant parties. Susan had met one of the original Beatles, Pete Best, and at one of our parties he played many Beatles songs for us. We had our fair share of famous visitors: music makers Herb Alpert, John Mayall, and Barry White all shared our home. The great character actor (and character!) Jack Palance did the same one-handed push-ups in our living room as he had done at the Academy Awards. Nicolas Cage and Jacqueline Bisset attended our Christmas parties.

Susan was an unbelievable beauty, and I'll admit I was egomaniacal about her. I had a huge poster made of her in a bikini, which I proudly displayed in my private office. It wasn't long after our marriage before Susan wanted to get back to working in films. Then, to my surprise, one afternoon one of my patients while in my office asked, "Who's that?" I told her it was my wife, Susan. "Is she an actress?"

"Yes. She just got here from England."

"I'm a casting agent working with Tom Laughlin, and he's planning a new film that she'd be perfect for. I'd like to take her to meet him."

Tom Laughlin was a very successful independent filmmaker. The film was never made, but Tom asked her to join his acting class and get involved with his production company, Billy Jack Enterprises. His classes were held at his private home. It was in an upscale neighborhood in Brentwood with a tennis court, and a lot of young film star wannabes.

Billy Jack Enterprises was formed by Tom and his actress wife, Delores Taylor, to exploit a character he had created, directed, and played in the movie *Born Losers*. This movie was a top box-office success and said to be one of the best biker films ever made. He followed that blockbuster with the film *Billy Jack*, which he made independently and with his own money. It was a very controversial anti-government type film, and the Catholic Church banned it. After much political squabbling he was finally able to release the film himself. It was another big box-office success, in fact, the most successful independent film made at the time.

Many young people including Susan were attracted to the excitement and controversy of Billy Jack, a character Tom Laughlin created in the image of his inner self. Tom Laughlin was a very creative and charismatic man that the young people respected. While attending his school Susan became interested in film editing and frequently expressed her opinions to Tom. One night at a huge screening at his home theater, with luminaries like Jane Fonda and Farah Fosset in attendance, Tom approached Susan as she was trying to sneak out. When he asked what she thought of his film *Billy Jack Goes to Washington*, she told him boldly that it "needed a lot of work."

"What don't you like about it?" he asked.

"A lot."

"OK - meet me at CBS Studios at 8 a.m. tomorrow," Tom said.

He then called in four of the town's top editors he had hired. They sat there disbelieving as this young upstart told them what she thought was wrong with the film. She especially didn't like the ending. None of them had the guts to change the ending, which was almost comical as Billy Jack with a breathing mask tries to kiss his love interest. Cleverly, Susan persuaded him to change the ending by saying, Billy Jack is like a Western hero and western heroes never get the girl. Instead, they ride off into the sunset. The editors were respectful but were unable to change very much. The film was a box-office failure. Even if they had made her changes, it might not have made much difference, audiences run hot and cold. They are fickle and unpredictable. It was there that she met and befriended Andy Scheinman, Tom Laughlin's attorney, and a great tennis player. He later became one of the founders of Castle Rock Entertainment, and remained a friend of Susan's.

While all this was happening, I found myself about to become a father once more. Susan was already nine and a half months pregnant the night we attended a party at the home of my patient, Denise Fraker, and her husband, the cinematographer, Bill Fraker. They lived up in the Hollywood Hills in a beautifully landscaped Spanish hacienda, and what a party! The place was full of famous people, I think we were the only nobodies there. When Susan found herself seated next to Steven Spielberg, he politely asked when the baby was due. Susan, who looked like she was going to burst, told him she was due any minute.

"My God," he said with alarm. "Maybe we should drive you to the hospital?" Steven was extremely relieved to learn that Susan was traveling with her own obstetrician.

To return to Liza for a moment, I'll always remember the time Susan and I were guests at one of her openings in Las Vegas. There we were, my wife, my daughter, Samantha, and I, third row center, watching in awe as Liza belted out her songs. Liza shimmied across the stage in a sparkling beaded gown, which Samantha loved (she whispered, "She looks so pretty.") Later backstage Liza showed Samantha how heavy the beaded dress was. It was forty pounds to be exact. Can you picture anyone carrying forty pounds of silver beads while doing leg kicks, twists, and twirls around on stage, while belting out song after song? I was reminded of the time I looked at the bottom of Liza's bare feet during her exam. Those calluses! I'd never seen calluses like that. Liza had to be one hell of a trouper. After all those years, her voice still rings like a bell, but her calluses are a testament to the innumerable hours she spent practicing and performing on the stage. I'd heard it said, but now that I've seen those calluses I really grasp the meaning: there is no substitute for hard work.

Sir Anthony Hopkins and my wife are both from Wales. After seeing him in Shakespeare's *The Tempest* at the Mark Taper Forum in Los Angeles, we had lunch with him at a mutual friend's house. Later we accompanied him to get an award for his film *Magic*. Susan and Hopkins spent the evening trading stories about Welsh guilt and negativity. Apparently, letters from relatives back home were littered with the ill-health of various neighbors, and news about the recently deceased. They got quite the kick out of impersonating their long-suffering relatives.

Christina Fulton, Nicholas Cage's ex, is a sometime writing partner and good friend of Susan's. Nicholas' son, Weston, and our daughter, Alexandra, grew up together. Nicholas Cage treated my wife and our children to a dream day at Disneyland. They got to enter all of the rides at the 'stage door' and stay on them as long as they pleased. They had their own tour guide for the day. Nicolas used to live in our neighborhood in a castle, but is now entrenched in Dean Martin's former estate in Bel Air.

Our second daughter, Alexandra, was beginning to have her own Hollywood adventures. She played Roxie in a production of *Chicago* at Stage Kids. Later at the premiere screening of the *Chicago* remake she got to meet Richard Gere (who was "sooo nice") Catherine Zeta-Jones (the second Mrs. Michael Douglas), and the wonderful Queen Latifah, whom she loved. When she was introduced to Alexandra, the Queen yelled out to Renee Zellweger, "Yo-Renee, come over here and meet the real Roxie!" That's how Alexandra's autographs from that day were signed—"To the real Roxie!"

Later when Susan was in London with Alexandra, they were walking down a street when they were suddenly surrounded by paparazzi. There must have been sixty people pushing and shoving, calling out, cameras flashing, and poor Alexandra didn't have the slightest idea of what was going on. They finally ran into a pub and out the back. As it turned out, the press had mistaken Susan for Madonna. My daughter was very young then and said, "Mommy are you really a movie star and you're not telling me?" Susan just smiled, "No. I wouldn't lie about that." Alexandra looked at her mother, "Mommy, I don't want you to be a movie star." Though Alexandra had been on TV and in the movies, and was a member of both guilds as a child. Today she doesn't want to be an actress.

In our house situated between Vince Vaughn and Brad Pitt, Susan has seen a lot more action than I have. I was either at the hospital or asleep when most of the Hollywood shenanigans played out, and I can sleep through a helicopter landing in the garden. When Vince moved in. Susan was positive some "Okie" had bought the property and was working on it. She heard all sorts of hammering and people calling out "Yo!" She insisted they must be on Barcelona time because they started the stereo at 2 a.m. I missed the whole thing. Susan called the police three different times. After several times being kept awake most of the night by loud music, she and Alexandra dragged two huge speakers across the dining room floor over to Vince's side of the house and played very loudly the insufferable kid-favorite "Hermie The Worm" over and over at six in the morning just as Vince and his friends were nodding off to sleep. Things quieted down next door after that.

When Christmas arrived, Susan sent Alexandra over to Vince's with an invitation. He accepted. In fact his whole family came. Everyone had a good time laughing when Susan admitted she'd called the police. It's a common problem when people move into the Hills for the first time. You have the feeling you're there all alone and anything goes. But not true. You have neighbors even if you can't see them through the trees, high fences and gates, and sound travels through the canyons. Living on the side of a hill is like having a box seat to the Hollywood Bowl.

Regarding Brad, I believe that he and his now ex-wife had several homes so we don't see much of them. But when Brad moved in, some of his fans followed him. Girls would show up at our house mistaking it for his home. They would peer through the hedges and try every way they could to see inside. If they caught sight of someone, they'd scream and scream. Unfortunately, they had the wrong house and were only screaming at my wife and daughter.

One morning when Susan was taking Alexandra to school, she noticed a girl sitting on the ground across the street from the entrance to Brad's house. The girl looked despondent. When Susan came home, the girl was still there. After her second trip out, Susan returned to find 2 police cars in front of Brad's residence. The girl was arrested for breaking and entering. Apparently she was found in Brad's bed fast asleep.

My friend, Al

16 SEXUAL ORIENTATION

Sexual intensity and preference is more born than bred. There is a wealth of information available today on the subject of same-sex partners and sexuality preference outside the mainstream. Some of us were simply born different. It's always been that way. For centuries the acceptance of being outside the majority has languished in the dark ages of disbelieve, superstition, and religious bigotry. In the hearts and minds of some it still exists.

I have known many, who didn't know that they were gay, but they knew that they were "different". Sexual preference develops well before birth in the first trimester of gestation, at around ten weeks of gestation. In the beginning of fetal life all forming brains start out as female. Early in fetal life the male fetus starts producing testosterone. His fetal brain needs testosterone in order to develop male orientation. Studies suggest that male sexual orientation of the brain is also dependent on the presence of the male hormone testosterone. Without it, his brain remains female. In the absence of early testosterone the brain will be female-orientated, while the rest of the body develops normally according to its genetic direction. Thus the brain becomes fixed in our sexual preference long before our sexual organs are created. The environment and social conditions play a minor role, if any in our sexual preference.

I don't think it's known why the fetal brain's orientation becomes fixed in the first trimester. Or why there is not enough testosterone in the early lives of some male fetuses. There is some evidence that some mothers produce an anti-testosterone. Maybe the male fetus just doesn't start producing enough testosterone soon enough to orient his brain toward being a male brain. Without getting too technical, there are many studies that support the correlation of other anatomical variations associated with or without testosterone. Early prenatal testosterone seems to play a role in the brain structural development as well the sexual orientation. There are parts of the brain that are a little different in males than in females. These variations are correlated with their sexual orientation not their gender. For example finger length ratios, clumps of neurons in the mid-brain, and the relative size of the chiastic structure connecting the left and right brain.

Some researchers believe that some mothers destroy the testosterone being produced by the fetus in early fetal life leading to permanent female brain orientation. Supporting this idea is the fact that women who have one homosexual male child have an increased chance of having another. Homosexual fathers do not have an increased chance of having a homosexual son. When a large study was done in Australia on twins, they found that if one of the twins is homosexual, there is an increased chance of the other being homosexual. This occurs more often in females than males. All this data is fascinating, but lacks full understanding or absolute proof.

There are female anatomic features in the brains of homosexual males. We have known that for years. Unfortunately, even in the modern world religious dogma is much stronger than scientific knowledge, and they are unwilling to acknowledge the facts that go against their beliefs. We have known for many years that there are differences in the anatomy of the brains of the different sexes in a variety of animals including humans. It has been thought for a long time that sexual difference in the brain causes sexual difference in behavior, and it's probably true, but it's controversial. It still has not been absolutely proven. It is proven that researchers have found structural difference in the male homosexual and heterosexual brains, but the brain is a complex organ. Many of its functions are poorly understood even today. The association between specific sexual behavior and structures in the brain has not been fully established. There is still a lot of work to be done. My position is that sexual orientation is made in the fetal brain, and there is a lot of research evidence to support that contention. Sexual activity may be learned, but sexual feelings are acquired for the most part.

During my teen years sexual orientation was rarely discussed, not in my world anyway. At that time, fiction was the name of the baby game. The stork brought the baby and all that baloney. I went to high school in a small town dominated by the Mormon Church. Sex education was not on the curriculum, except to advise that having sex before marriage was sinful. In fact, representatives from the church would come to our homes and advise our families that both girls and boys should remain virgins until their wedding bed. That was the extent of my early sexual education. Oh, some young people were already having sex, but they were "sinners". So when I went into the Air Corps right after my eighteenth birthday, to say that I was naive about sex would be an understatement.

Being a loner from a small town I spent most of my free time by myself doing my favorite thing, going to the movies. Stationed at the Stevens Hotel in Chicago, I had quite a hike from there to the Loop downtown where the major theaters and nightclubs were located. One late night I was coming back to the hotel after a movie when a man approached me. I didn't know what he wanted, but I knew enough to get the hell away from him. Later, when I told my bunkmate about it, he laughed his head off. He was from New York and knew all about such matters. I don't think he believed me when I told him I'd never even heard of homosexuality, and that I was still a virgin at eighteen. From that day on they all called me a "hayseed". I didn't care and didn't want to know about homosexuality. It sounded disgusting to me. That was a long time ago and I've learned a lot since then, especially from some of my close gay friends.

It's astonishing now to recall when I went to medical school, we were taught that homosexuality was a disease, and the American Psychiatric Association listed it that way until 1974.

No one has the power to change their sexual attractions. What turns someone on and pushes their buttons has nothing to do with their families, or the church, not even themselves. The fact is they may be able to control what they do, but they cannot control how they feel.

Sexual drive is also variable and important. Some have insatiable appetites while others could care less. Behavior is not always consistent with sexual orientation. A homosexual may have heterosexual relations for several reasons: to maintain a marriage, to keep a secret, or even for financial or emotional security. Straight people are capable of the same thing. Some people prefer monogamy. Others have a strong sexual drive and will have sex with whoever and whatever is available. To take a page from American singer Stephen Stills, "...if you can't be with the one you love, honey, love the one you're with."

Medical doctors have been trying to understand sexual orientation ever since the science of psychology was developed. Famed sex researcher Alfred Kinsey based his early work on twelve thousand cases from the 1930s and 1940s and there have been many serious studies done since then. Based on his original work, Kinsey estimated that three to eight percent of women and thirteen percent of men preferred their own sex as partners throughout most of their lives. Since then many studies have been done and today it is estimated that about five percent for both men and women are homosexuals. That number is way too small for Hollywood.

One might expect bisexuality to be more common than homosexuality, but it's not. Most of today's studies indicate that the number of bisexuals is about half that of homosexuals when adults. Bisexuals tend to pick one sex or the other, as they grow older.

It is interesting to note that in the last 45 years, the percentage of homosexuality has not increased in spite of the sexual revolution and greater social acceptance of coming out of the closet (so to speak). This further indicates that homosexuals don't choose their sexual desire. It was chosen for them before they were born.

Despite an increased degree of acceptance, I don't believe that most homosexuals have an easy life. They are outside the majority erotically and that can make their behavior different. Society rejects anything that's different. Many homosexuals make their adjustments and live a happy or reasonably happy existence, but I believe there are many who remain troubled most of their lives. In my years of practice, I've had close contact with individuals from both categories.

CHARLEY

Charley was nineteen when I first met her. She was tall, trim, blonde and very sexy -- at least I thought so. I recognized her from television, where I'd seen her doing commercials. Striking and self-assured, she hadn't been in my office more than five minutes when she announced to me, "I'm a lesbian."

This was a bit of a shock to me because she was very feminine and sexy to me, but I told her, "That doesn't make any difference to me. That's your business and none of mine." My reaction seemed to please her, and we got on with the purpose of her visit.

Charley and I became very good friends through the next couple of years, to the point where I invited her to a party at my home. Being so exciting and full of energy, she was the life of that party. All my friends loved her. It was a little strange though, as she came alone. The older woman she was living with didn't want to come. In fact, I never did meet her.

Charley was always perplexing and a little disappointing to me. She was a lot of woman and turned me on, yet she professed no interest in men. I realize it might be my male ego talking to me. I knew women who went with homosexual men thinking that they could change them.

One day Charley came to my office and informed me that she was leaving for Northern California to work on a ranch and wouldn't be seeing me anymore. I was very sorry to hear that. I liked her a lot and I would miss her.

I didn't see Charley for about ten years, but I always wondered what happened to her. One bright morning she came by my office to introduce me to her two sons, Billy and Thomas. I was surprised again, but happy for her. She had married a rancher and loved rural life. She spent most of her time working outdoors with the livestock and her pets. She said her old sexual feelings had not changed, but preferred the life she had on the ranch. Though very sexy, her sexual drive was low. All the same, her maternal instinct was very strong. Her boys gave her great joy and she was very proud of them.

AL

I got embroiled in the anti-abortion laws and started writing a book about it. The publisher hired a ghostwriter, Lady Brett Howard, to work with me. Brett was an author in her own right, a very interesting lady and her friends were fascinating intellectuals. I was glad to have the chance to meet her friends. One friend, Al, was from New York City and was about fifty years old, but looked much younger. He was quiet, clean and spent most of his free time with his homosexual friends. Prior to the war Al had been the headwaiter at the famous New York City restaurant and night club, 21. He was and interesting guy, and knew everyone who was anyone.

As it happened Al needed a place to stay. Our extra room was empty, and as always, generous Irene (my second wife) agreed to allow Al to move in. He stay with us for nearly ten years, but had one serious problem. One of his arms was partially paralyzed from a WWII head wound. So Irene got him into the pool to teach him to swim, and forced him to work with his disabled arm, day after day. Like magic most of the normal function gradually returned to his arm. As a New Yorker, Al had never learned how to drive a car. She taught him and made him get his driver's license. Sol (our neighbor) gave him an old car. Later he was able to trade it for a small, new Toyota. Al was set free for the first time since the war. During that time Irene ultimately helped him regain the life-skills he felt he had lost forever. He used many of his newfound skills to be of service to our family.

Over the years, Al and I also became good friends. I started going to some of his friend's parties where I met editors, writers, lawyers, and other professionals. They were very interesting people who knew a great deal about the arts. I was fascinated by their knowledge and cleverness and on several occasions, invited them to my home. There we sat around drinking wine and talking about writing, the cinema and art. They also talked extensively about their homosexuality, and I learned a great deal from those conversations.

This was a very new experience for me, I love medicine and science, but this was different. This was a broadening of my horizons, and in many ways against my Mormon up bringing. It was a time of personal growth, the birthplace of new ideas. I was hoping to one day become a writer myself. Something I had never even considered during my college years.

Of all the writers I was to meet in that group, Tennessee Williams was the standout. Al had known Tennessee Williams from his days in New York at "21." When I heard he was coming to LA on a visit, I was excited and hoped I might have a chance to meet him. I'd been reading his works, seen his plays, and films for years.

When Al did introduce Tennessee to me, the meeting was brief. He was extremely shy and polite. I remember looking at this quiet man and thinking of all the very unquiet words and ideas that had exploded out of him. Al later told me that Tennessee had endured a very chaotic and disturbed life. His childhood had been difficult. His sexual preference was a sin where he came from and when he did find personal happiness, his lifetime lover and manager developed cancer and died a horrible prolonged death. Though famous, Tennessee seemed to be a lonely unhappy man.

As far as I understood, Al never had a partner or sexual encounters while he stayed with us. He simply had a very low sex drive, and even though he had a preference for men - he was practically asexual. Eventually he moved back East to live with his sister, and died shortly thereafter. I will always be grateful for his assistance to my family, he is a friend I love and treasure.

LORA & JACKY

Lora and Jacky had been living a quiet, private life together in a small house in the San Fernando Valley for six years when they visited my office together. Both had already been patients of mine for several years when they announced that they wanted to have a baby. They had decided that Lora would be the one who would carry the baby after artificial insemination. They wanted to know if I would help them.

Wow! This was early in the baby game for me, and I'd never had a request like this, but I forged ahead. They went on to say that Jacky didn't want Lora to have sex with a man, but they knew a man who was willing to be the sperm donor.

"Good," I said, "That solves the problem, but he may have to give several specimens." They both looked at me with a frown. "Almost no one gets pregnant from one shot. That only happens in the movies." Then I added, "And you don't need me."

They both stared at me like I was out of my mind. "Just use a turkey baster," I continued. "Have your donor collect the sperm in a clean glass, suck the specimen up in a clean turkey baster, insert the turkey baster in Lora and squeeze the specimen inside. If you like you can do this during love making." They smiled, did exactly that and in time Lora got pregnant. I delivered Lora's baby, a little girl, and they were both very happy.

About a year later, Lora came to my office to tell me that she and Jacky were no longer together, and that she was marrying a member of the opposite sex. She said, "Having the baby changed things. I still love Jacky, but I didn't want to live that way any more, it didn't feel right for the baby."

Her maternal instincts were strong, and with the birth of her little girl her desire to be a routine mother was overwhelming. I felt sorry for poor Jacky and hoped she would find some happiness in her future life, but I never did find out what happened as I never saw either of them after that.

MARIA

Maria was a petite quiet girl in her early thirties. She came into my office frequently with many minor problems. She worried about everything. She was very hard to get close to, but I tried. One night a neighbor of hers called me and wanted me to make a house call to see Maria. The caller said, "Your patient is very sick and really needs your help."

Concerned, I went to her home, but I wasn't prepared for what I found. She was sitting on the balcony of her apartment, staring into outer space as if she were in some sort of trance. I looked down at her wrists and they were both sliced open and bleeding.

"What happened?" I asked. She just looked at me and did not answer. As I carefully examined her wrists, her arms gave me no resistance. They were almost plastic. Both wrists were cut, but not very deeply. I was able to stop the bleeding and close the cuts with butterfly bandages. While I was bandaging her wrists, she just looked at her hands as though she didn't know what had taken place. She still said nothing. I asked her neighbor, "What happened?"

She answered, "She's a lesbian you know."

I said, "No, I didn't know. But what does that have to do with this?"

The neighbor shook her head sadly. "They have been together for years and they just broke up. She was upset."

I never did learn the details of the relationship. She needed mental help, more than I could give, so I took Maria to a small lockup hospital where she could be under the care of a psychiatrist.

I hope that my case histories haven't made the reader feel as if I have had no positive experience with people of alternative sexuality.

This is certainly not the case. I'm also not suggesting that heterosexuals don't experience these same problems, but it seems to me that heterosexuals have more emotional support from family, church and society. Homosexuals are too often without these comforts. They have their friends, and they can go to various gay centers and support groups, but only where such things exist. Sad to say, there are many (make that many, many) areas where these comforts are simply not available for anyone whom is "different".

(front from left) Clint Eastwood, Kitty Lee, Dick Lee
(back from left) Maggie Eastwood, James Brolin & Jane Brolin

17 **KITTY, MY UNFORGETTABLE PATIENT**

Get ready to meet Kitty, a fantasy woman in a fantasy world. Getting to know Kitty was an honest-to-goodness Hollywood experience. We all had fun at Kitty's Hollywood Christmas parties. Every year, hundreds of beautiful girls from all over the globe swarm into Hollywood with hopes and dreams of making it to stardom. Some succeed, most fail, only to move on and remain wannabes. Then there is Kitty. She looked exactly like Kim Novak, a platinum blonde with mesmerizing blue eyes. She had a breathy, husky, velvety voice, and boy could she belt out a song.

Kitty was a small-town Texan, who at the age of fourteen, was the opening act for the yet-to-be-discovered Elvis Presley (he was all of eighteen himself). They became close friends and remained that way until his death. Shortly after I opened my office in Hollywood, Kitty Lee Jones became a patient and helped fill my office with other upscale patients, too. I also had the great pleasure of being her friend. Once I met her, my life was never quite the same. And I'm sure I'm not the only one.

While singing at a nightclub in Houston, Texas, Kitty became friendly with the first astronauts. She dreamed of coming to Hollywood to be somebody, and if she couldn't attain celebrity herself, she sure as hell was going to get to know as many of them as possible. She did exactly that, in spades. Kitty began building her Hollywood celebrity foundation by performing at small but "in" clubs like Riggio's and Villa Capri. Besides her great looks, voice, and her heart of gold, Kitty had what she called "balls of steel". Nothing scared her, least of which rejection. So, she fearlessly made her way into the lives and phone books of the crème de la crème of Hollywood. As she put it, "With more cojones than brains, I maneuvered and manipulated my way into the top echelon of Hollywood." Kitty added, "I would do whatever it took to win."

She socialized with motion picture and television stars, astronauts, and political figures. Kitty knew everyone. Clint and Maggie Eastwood were her friends for much of her life and she was a close companion of Troy Donahue, a big star in the 60's. She told me she was friends with Burt Reynolds, Cary Grant, Glenn Ford, Brian Keith, Andrew Pine, Chill Wills, James Arness, Michael Landon, Robert Vaughn, Warren Beatty, Richard Burton, Robert Lansing and Kenny Rogers to mention a few. Some of it must have been truth; I met many of them in her presence.

When Kitty told me she was planning to throw a huge Christmas Party for Hollywood's major players, I was very dubious. I knew she had no money, but I also knew Kitty well enough to know if anyone could pull it off it would be her. All I wondered about was *how*. Well, she told me:

The thought of throwing a big Christmas party came into my mind in a flash one September day. It all started at Warner Brothers Studio. I was there visiting my friend Ty Hardin, who was starring in the television series, Bronco.

Ty was from my hometown of Houston, Texas and I had known his mother, Gwen Hungerford, for some time. I met her while I was singing with Kenny Rogers, and other unknowns (at the time) at a club called the Showbiz Lounge across from the Shamrock Hilton. Ty and I hit it off right away. What a mixture he was, sometimes very religious, and preached to all his friends about God, the evil of drinking, sex, and living the good life in Hollywood. He even led the meetings of the Hollywood Christian Group with members like Ann Margaret, Margie Regan, and many others. Other times he was screwing girls left and right. Then he'd go back into remission and blame it on the devil. The devil made him do it, he would pray and make a big deal of asking God to forgive him. I never knew what the day would bring with Ty Hardin.

One day he was in a sour mood, probably not the perfect time to tell him that I just had to meet Troy Donahue, then the biggest star on the Warner lot. When I begged him to introduce me, he said, "Kitty, go over to the Surfside 6 set and introduce yourself to Troy. Tell him you're a friend of mine." Other than that, he couldn't be bothered.

Well, that was all I needed. I rushed to the set where Troy was working, and was told he was in his dressing room. Very secure, with balls of steel, I approached the dressing room door and knocked. From inside, in this very sexy voice, Troy said, "Come on in." I obviously wasn't whom he was expecting and he was a little shocked at seeing a perfect stranger, but I went into my routine. "I'm Kitty Jones from Houston," I bubbled fearlessly. "My friend Ty Hardin sent me over here to introduce myself. I told him I just had meet you. Hope you don't mind."

Troy smiled that famous smile. "Not at all." he answered graciously. "Come on in and help me with my lines." He was so gorgeous! Anyway, for the next twenty minutes I read his script and cued him until they called him back to the set.

After he finished filming, we finished our conversation. "I came here to become a singing star on TV," I admitted. "I was supposed to test for a series called Frontier Circus, but it's been cancelled. I'm looking for a singing job, or really anything to pay the rent."

Troy looked very thoughtful. "Can you drive?" he asked.

"Of course I can drive," I answered. Then he handed

me a set of keys and said, "My black Cadillac convertible is parked right outside the sound stage. This is my address," he added, writing 1234 Weatherly Dr. in Beverly Hills on a pad. He also wrote down his private phone number.

"Okay Kitty, go to this address and pick up my maid, Jeannie Lewis. I want you to take her shopping, to the cleaners, and wherever else she needs to go. Here's my gas card and some money. You now have a job as my secretary. I'll give you 50 bucks a week. Now hurry! I'll call Jeannie to tell her to expect you."

I was in shock. I suddenly had a job working for the heartthrob of America! I rushed to the Bronco set and told Ty of my good fortune. I hurried off to the address Troy had given me. Troy's maid, Jeannie, and I got along from the first day. That was the beginning of a long-term relationship for both of us.

A few days later, I had dropped Troy off at Warner Brothers, and was hanging around with some of the contract actors at the studio: Joe Gallison (who at the time was known as Evan McCord), Connie Stevens, Efrem Zimbalist, James Garner, Will Hutchins, Jack Kelly, Ed "Kookie" Burns, Diane McBain, and all the other Warner players. I'd become very friendly with these people in a short period of time. It is who you know, not who you are, that gets you into these circles. Take it from a professional. That same morning, Troy summoned me to his dressing room. "Kitty, run up to Jack Warner's office and pick up the contracts he wants me to read, will-ya?"

I rushed over to the executive offices stopping to yell, "Hi" to Bill Orr, playboy son-in-law of Mr. Warner to Tibby Tibedow from casting. I saw producers and directors like Jerry Davis and Charlie Rondo. And then there was Michael O'Herlihy.

I proceeded to do what Troy had asked. When I arrived at Mr. Warner's office, his secretary was heading for the bathroom. She asked me to get the phone for her until she got back.

As I picked up the contracts from Mr. Warner's desk, his address book caught my eye. It had to be crammed with phone numbers and addresses of anyone who was anyone, I thought. I knew Jack Warner was out of town, so I slipped the address book into my large bag. Then I moved over to the secretary's desk to wait for her. I was very nervous to say the least.

"When is Mr. Warner due home?" I asked, when she returned and got herself situated.

When she said not for a week or so, I thought 'Great!' That would give me time to copy the whole book and get it back before he resurfaced on the lot. "Call me on the set if you need a break," I offered and got out of there quick.

Shortly thereafter is when the idea of the party hit me. I'll have a star-studded party like the ones they have only in Hollywood I thought. Then my mind began clicking away on how to do it with little or no money and no place to have it.

It would be a Christmas party, which meant December. That gave me two months to plan and arrange it. Could I do it? You bet I could! Just watch me. When I got home from the studio that day and discussed the party idea with my roommate, June Ellis, she was very excited. She knew how crazy I was, and that I could probably pull this off.

One thing I'd done over the years was make good friends and keep them. And I'd always left them owing me a favor. So, in the short time I'd been in Hollywood, I'd already met several people now in my "owe-me" column.

I started writing pages of things I'd need: a location, lights for the outside, (so it would look like a real Hollywood party), security, valet parking, a fantastic band. I'd also need Christmas decorations, etc. My mind clicked on and on. After I made a list, I checked it twice and re-did it. Then I started copying Mr. Warner's address book.

By then I had taken an additional job, working for an answering service in Beverly Hills. I had met the owner, Dianna, at Turner's Liquor Store on the Sunset Strip when I was picking up something for Troy. When I told her I could use a few hours, she suggested that I help her out on the night shift. She offered me free service on my home phone plus a salary and I agreed. I didn't know how long I would be able to keep it up, I was already getting only four or five hours of sleep a night. This job started at 2:30 a.m. and went through early morning after which I had to go back to Troy's to work, but I decided to give it a shot. I made up my mind when I realized that every person on the service was a movie star! This list included Barbara Streisand, who was just getting famous at the time, and numerous others. That was thrilling enough, but I would also be able to get their addresses and phone numbers from the card file. I spent several nights copying that information (by hand, this was before every office had a Xerox machine). This netted me another 200 names, private numbers and addresses.

When I went off shift at the answering service, I would take Troy to work, then pick up a couple hours of sleep at his house before Jeanie came. That's the way it went for some time.

As soon as I had all of my copied addresses in hand, I knew I'd better get busy and find a place to have this bloody party. So I started thinking. My ex-husband (my first husband, the dancer) had bragged that he now had this really gorgeous dance studio in Beverly Hills. I finally decided I'd call him, as much as I hated to, so I met him for lunch. I gave him this whole line of bull about how I was having this big party with all of these movie stars. Of course, I didn't tell him I didn't know any of these people, and had no idea how I was going to do it.

I promised him that if he let me use his Beverly Hills studio and ballroom, I'd let him be one of the guests. At first he laughed at my "generosity". It was his place so he would have come to the party anyway. But he finally agreed.

I left our lunch beaming because now I had a fantastic party location on Robertson Boulevard. My next thought was where and how to get the invitations. When I began thinking that over, I recalled a printer I had met at a party about a week before. I went over to see him and told him that I was having this great party, but couldn't afford the caliber of invitations I wanted: gold embossed, very *expensive-looking invitations. Then came my bargaining chip. "How'd you like to meet Marilyn Monroe?" (At that time I didn't know Marilyn Monroe, but I had her address and that was a start!)*

The printer all but panted. "I'd love to meet Marilyn Monroe," he croaked.

"Tell you what," I said. "If you'll donate these 500 invitations, and print them up for me, along with some business cards in my name, you can come to the party and I'll introduce you to Marilyn."

"You've got to be kidding," he said. "I'd actually get to meet her?" Needless to say, he agreed to my terms. I left beaming again, of course, and loving every minute of this challenge.

My next quest was to get those invitations mailed. Fortunately, I knew a guy who worked at the post office, someone I'd met through my mailman. So I went to the post office and I had a little chat with Jerry.

I said, "'Jerry, I've got this little problem. I'm giving this big Christmas party with all these big stars coming, but I've run out of money. I was wondering if there was any way you could slip some invitations through your machine back there and get away with it?" Jerry turned red and made sure that no one was listening. "Well, maybe a few, how many are there?" When I told him about 500, he exclaimed, "That's not a few!"

I told him to do as many as he could, a few every day for the next couple of weeks. Then, when party-time came around, he would get to attend and also, you guessed it, meet Marilyn Monroe! That was all the incentive he needed and I left all the invitations in his care.

My next worry was the band. Again, I used the same plan. I had heard this band that was really dynamite. Since I was a singer myself, I'd done a couple of songs with them. Well, I talked them in to performing at my party for nothing. I told them they'd meet record producers and record company VIP's.

My neighbors at the time were Bob Skaff (Paul Anka's cousin, he looked just like him) and Bud Dane, who were executives at Liberty Records. I now knew I must invite them, because there would be a band at the party, a good one, in the market for a label.

So my mind was clicking, clicking, and the next thing I did was visit a friend who worked parties and knew a lot of the caterers. .She told me she really couldn't help, but she recommended a woman named Beverly who had her own company. She suggested I go talk to her because Beverly was really star crazy.

Again I was all excited as I went and gave Beverly the whole song and dance. I told her a great party had to have great food, and if she would furnish it, she'd meet all the famous stars. She said that would cost her a lot of money, and I agreed but I told her, "Just think what you're going to make out of it. You're trying to build your business, and now you'll be able to. All these movie stars will eat your food, love it, and call you for their next party!"

When Beverly agreed, I went to my neighborhood liquor store, where I was friendly with the owner. I told him my plight. I told him I needed a full bar with all the top liquors. I watched him thinking, 'Oh great,' knowing he was going to make money. That's when I said, "There's just one catch, Bill." When he found out what it was, I followed my confession with my usual offer. I closed with, "And you'll even get to meet Marilyn Monroe!"

"Do I have to bartend" he asked, weakening. I told him I could probably get somebody else to do that, but if he did it himself, he'd meet all the stars when they came up to ask for their drinks.

He got pretty shook up when he found out how many people were coming, and said it would cost him a fortune, but I kept dangling my celebrity hook in front of him until he finally bit. By the time I left, I'd talked him into arranging for everything, including the ice.

After that I talked to another friend of mine who worked at Abbey Rents into giving me free glasses and tableware.

So, in a period of a week I arranged almost everything. The only thing that I hadn't done at that point was to get the decorations I needed. I had to wait awhile on the Christmas tree, that happened shortly before my party.

When the beautiful invitations started going out, I began getting the RSVP calls at the answering service (I'd used that number with Dianna's permission. She was coming to the party, too). There were also a lot of messages from star to star, all of who must have thought they knew me because they were saying things like, "Are you going to Kitty Jones's party?" The reply was almost always, "Yes, are you?" So word of mouth was another way the news of the party got around town.

Esther Williams, Lana Turner, Dorothy Manners, Louella Parsons, Hedda Hopper, Rona Barrett, Frankie Avalon: they were among the celebrities talking to each other and nobody took the time to ask, "Whom is this Kitty Jones? Do you know her?" They thought I was somebody, and it worked.

Money was growing short before the party. Fortunately, I'm very good at organizing (remember, I was also working day and night while pulling off this caper). I was able to get a dress shop to loan me a gorgeous outfit by assuring them I'd tell everyone where I got it, of course, and inviting them to the party.

About two days before the party, I found the perfect Christmas tree in a lot manned by a young guy, about thirty years old, who was really nice. So I went up to him and said, "Listen. I'm having this big Christmas party down the street for all these famous celebrities, and I'd like to invite you. But the only way I can is if you donate the Christmas tree. You can even bring someone with you!" Well, he just flipped out. It was no big deal, he carried the tree over to the party while the band set up, and totally decorated it himself. It was the most beautiful Christmas tree anyone had ever seen.

Oh, it was all put together. I had arranged to take the night off before the party, so I would be fully able to function. As for the "Who's Kitty?" factor, my roommate June and I worked this out.

About four hundred people had RSVP'd by this time. They hadn't asked a thing because the party was in a *great location, the invitations were very upscale, and after all, it was the season of good will. But just in case somebody got suspicious at the last minute, realizing they didn't even know their hostess, June and I came up with a plan. I would greet people at the door, as if I knew them, not even mentioning my name. If someone looked too confused, about to ask questions, June would call "Kitty, I need to speak to you," loudly enough for them to hear my name. That way they would at least know who I was and hopefully just think they'd forgotten my face (stars meet so many people, they often don't know whether they've met you or not).*

This is exactly what happened when the first celebrity walked in with a group of people. It was Ernest Borgnine, and he stopped and gave me a puzzled look. June chimed in right on cue, and I said "Oh, Ernie, it's so nice to see you again. How have you been?"

"I'm fine, Kitty," he answered. "How are you"' Then he went happily on into the party. Then everyone started showing up, every big star in Hollywood. Nobody said a word about who I was except Marilyn Monroe. When she arrived with her agent, Johnny Hyde, I walked up and said hello to her. She gave me an odd look and said, "I don't know you."

I laughed merrily and said, "Oh, don't you remember..." Remember what, I had no idea, but just then June broke in calling "Kitty! Kitty!" She'd seen what was happening, and when I had to conveniently excuse myself, Marilyn and her escort stood there a moment. They came in anyway, so I got pust that one. But she was the only one who said anything."

Needless to say, Kitty's party was successful. The food was wonderful, the booze flowed fully, and the stars were numerous. Since everyone knew, or knew of, everyone else they had a ball while dancing and hustling each other. The biggest hustler of them all was their hostess, Kitty. She convinced many stars, producers and top columnists that they all they knew her. It was a great party and it went on until the wee hours of the morning. By the time it was over she'd become a best friend of a majority of those beautiful people. Many said, "You'll have to come to my next party, Kitty!"

Kitty told me, "I returned Jack Warner's phone book without anyone being the wiser. I even invited him to the party. He didn't come. It was his loss."

I honestly don't know how much of Kitty's story is true, but I did meet many of them through her. I was at her party and talked with June Graham, who became a lifelong friend. Three of the original astronauts were there -- I saw them. I spent half an hour talking to Wally Schirra. If Marilyn Monroe was there, I didn't see her.

Kitty lived a fast fanciful soap opera life, but with a tragic ending of enormous proportions. All the same, she did become somebody. She once told me, "My first child died, I had many forgettable lovers, and I had three horrible marriages."

The death of her first child happened before I met her, but it was my pleasure delivering her two sons Ricky and Michael. When Michael, her youngest was sixteen he was thrown from the back of a pickup, landed on his head, and broke his neck. Suddenly her baby was a dependent quadriplegic. Then in midlife she developed sever kidney disease and spent the next eight years on dialysis, which meant hooking her up to a machine every week so the machine could do the cleansing that her kidneys could no longer do.

Kitty was a fighter and didn't let that stop her. She didn't like spending a day out of every week at the hospital, so she got a large four door Cadillac and converted the backseat to a small hospital room. She learned how to do her-own dialysis. She carried extra therapeutic solutions with her and went everywhere. Whenever she needed dialysis she jumped into the backseat and did it no matter wherever she was located.

After eight years of waiting she received a kidney, and no longer had to do dialysis. Kidney transplants are wonderful, and they save thousands of lives every year, but they're no panacea. The recipient is forced to take drugs to prevent rejection of the new kidney. Unfortunately it also weakens the body's ability to fight off infection. Within a year Kitty died of an overwhelming infection. I shared those last few days with Kitty along with many other physicians. We tried everything but to no avail.

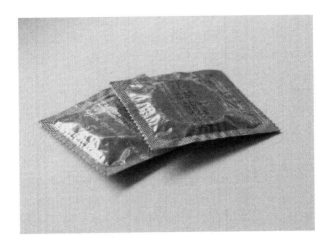

18 ARE WE KIDDING OURSELVES ABOUT FREE SEX?

Suddenly the sexual revolution was upon us. It didn't happen overnight, but it almost seemed that way. Sexual rules of conduct had changed. Things that had gone on in secret since time immemorial were suddenly guiltless and out in the open. The pill was in full use, antibiotics controlled venereal disease, and sexual activity no longer carried the fears of disease or unwanted pregnancy. In many quarters it was no longer the incentive to hold back.

In those early days women began to liberalize their attitudes towards sex and men loved it. A far more casual attitude of living together was out in the open. Communes were dedicated to making love not war. They were advocating free sex, harmony with nature and raising organic food. They were more likely to smoke pot along with liberal drug experimentation. Then there was activities the more sophisticated indoor sports at places like the infamous Sandstone. This was a posh sex club in the Hollywood Hills that played host to a clientele of the rich, famous, and horny. If it felt good, you did it, in twos, threes, and group gropes, whatever -- all performed in more upscale surroundings.

Several of my patients were members of Sandstone, and I was invited to join the festivities more than once, guests were encouraged to come. I declined. Not only was I married, but I am admittedly the old-fashioned sort who would never be able to raise the necessary weapon in a crowd. One of my patients and her disc jockey husband were more adventurous. They were invited to Sandstone and went together, in hopes of getting to better know themselves and one another sexually. However, the trip was pretty much a flop. The wife took one look at the proceedings inside the main hall (lots of mattresses and lots of sex in progress) and ran out to wait in the car. The man was taken aback as well, but he was fascinated, so he disrobed, laid down on one of the mattresses and looked on as the couple right beside him went to town.

After this experience, he told me, "I couldn't have risen to the occasion if my life depended on it, and I wonder if I'll ever be able to again." But he was grinning as he said it, so I asked him to explain himself. "The couple next to me changed positions about eight times without stopping and kept on going for 45 minutes!" he said. "I do about three minutes of serious fuckin'. Then I need eight hours of sleep! And a bowl of Wheaties!" We both laughed at that great old Richard Pryor line.

I never heard of anyone getting hurt at Sandstone, other than their egos, but something happened that caused activities of this nature to start petering out (you should pardon the expression). With the upsurge in sexual activity, new sexually transmitted diseases began to surface. Especially to young people who had begun their sex lives in the heyday of the revolution and just weren't prepared to start paying the piper. Hearing of this, or discovering it firsthand, women began getting spooked.

ROBBIE

When Robbie, then only eighteen, had sex for the first time with a rock star she was crazy about, she woke up the next morning with fire down below. She not only itched on the outside, but inside as well. Terrified that she had picked up one of the new varieties of venereal disease (in those days it was called VD, a gift from the love goddess Venus), she douched frantically with some kind of strong laundry detergent! She came to my office in terrible pain, and a swollen, bright red vagina. She was lucky. She healed without leaving any scars, but she was one miserable human being for a while. It was really all for not, her only maladies were a guilty conscious and a simple yeast infection. Ten years later, I delivered her a healthy baby boy. By then, she was a star in her own right, but she never lost her sense of humor. We had more than one good laugh about her awful experience, although a better word would probably be inexperience.

Another patient went through a similar trauma. She had been sexually involved with a famous actor for several months and one morning she woke up in his bed in a panic. She felt like something was crawling on her, and biting her in the most personal of areas. She'd heard about the current crop of sexual bugaboos and upon inspection, that's exactly what she discovered. Bugs! At this point she was alone in his bed. Her lover had already left for the studio.

In the days when attitudes toward sex weren't so offhanded, everyone knew about crabs. There were all sorts of jokes about the little devils, even song lyrics that went, "Get out the blue ointment to the crab's disappointment." It's my guess that people talked about such subjects then because they couldn't talk openly about sex, so topics like crabs were titillating. It was something that only happened to others. This poor girl had never heard of crabs. Nor did she have any idea of what to do about them.

The creepy crawlers were driving her nuts, and nuts is the word for what she decided, in her ignorance, to do about them. Grabbing a can of bug spray from under the sink, she took aim and fired. She was in my office the next day, with her bright red response. She suffered, believe me, but she came through it far wiser, and now knew what not to do. She also wised up about the actor. Through one of her friends, she discovered that the night before her infestation, he had been romping in that same bed with a flight attendant!

As more and more sexually transmitted problems began to occur, far more serious ones than those just discussed, public attitudes began to change. There was no way around it. There were previously unknown health problems coming from widespread sexual freedom. Genital herpes was probably the first huge scare, the disease manifesting itself in a very dramatic way. Patients started developing very painful blisters in the genital area and we doctors were not familiar with the problem. This was a new disease even to us. Don't misunderstand, herpes was no secret. We knew about it. We just hadn't seen it this severe and this commonplace. And frankly, we didn't know how to treat it. The little virus loves moist areas and the female genitals are a greenhouse for such growth. Moist women are more susceptible than dry men. I have seen ulcers extending from the clitoris down through the vulva to far back beyond the rectum.

This sudden virulent virus strain, Herpes Simplex Progenatalis, was not fatal but it could be so painful, it could make you wish you were dead. Some of these women were in so much pain that they had to be hospitalized. There was no definitive treatment available, so we tried everything. Once it develops, it can be spread to others, and for some it may reoccur forever. Treatment has improved greatly because we have learned more about the disease and many new anti-viral drugs are more effective. They do not work all the time for every patient, but if given at the onset of the primary infection, the disease can frequently be cured. Others remain infectious and must take prophylactic drugs to prevent spreading it to others. The development of herpes was the first sign that maybe free sex was not so free. Herpes became such an epidemic that fifty percent of young people had had it! Their blood test for it remains positive. Fortunately, as the disease spread, it changed and became less virulent. People became more relaxed again and we were back to the revolution, but maybe with a little more caution.

The two most common STD's are gonorrhea and chlamydia, both easily diagnosed and treated. A simple microscopic slide taken from the genital area and the appropriate antibiotics are usually all it takes. The problem is it's far too easy for a person who has either of these diseases to be totally unaware of it. A man may have a minor discharge or some burning upon urination. A woman may have no symptoms at all or maybe some vaginal discharge. But vaginal discharges are common in women and may be completely normal. Therefore it is quite easy for the disease to go undetected in both sexes. Ignorance of the problem may continue for weeks, even months, resulting in a slow spread of the disease to deeper pelvic organs, not to mention it being given to other individuals. This can lead to serious problems including sterility.

But in all honesty, neither of these two diseases deserves the infamy that was attached to them. The diseases must be diagnosed and treated, but victims don't drop dead or rot away from them. The same cannot be said of syphilis. This disease can be diagnosed by a simple blood test, however the symptoms are very insidious. The first warning of syphilis, which usually shows up about two to three weeks after exposure, is a hard sore (chancre) in the genital area or mouth. It is painless and disappears in a few days without treatment. Then, unfortunately, blood tests remain negative for six to eight weeks after exposure.

This makes it all too easy for the patient to wander right through the symptomatic phase, oblivious to the problem, and not obtain treatment at all. When that happens, the disease settles deeper into the vital organs of the unsuspecting patient, where it can do substantial damage. Often by the time the individual is aware of this damage, it's too late. Syphilis never gives up. It will stay with you as long as you live or until it's treated. Today people are wiser, and syphilis is on the wane.

That old crop of disorders, now called STD's (Sexually Transmitted Diseases), are still a universal problem. Who gets an STD? Most would singled out the young, the poor, the promiscuous, street-workers, and people on drugs. However, anyone having unprotected sex can get it, and this adds up to quite a segment of our total population. The result is an out-of-control problem and a regrettable byproduct of sexual freedom.

Before any disease can be treated, it must be detected. Our detection record for STD's is not that great in the United States, let alone less advanced countries. This is partially because the infection frequently presents itself with such innocuous symptoms, and they are easily ignored. Another consideration may be because the most vulnerable people may be too ignorant or nonchalant to seek help. The lack of detection is also due in part to our public health system. It's diligent, but not very effective. Their services are free, yet for some reason they are under-utilized. Perhaps it's due to the social stigma attached to these diseases. An STD can signal promiscuity or infidelity. This can make many people reluctant to present themselves for treatment.

Then in the late 1970's it all changed again. HIV-AIDS made its first awesome appearance. Many previously healthy young homosexuals, especially those frequenting bathhouses, became gravely ill. In my hospital, we all became very concerned when one of our young laboratory technicians (a personal friend of mine) came down with a new kind of pneumonia: Pneumocystis Carinii. Six weeks later he died. I had not even heard of Pneumocystis Carinii; it had been around, but was very rare.

Then a forty-two year old active homosexual was admitted to the hospital with Kaposi's sarcoma. This is a rare cancer. I had never seen a single case in all my years of going to the county hospital. Shortly after admission he also died. This strange new malady, AIDS, was suddenly cause for alarm. Many young men were dying, but of exactly what? Did it have something to do with homosexuality? Did it have something to do with sex? After AIDS appeared, people and women in particular became a great deal more conservative sexually. Some even stopped having sex altogether. The sexual revolution wasn't just in trouble. Essentially, it was over.

It wasn't until the mid 80's before the AIDS virus was properly diagnosed. AIDS is still very much with us today, and although we have discovered medication to control it the drugs are very expensive. We can't cure it yet, but in the US, we can prolong the lives of its victims for years, even decades. Several medications must be taken more than once a day adding up to a dozen or more pills daily. We have yet to find a cure. Many vaccines have been tried but have failed.

All of these diseases are relatively treatable if one has the time, the money and the desire. Unfortunately, this is not true in third world countries. Drug treatment is so expensive and there are so many cases that some African nations cannot afford to treat their victims. Given the astronomical economic burden of AIDS, some African nations deny the existence of the disease. In Botswana, thirty-six percent of the adult population is HIV positive, twenty percent in South Africa. Twenty five million or more *human beings* have died of AIDS by the year 2007. The AIDS epidemic is worse than the Black Death of the Middle Ages. And many poor children are living with AIDS. In 2007 there were three hundred and seventy thousand newly infected children. Africa has 11.6 million orphans from AIDS. It is the most lethal epidemic in recorded history.

It need not be that way. We can treat AIDS effectively. If the mother is treated with inexpensive drugs during her pregnancy less than one percent pass the disease to their babies. If not treated one third will have AIDS. AIDS is a global problem and even the poorest person in the poorest setting ought not to be condemned to a vile and premature death, leaving families for others to care for. I know one such family where a grandfather, at the age of seventy-three, was trying to raise thirty-two grandchildren. Their parents, his sons and daughters, were all dead from AIDS.

MONA AND MARIAN

The day was the same as the day my daughter Samantha was born. It was a very happy occasion for me. It was also a happy day for one of my dear friends Mona who also gave birth. Mona had been under my care for many years. Like many of my patients, I first met her when she was in her teens, a happy carefree kid. During the ensuing years her life went through many ups and downs. At one time, she becomes rather promiscuous, and concerned for her health, so she came to see me often. She was lucky and never had any serious diseases. In her early thirties, Mona met and married Tim. It was wedded bliss and soon there was a baby on the way. My wife Susan was pregnant at the same time and Mona and I compared the pregnancies with each prenatal visit. We were both having little girls. Tim and Mona were very happy, but when Mona was six months pregnant, Tim was killed in an awful automobile accident. It was devastating to Mona, but there was some salvation for her sorrow with the delivery of her little girl, Marian. Mona devoted her whole life to her child. She lived through the loss of Tim by immersing herself in Marian.

We both had healthy daughters of the same age, and as the years went by, we continued our comparisons. Hers was always a joyous office visit. When our daughters reached their late teens, Marian also became my patient. She was a lovely girl, still a virgin and planning to remain that way until marriage.

When Marian was 19, Mona came to my office very distraught. Marion was HIV positive! I was shocked, how could that be? I had seen her just a few months before. Mona surprised me again by saying, "She's been having sex with Robert, the boy next door."

Marian had talked to me about Robert and I understood that he was as virginal as she was. But Mona went on to explain, "It was first love for both and they've been dating for several months. Sex just started recently." Marian and Robert were both young adults, and pairing off sexually was part of the normal progression of their love, but not for one terrible fact. Robert was a hemophiliac. He had been under treatment at Children's Hospital since birth and had received many transfusions of concentrated blood products (concentrated from many different donors) long before we knew about AIDS.

Robert had contracted AIDS through the blood products he'd received from multitudes of donors, which is not surprising now. Ninety percent of the hemophiliacs who were treated before the 1980s are now dead from AIDS. Sadly, Robert told no one, including Marian, that he had AIDS. His doctor repeatedly asked the teenager if he was having sex, and the answer was always no. Then the day came when Robert finally admitted to his doctor that he was having sex with the girl next door. When the doctor called Marian to come in for testing, she tested positive.

Poor Mona, as if she hadn't had enough. Now the only thing in life that she loved was fatally wounded. Then came more bad news. Marian came in to see me. She wanted an AIDS test. I was perplexed and asked why. She said, "I don't have AIDS." I assured her that she was indeed HIV positive, but she still wanted me to repeat the tests, which I did. No surprise there, she was still positive. But when I gave her the results, she cried, "No! The test is wrong. I do not have AIDS and I have stopped taking all those awful drugs. They are dangerous."

I tried to change her mind but it didn't work. All I could do was give her a hug and wish her well. That was the last time I saw Marian. These diseases change the lives of real people, even the innocent. Unknowingly, Marian made a mistake tantamount to a Shakespearean tragedy, and her life was never be the same.

Although that probability is not nearly as grave as it once was, AIDS and STD's can infect anyone, including the newborn. Most babies in this country are delivered in hospitals, after having proper prenatal care. Unfortunately, this is not the case for all babies. At this very moment, there are still babies being born outside of hospitals, in unsafe conditions, often by well-meaning parents who want to save money or be more natural. This can be disastrous if the mother is infected. Gonorrhea alone can cause immediate blindness when the infant passes through the birth canal.

When I was a medical student at the county hospital in Los Angeles, a mother brought in her three-year-old daughter with a vaginal discharge. I checked the secretion under the microscope and it was positive for gonorrhea. This really blew my mind! How could it be? When I asked the mother how on earth this was possible, this was her shameful reply: "I think my husband is having sex with her."

I was horrified, an adult having intercourse with a three year old? Not only was I furious with the father, but with the mother as well. She had known this was going on and had told no one until me. Of course, the police were called and justice was done, but I still wonder what justice the little girl got out of the deal.

Babies can contract syphilis from an infected mother in the last trimester of her pregnancy. Congenital syphilis is no longer a statistically significant problem for the most part, but cases still do occur. And with the upswing in the number of reported cases, more and more infants are likely to suffer. Proper diagnosis and use of antibiotics could prevent these little babies' problems.

In this country, STD's are far more prevalent than AIDS, but are controllable with our current resources, if we'd just use them. Efforts are being made to create more public awareness of STD's, and as often happens, some people become not only concerned, but in a state of panic. Those most frightened are often least likely to be infected. I have had patients, for example, who have never had sexual exposure, but were terrified by what they read in the newspaper or see on television. They suspect that the neighbor in the next apartment may be spreading disease, or the checker at the supermarket, or perhaps the pimply-faced youngster at the Laundromat.

Believe me, it has taken some persuasion on my part to assure these women that they are not endangered by a fleeting non-sexual exposure. Other patients have called me with symptoms that could reasonably be considered alarming, but often they are not indicators of a serious problem. Many very common vaginal disorders such as trichomonas and moniliasis present themselves as discharges that a layperson can easily misread. Maybe the woman has a simple skin eruption in the genital area or pimples on the labia, neither of which are immediately symptoms of STD's. What worries me about these misleading symptoms are the fact that the patient may be so frightened they avoid seeking proper diagnosis and treatment.

The symptoms of STD's can be very misleading, even for a trained doctor. It was not at all uncommon in public health clinics to routinely give antibiotics to the patients who come in with suspicious symptoms while still awaiting the test results. Many of these patients would never return for the results and if necessary, further treatment. At one end of the patient spectrum, I see fearful and panic-stricken women and at the other end the neglectful and irresponsible. In the middle is a large cluster of women, whose reaction to a diagnosis of a STD is at first, "How could that happen to me?" Then, "That no-good bastard!"

JAN AND HERB

Jan and Herb, both in their late twenties, worked in the public relations department of a record company, both unmarried. They had been lovers for three years. When Jan grew careless with taking her birth control pills and became pregnant. They were devoted to each other, and unencumbered elsewhere, but they were not interested in parenthood. There was no question that they both wanted Jan to have an abortion, which she did, with no regrets and few, if any, afterthoughts.

Their relationship continued until it ran into an unforeseen complication. Jan's professional life blossomed and Herb could not handle the competition. He was openly resentful at the office, and it spilled over into the bedroom. After a few months of bickering, they decided to go their separate ways. Herb, whose ego was battered, sought solace with other women, many of them in succession. Jan was much too busy forging ahead in her career to look for a replacement. Four months after their separation and four chaste months for Jan -- they drifted back into bed again. It was one of those for-old-time's-sake encounters. A week later, Jan was in my office. She had gonorrhea, and an informed, sophisticated person like Herb didn't have the remotest idea that he had infected her. Jan was in a rage. Obviously remorseful, Herb paid for her medical bills, but this did not assuage her anger. As we talked about it, she said (with some amazement of her own feelings), she was experiencing more resentment over his active sexual life than the gonorrhea itself.

Judgmental attitudes toward sexual activity are probably the major stumbling block in our drive to conquer STD's. But many people (maybe most) have trouble thinking clearly when aroused sexually. The case of Herb and Jan is a classic example. Herb was behaving immaturely by resenting his lover's success. But was Jan any better for feeling she had a right to harshly judge his behavior after they'd parted? She said she was "resentful", which implies she had been victimized, but both of them had to participate to get gonorrhea. Since it was an honest mistake, it would have been healthier for her to be more understanding of Herb's sexual needs and less angry. However, jealousy and territorial emotionalism, on the part of both men and women are never more rampant than they are on the subject of sex.

Therefore society considers STD's more than an infection. It is proof of sexual activity, sometimes infidelity, and that's an unforgivable sin in the minds of many people. Deep in their hearts, these same people, mostly the old, righteous and powerful think disease is exactly what our promiscuous populace deserves. They don't seem to understand that a different attitude toward sex now exists! The genie is out of the bottle. All the pamphlets, abstinence lectures and scare tactics are not likely to sway the liberated young people who make up the STD population.

Public health authorities are doing a noteworthy job. It is their responsibility to diagnose and treat STD's without charge. They have many clinics that provide just that service. Were that not true, I'm convinced that our STD problem would be infinitely worse. The public health system is committed to a follow-up program. Officials feel that treatment of infected patients is not enough that they must track down the source of the infection and extend the treatment to that person as well. Accordingly, everyone treated at public health facilities are asked to cooperate by providing the names of all their sexual contacts. In this way their contacts are identified and sought out and treated. This method is a fine idea on paper, but in the real world, it can often backfire. Many people avoid seeking treatment, for fear of having to expose their personal lives. It can also be used to victimize others.

BARBARA

I got a call one day from Barbara's mother in San Francisco. I had met her a few weeks previously when I delivered her daughter's first baby. Barbara's mother had a very strange and surprising request. She wanted me to check her daughter for syphilis and furthermore keep the request secret from Barbara's husband.

Barbara worked for a very successful rock group, and I thought, well, musicians will be musicians, and after all, this is Hollywood. On the other hand, Barbara appeared to be very happily married. The fact that she might be suffering from a serious venereal disease just didn't seem right to me. When I did a bit of sleuthing, I came up with a chilling story. While on tour in Florida, one of the musicians developed syphilis. When he was asked to provide the names of his contacts, he included Barbara's. The Florida public health notified the public health authority in San Francisco, who in turn passed the word on to Barbara's parents. When I spoke to Barbara about the matter, she said she hadn't even seen the musician in over a year, and had never had sex with him. To really blast his story, Barbara was in the hospital under my care when the contact was reported to have taken place. Pure mischief making on the part of one man could have spelled disaster for Barbara's marriage.

LORETTA

A forty-five year old virgin, Loretta, was the executive vice-president of a large business organization. With Loretta, I was quite sure from the beginning of her problem that she was being victimized. She had been my patient for years and as of the last time I'd checked her -- still a virgin. I was quite unprepared, then, for Loretta's distraught phone call. She wanted an urgent appointment. A public health worker had just notified her that she had syphilis and was spreading it to others.

That didn't sound like what I would expect from the public service, but I saw her that very day. The results of my exam concluded she did not have syphilis, and indeed was still a virgin. I also found, on subsequent investigation, that a salesman for her company had been fired. Convinced that Loretta had been responsible for his dismissal, he furnished her name as a contact for his own syphilis. I have stopped wondering why people resort to such tactics. Some people are simply vicious.

Neither the case of Barbara nor Loretta is typical of the day-to-day activity of diligent and responsible public health workers. The fact is, sometimes the system does not work the way it was intended. These cases are real and did occur. I wonder if the push for prevention would not be infinitely more effective if STD's did not carry with it the overtones of immorality.

In the early 1920's, conservative religious leaders battled against the use of contraceptives. A battle the Woman's Suffrage Movement won, thanks to Margaret Sanger, though she went to prison for giving contraceptive advise. Religious leaders, mostly old men, were fearful that the liberalization of females would promote promiscuity, and give women a new sense of freedom and worth. The same occurred with the development of the pill and abortion is still being vigorously opposed. People all the way from the "Religious Right" to total fanatics are still fighting Row v. Wade. They believe abortion, no matter how early, is the taking of a human life, not that they seem to give a damn what happens to it once it's born. Abortion is the termination of a potential life, but even more frightening to many of these groups is the fact that it further liberalizes women, giving them substantially more sexual freedom and personal choice.

I worry that these same pious, tunnel-visioned zealots might target the fight against STD. As a case in point, we have spermicidal suppositories, why not suppositories that kill sexually transmittable diseases? There has been some research done but there needs to be a lot more and why isn't it happening? Most of these organisms are very fragile and must be spread from one moist part of the body to another. If they dry out, they die. To develop such a suppository would not require a major scientific breakthrough, so what are we waiting for? Or, better yet, why are we waiting at all?

Until STD eradication is a reality, I suggest we employ simple common sense measures. First, the good old-fashioned condom is still one of the best ways of preventing the spread of disease. Casual sex partners should both insist on condom usage, not only as a contraceptive but also as prophylaxis against STD. Even if a woman is on the pill and not worried about getting pregnant, this precaution should be taken. The man, who may be equally uneasy about possible infection, ought to consider this a fair bargain. Same-sex partners should also use condoms. This was a given at first, but now that AIDS has become a treatable disease, many of the high-risk populations have become complacent and are no longer practicing safe sex. Sadly, this has led to a "rebound" in the number of new AIDS cases.

Second, and this may sound capricious and unromantic, please examine your partner. Make sure there are no obvious evidences of infection in the genital areas. This need not be as crass a procedure as it sounds. This effort does not necessarily differ from the usual sexual foreplay. Just pay attention to what you see. The significant difference is that you are on the lookout for warning signs: a cream-like discharge from the end of the penis, sores or warts on the labia or shaft of the penis. If you see anything suspicious, cancel the entire encounter.

If you find nothing out of order and decide to forge ahead, both partners should take one final precaution. Cleanse themselves thoroughly after the rendezvous, women both internally and externally. Soap and water won't kill many germs, but they wash lots of them away. If you feel this routine would take some of the magic out of sex, I assure you there is nothing magical about an STD. Remember, you could pass it on to others, perhaps someone you love. Any good prostitute practices a routine very much like the one just suggested. She does it because her livelihood and health are at stake. We would be smart to adopt their ground rules.

Sexual activity outside of marriage was not invented recently, it has merely become more acceptable. We can wipe out STD's, but we can't rely on a small corps of civil servants to do it for us. It will have to be done boldly and definitively, under the leadership of medical scientists, with not only aggressive public support but with public insistence. We will have to overrule the squeamish, the prudish, and the serve-em-righters. Considering sex can create physical disease, mental anguish, and last but scarcely least, **PEOPLE**; I would say sex is anything but free.

HAPPY MARRIAGE: TRY, TRY AGAIN

Continued from First Page

openly with their friends, doctors and even their husbands.

"Infidelity is not the major threat to marriage today," he insists. "That threat is boredom. Most marriages do not really succeed; they survive.

"Some of the freedom that is characteristic of many affairs would infinitely strengthen most marriages. No one expects an affair to last forever."

Cooper said that those who divorce and remarry should not be subject to social disapproval.

Sexual Revolution

"We should encourage the alternative of multiple

Dr. Boyd Cooper
Times photo

Los Angeles Times Article | 1972

19 FIDELITY IS FOR EVERYONE

Most human beings would probably agree that monogamy, one of the cornerstones of civilization, is the most ideal method of human cohabitation. Yet for many people it doesn't work in their world. In my early days of practice it was estimated that infidelity occurs in fifty percent of marriages. There are any numbers of reasons why people stray. The same old position in the same old bed during the *Tonight Show* has a short shelf life. Sexual boredom, the seeking of sexual excitement, or just plain relief sounds exciting, but it seldom is after a brief interval. Another is non-existent sex at home. There are an appalling number of sexless marriages that go on forever. I have known many. There are many other reasons for divorces, and all sorts of reasons for bonds breaking between two people. Frequently the marriage was a mistake from the beginning.

Sex outside of marriage is much easier to come by today. Women work and are no longer confined to their homes. Sex is all around us now, in the open, and since everyone else seems to be getting some, there will be those who decide, hey, why not me too? Cheating is not as socially repugnant as it once was. Married people also fall in love with others, or make mistakes in judgment, or both. Many individuals choose a life partner before they even begin to live, and I'm certain this has a massive effect on both the divorce and infidelity statistics.

Then there is the insecure person, one who hasn't matured yet when they validate their sexual behavior with marriage. Or the player who takes an amoral point of view, and gets a lot of action but not much satisfaction out of his or her sex life, but they keep searching.

There are a lot of other possibilities, but one of the most important factors is that we, like all other living creatures, are hard wired for sex. We often desire different experiences, thus leading to extra-curricular sexual behavior. We are driven by primordial urges to procreate, and although we have civilized ourselves (to a point) and have risen above those urges, or learned to live with them, the fact remains that these primitive urges still play a big part in contemporary sexuality. Consider the fact that most males generate millions of sperm each day. Man's basic primordial drive is to spread that sperm as far and wide as possible, unload them and hurry off to procreate with the next available female. Many animals are willing to die for that right (even some men). It's the strongest drive mankind has, second only to his own survival. We are not necessarily conscious of the origin of this drive, but it's built into the motherboards.

Where men are concerned, their reaction to these urges go from one end of the spectrum to the other. At one end they live in denial of their urges and find other outlets for additional sexual expression. They can range from sports and hobbies to aberrant behavior like excessive neatness, acquisition of material things or money, or whatever else turns him "on". At the other end, we have the man who wants complete freedom to fulfill his animal longings, the old "eat and run" concept. In order to pull this off he has to have the charisma and/or necessary wealth to attract numerous females while totally avoiding commitment. Most men lie somewhere in between.

Some men and women never wander astray, finding satisfaction with fantasy. Whether that be like an HBO's series on the internal struggle to stay faithful, *The Mind of the Man Married*, or surfing the internet for porn -- most men and women are willing to accept monogamy provided they are able to sneak a little on the side every once in a while.

However, contrary to what may still be the opinion in some circles, females are statistically just as likely to engage in extra-marital sex as males. Recent studies indicate an equal percentage stray. Many human behavior studies clearly demonstrate that the inclination towards multiple partners is more natural than fidelity.

Further, our sex drive demands that we produce the best possible offspring. Both sexes want their progeny to survive. They just have different ways of trying to achieve it. As for women, with eggs being scarce -- one a month at best -- the primitive female had to select her mate very carefully. Although men have many sperm, it is just one of her comparatively few eggs that will lead to carrying a child for nine months and in turn spend many years raising. Often times women make a mistake and pick the wrong partner, leaving her stuck for many years with the choice she made.

In a recent retrospective study it was determined that if a woman was having periodic sex with a lover in addition to her husband she was more likely to have sex with her lover during her fertile period. Most of these women in this study did not connect their sexual activity with their ovulation cycle, but the connection was there unconsciously. So, when it comes to our instinctive urges, women are just as primitive as men. They just have different aims for their primitive urges.

In the early seventies I did thousands of abortions and during that time I conducted a little case study of my own. I was amazed to discover that I had performed abortions on seventeen women over the age of forty whose husbands had had vasectomies. Many of the husbands never knew. I certainly never told them, anymore than I discussed the many male patients and "friends" I helped get rid of the products they produced outside of their marriages.

Another reason why women have joined the infidelity movement is that the consequences of sex, outside of marriage have changed. That playing field has leveled off a bit allowing women to have fun, too. And now with the availability of DNA testing, fathers have to take responsibility for their offspring, in or out of wedlock. As for the myriad of sexual diseases lurking out there, they affect both men and woman alike, but it's no longer an international scandal for a woman to get one.

Until forty or so years ago, objects and avenues of sexual pleasure were generally thought of as a male province. They still are to a great degree. At least a majority of sexual enterprise is still aimed at the male consumer. Sex is the carrot used by businesses to pique the interest in everything men buy from the car they drive to the beverage they drink. Even if a man is not inclined to avail himself of outside sex, that can change during male menopause, or mid-life crisis, or whatever the current term for the condition may be. It's no longer considered an outrage and has become only an embarrassment for Mr. Stable to suddenly find himself buying a sports car and a tootsie to match. Not to mention the availability of pole dancers, lap dancers, prostitution, pornography, massage parlors, peep shows, 1-800-Fuck-Me phone lines, etc.

But what's good for the gander has also become good for the goose. Women can find their own massage therapists and personal trainers who double as sexual partners, and even their high-buck male prostitutes are available for a price. As for the sale of vibrators, we are talking big business, worldwide. Where they are legal, of course, as there are many countries where they are not allowed to be sold. To my knowledge, in America, they're available in every state except Alabama. I believe that masturbation is on the increase in general, by both males and females. I cannot prove it, but I believe it to be true. Don't misunderstand, masturbation is alright, but I still think sex is better.

Most sexual humor is still at the female's expense; of the men are from Mars and women from Venus theme. Some have come up with this sexist (but funny in a totally politically incorrect way) "explanation" for it all: "Women have sex with men so they can talk. Men talk to women so they can have sex." Unfortunately, in too many cases, nothing could be more accurate. There are women who so desperately long for any sign of communication with a man, that they will try getting it through sex. And there are some men whose personal growth is so stunted, they find no use for a women but a quiver for their arrow.

Another popular joke that's funny, but sexist as hell, has more than a grain of truth. A man feels it's important to find a woman who works around the house, cleans, occasionally cooks, and has a job. He needs a woman who makes him laugh. It's very important to find a woman who is dependable and doesn't lie. It's important to find a woman good in bed that constantly loves to have sex. It's also extremely important to him that these four women never meet!

It's true. Men do tend to want it all. But then, come to think of it, don't we all want it all? It's just still more socially acceptable for men to go after it. And they have a low resistance to sexual stimuli. Let's face it, most men are easy. It's been stated that males think of sex every ten seconds or three minutes or whatever the number is. I don't think that's true in today's world when we have so many other things on our minds and in our lives. I know I certainly didn't think about sex while I was delivering a baby despite the location of my job site. However, it's definitely on our minds. A very clever comic named Dana Carvey, once said that the three sexiest words in the English language are "white cotton panties". My friend Theodore Sturgeon, a famous fantasy writer whose young son, Andros, I delivered, took it one step further: "There's nothing as exciting to a man as two little words: new pussy." Women are coming back with their own bon mots on the subject, beginning with "A woman needs a man like a fish needs a bicycle."

ART

Men are easy marks. Loretta, a patient of mine, was a sexy young woman from Argentina. Her parents had moved to Argentina following WWII. Loretta and her mother had recently left her father and moved to Los Angeles. She had some connections with the entertainment business -- many of her friends were in showbiz and she was a wanna-be movie star. Loretta, who was never serious about any man, surprised me when she brought in Art and told me that they were getting married and invited me to their wedding. I went and was very happy for them. Art and Loretta became my dearest friends. I was new in practice at the time and had a brand new house in the Los Angeles. It was a swell house but it had no furniture! We had a king-sized bed with no headboard, but no furniture at all in the living room. Loretta and Art gave us our first sofa. Later I delivered their two beautiful boys.

One day when the boys were in their late teens, Art called, very distraught. He wanted to meet me on an urgent mater. After a drink and a bit of polite small talk he said, "I have to get a divorce." I was shocked! I thought they had everything and were very happy together.

"What happened?' I asked, "Are you and Loretta having problems?"

"No, Loretta is fine," Art replied. "It's me. I have to be free. I can't go on like this any longer." At this point I was stunned into silence as Art started pacing around the room. "I met this wonderful woman," he said finally. "I spent the afternoon and evening with her. She's absolutely the best. The very best and I'm the best when I'm with her." He stopped for a moment, then with a big smile on his face, he added, "I came three times! I'm over forty years of age and I came three times. Do you know how long it's been since I came three times?"

I shook my head. I knew I had to be careful what I said. If I began moralizing (Loretta was my friend, too) I wouldn't be able to help him. In order to be helpful, I first had to find out exactly what was going on. "Wow," I said. "It sounds exciting. Tell me more. Who is she? Is she young - and gorgeous?"

"She's a client of mine in her thirties," he said. "She's wonderful and if you can believe this -- she came on to me."

I begin to ease gently into the reality of the situation. "Are you and Loretta having sex problems?"

"No, but we don't have much sex anymore. It's so different with this woman. The only problem is, she's married and has three kids."

Oh, boy, I thought, but I stayed cool. "So, what are you going to do about it?"

"I want to get a divorce so I can spend the rest of my life with her," Art said firmly. "I haven't felt like this since I was a kid. I feel so alive, it's so exciting." But there was a look on his face, one that had been growing since the moment he began this confession. Suddenly I knew why he had called me. He knew this was wrong and he wanted me to talk him out of it. I was ready.

Looking him squarely in the eye I said, "If I understand you correctly, you're willing to throw away the lives of five children and four adults because you came three times? Your new-found sex life must be very important to you." Art just stared at me. "You want my advice?" I continued. "And you must or you wouldn't be here. Why don't you just cool it for a while and see where it goes? Don't talk about divorce, not now. Don't even think about it. And don't make Loretta suffer from your little adventure."

In the end the new girlfriend moved on to her next seducible male. Some men in their forties and fifties are uncertain of their future potency and sexual desirability, so they are easy targets. Art was no different. Loretta fortunately was able to survive the affair and they're still happily married. The girlfriend bruised Art a little, but he survived.

Women are generally more careful in their choice of playmates. It's part of their DNA. Men are admittedly very tricky (they lie a lot where sex is concerned) so her careful selection is not always easy. But all is fair in love and war, and make no mistake, this is both love and war.

Sometime the female simply finds a better mate. Couples can grow apart as they grow up, or perhaps the mate she selected earlier was not what he advertised. Unfortunately, she can learn this truth at any time, at any age, or at any time in the marriage. Modern women are having real problems with the selection process. The feminist revolution strengthened the female role and in so doing weakened the males'. It is acceptable for the women to be making the choices, but there doesn't seem to be that much of a selection for them. Men are not what they used to be. They are no longer willing or able to slay the fire-spewing dragon for the woman they love, so a lot of women don't want the men they meet. There are not fire-spewing dragons to slay nowadays anyhow. Physically strong men are no longer needed in modern society. I often hear from women that men are not aggressive enough. He is no longer the hunter. Women are disappointed. Some question their own femininity and sexual appeal. Still, many women have the fantasy of the white knight carrying them off on high to his wind swept castle in the sky. It's seemingly part of their DNA.

Many years ago a study was done at UCLA in which a group of rats were given a wonderful home with everything a rat could need: an acceptable male-female ratio, large clean cages free from disease and plenty of food. The only thing limited was space. They increased their numbers and were a very happy colony until they out-grew their space. At that point there were dramatic social changes. Some males became homosexual and some became vicious and started killing other rats. Gangs of young rats roamed around the bottom of the cage killing others indiscriminately. The social interaction between males and females became strained. Eventually the rats forgot how to relate to one another. The females became infertile and in time they stopped reproducing. Ultimately the colony died.

I realize that humans are not rats, but that study has always worried me. We humans crowd ourselves into larger and larger cities only to become more and more isolated from one another. The internet, voicemail and texting have given us the opportunity to isolate ourselves even more. What we will be doing in the future I don't know. The rules and behavioral studies will probably be different, too. We live in a dynamic world that is changing more rapidly as time progresses. We have to make room for one another even if we have different beliefs. We have to learn to be more tolerant of one another and not insist that everyone's sexual choices are the same as ours. People change as they go through their lives. The person you were may not be the person you will become. The same applies to your spouse. Buried primitive urges are unleashed. Personal needs, long tampered, rise to the surface. We certainly could and frequently do grow apart as we go through our very long lives. But with all of this fidelity is it still possible, and practiced by most.

Modern man lives and remains healthy for a much longer time than the days of old. Fidelity was more important and much simpler for those who lived in the time of the Bible, the time the rules of sexual behavior were established. Life was much shorter and survival more questionable. The average human being was dead at the age of forty-five. In those days, survival of the species was best sustained in monogamous relationships. But they cheated on their spouses in those days too. Read the Bible.

When someone strays from the ideal path, it's not the end of the world either, and need not be the end of a partnership. Not if the couple really care about each other, and understands the other person's drives and needs. In order to do that, we must understand our own needs, and be honest with ourselves. We are all different. Might we not have done the same thing if we'd been walking that proverbial mile in the other person's shoes? I'm certainly not recommending affairs or one-night flings. But if this happens to someone we care for, and who cares for us, or if this happens to us personally, here is a pertinent question to ask ourselves when trying to cope with the transgression: in Tina Turner's words, "What's love got to do with it?"

Ninety-nine times out of a hundred, the answer is *not a damn thing!* Having sex outside of marriage does not mean we do not love our partner, certainly not in every case. Remember, people have different ways of handling their own needs. Our primordial urges may account for how we feel, but what we do about them is up to us and is highly individual. Obviously sexual verity is desired by many, both men and women, but is that verity worth it in the long run? Frankly I really don't know. In some partnerships, fidelity, which is another word for loyalty, may be more a matter of heart than of body.

The Bluebird Inn | Cambria, California

20 THE BLUEBIRD INN

I knew I would have to stop doing surgery long before I'd be ready to stop working all together. Unlike some doctors I didn't choose to do surgery after my skills started to wane. Surgery is like any other athletic event. The surgeon should be at his best -- quick of mind and operative skill, yet able to stand operating at the patient's side for hours without weakening. I'd been a doctor for over forty years, and was getting very upset with the way medical practice was going anyway. Malpractice fees were becoming unaffordable, especially for obstetricians. I knew I'd have to find something else to do soon.

By that time my practice was growing and I had taken on an associate. I was making good money, but I was fed up with giving a large part of what I earned to the government. My youngest brother, Ken, was also doing psychotherapy in my office part time. The three of us, Ken, my associate and I agreed to start building apartments with our money instead of giving it to the IRS. In addition to seeing his patients, Ken was managing the office while starting to look for properties for us to buy and build. My partner and I would furnish the seed money as I already had a large line of credit at the bank. We agreed to split the profit three ways. It was very profitable and by trading up we stopped giving the money to the IRS.

What I didn't expect was that my associate would start stealing my money. He was already making more money than he'd ever made before coming to work for me. Money does that to some people, the more they have the more they want. I was encouraged to prosecute him, but I didn't. He had a wife and children and for him to lose his medical license would have hurt his innocent family. All our hospital colleagues knew about it, and that was punishment enough for me.

I love dealing with people and told Ken to try to find us a business with more day-to-day involvement with people. I was tired of building apartments. "Okay," he said, "I'm tired of dealing with other people's problems all day long and sometimes half the night myself." In his search he found a motel for sale in Cambria, California. Cambria is on the central coast halfway between Los Angeles and San Francisco. I liked the idea of running a resort hotel, and so did Susan. We decided to drive up the coast and look at the Bluebird Inn. Maybe we could even visit the Hearst Castle, media giant William Randolph Hearst's incredible estate. So we drove up Pacific Coast Highway 1.

Cambria is an enchanting village nestled between the mountains and the sea. People call it Camelot because the sun always shines there and it only rains while people are sleeping. Main Street goes right through East Town and West Town back to the sea, and a large creek runs across the back. It should be called Old Town and New Town, as the old part of town was built decades before. The tallest and most magnificent old oak tree stood at the front of the Bluebird at 1880 Maine Street. The Bluebird Inn's central building was the first building built in Cambria in 1880.

As we pulled into the Bluebird driveway we could see it was a bit rundown and retained a 1960's look. Still it had its own charm. It had been rebuilt and was now a little two story white house with more modern buildings all around it. The lobby was a large warm room with leaded glass windows and a huge rock fireplace. The carpet was red and the drapes were also red with white flowers. The atmosphere of the lobby was warm and inviting.

We looked at the accounting ledger. The rooms were renting well below resort prices. This gave it a lot of potential as a moneymaking yet fun investment. We decided to trade in our apartment building, and with my line of credit we were able to make the purchase.

Ken and his wife Gisela sold their home and moved to Cambria. They would live there and be the new managers for which they would be paid a salary. If we made any money it would be put right back into the motel to upgrade, and do the necessary alterations and repairs.

At first the business was marginal, and on the second year I had to take money out of my office practice to pay the Bluebird's bills. After that slow beginning the motel did well, and we put all the money we made back into the property. We rebuilt the roofs on all the buildings and replaced all the windows and doors. Ken used the money from selling their house to remodel their new living space in the main building. The motel was beginning to look a lot classier, and we raised the prices accordingly. Ken and Gisela were good managers.

At the back of the property there was a large space next to the creek and room to add six new units overlooking it. We decided to build the new units, and I put up the money to build them, but this money was a loan to the Bluebird and had to be repaid. The new rooms were beautiful. My family stayed in the new unit when we went to the motel on the weekends. My youngest daughter, Alexandria, loved going to Cambria and frequently brought her little friend, Lora, with her. We planned to move to Cambria after my retirement, but as my time for retirement came closer I became uncertain about my initial decision. Cambria is a lovely retirement community -- quiet, restful and things change very slowly there. Therefore it was outside the mainstream of an active society I was used too. I was older, but not dead. I still wanted to be where there was some action. So did my wife. We wanted to make films and spend time with the movers and shakers. I don't think Ken and Gisela wanted us there either. Four people, two families running a business, that's like two women in a kitchen. History has taught us that it doesn't work.

Ken offered to buy me out. I knew it was the right thing to do, but now I had no plans for my retirement. I still needed to be busy doing something. Oh, we tried to buy other motels, but none of that worked out. So I agreed to sell. We unfortunately had a disagreement on the price. I expected the Bluebird to pay me back for the cash I'd put up to build the new units. The rental on the new units had already paid the Bluebird more than I had lent them. The thought of my brother trying to not pay me back the money after all I'd done for him made my wife go ballistic. I was hurt, but after a period of time we came to an agreement.

I wish I had known that going into business with your kin and living with each others wives is like living with unexploded dynamite. Ken and I had grown up together and had been businessmen together, but he was first and foremost my baby brother. I'd always been in charge.

When Ken was born I was thirteen. Our lives were bound together from the beginning. When he was learning to walk he was afraid of walking without holding onto something. I was happy to see the joy on his little face when I walked him around the house with his little hand wrapped around my finger. One day while we were walking across a big room I slowly slipped his little hand off my finger, and continued to walk with him. When he realized he was walking without assistance he took off as if he'd just been released from bondage -- running, laughing, and looking up at me. He was proud of himself and so was I.

Ken was special to all of us, especially to dad. Dad had been rough and wanted us all to be strong, but not his baby Ken. He was our special, little brother. From that early beginning he certainly was special for me.

I opened the drive-in when Ken was sixteen, and he came to work for me. He began his adult life peeling and dicing potatoes for french-fries, hundreds of pounds of them. It must have been a boring job for a teenager, but he did more than his job. He became a fry cook, and learned how to manage the place. Later when he went to college he was able to get a job as a night manager at a small fast-food place.

Later when many of us had just returned home from the war, and ill-prepared for a normal adult life let alone the new technological world that had just been created, the GI bill was created. We were under-educated and both ourselves and the government knew it. Everyone was eager to help the veterans get on with their lives. When Irene and I moved to Seattle, Ken joined us. I had the GI bill, Ken and Irene worked, and we all took turns looking after my son, Lonny, who was now three. Later when we moved to Washington D.C. for med school Ken stayed at the University in Seattle to finish his education.

We went our separate ways for a few years. He became a psychologist, got married, and moved to Orange County. At that point I had opened my office in Hollywood. We were family and continued to see one another from time to time. At the time I opened my practice, Ken was working for the state of California. Governor Ronald Reagan was technically his boss. When Reagan began his campaign to run for president, he invited Ken to become a member of his team, but Ken didn't join him. He thought Reagan was too old and would never get elected, so Ken went into private practice instead. He needed an office, and I needed a psychologist.

When I started doing abortions I was worried about the possible emotional effects it might have on my patients. The literature seemed to indicate that having an abortion would damage a woman psychologically for the rest of her life. As I previously mentioned, I decided to have all the women who were having abortions receive psychological evaluations before and after their procedure. I asked him to join me and perform the patient psychological evaluations. It turned out to be a good move for both of us.

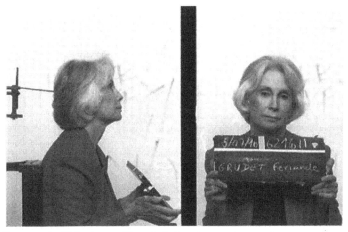

Fernande "Madame Claude" Grudet - whose clients included
President John F. Kennedy and Marlon Brando, fled from France to
Los Angeles in the 1970's to avoid the authorities for tax evasion.

21 HOOKERS

When I first opened my office, prostitutes soon discovered there
was a new gynecologist in town. I was amazed at the large number of
prostitutes who suddenly appeared with their hands full of cash. All
they wanted was to be treated like any other patient with an honest,
quick exam and my signature on a health certificate. They didn't want to
waste my time or theirs. I tried to oblige them, so they sent their
friends. They network just like members of any other profession. They
considered themselves to be professionals, just like me. They had
appointments just as I did, and wanted to get back to work so they
could pay their bills. In those early days, I was happy to accommodate
them because I too, had bills to pay and had very few patients in the
beginning.

From the beginning, I was mystified by how young and beautiful
they were. I wondered why such lovely young women would sell their
bodies to men for sex. It all seemed so contrary to my upbringing and so
unnecessary. I, like many others, was of the opinion that prostitutes
were either too lazy or unable to get real jobs. Or maybe they were sex

addicts, and experienced greater sexual satisfaction than other women. Maybe even to the point of being perverse. Of course, being a caring and somewhat inexperienced doctor, I wanted to save them all from themselves, from what I perceived as their depraved lifestyle. I wanted to help them become "normal". Little did I know that it was not that easy to understand or to reform them, but I kept wondering why. Why did they choose this life and all the danger and social condemnation that went with it? The truth was I didn't have a clue. They clearly preferred the way they were living, and did not want to change. That seemed bizarre, but if I wanted to reform them, first I had to understand them.

The sheer seediness of prostitution, street-walkers and hookers is just one reason governments have long sought to outlaw it. Some to a lesser degree have tried to corral it in licensed brothels or specific areas. Prostitution is the oldest known profession. Why have there been prostitutes since the first cave woman turned her first trick? And why did that fact of life upset just about everyone, including me? Even liberal Hollywood was prejudiced against hookers. Often, they are the real victims, they take the risk of infection and injury. Many of them end up in hospital emergency rooms. When unable to work they are frequently abandoned by their pimp. Many hookers do indeed suffer from trafficking, exploitation and violence. It's their abusive pimps that should be put in jail. To the powers that be, ladies of the evening were simply whores, bad girls, a menace to society, and the propagators of STD's or even worse -- AIDS.

Many Christians still believe that sex for sheer pleasure is immoral. Even Aristotle equated women with the material principle (flesh) and men with the rational principle (thought). In Aristotle's time, thought must over rule the flesh. Most theologians have decreed that sex just for the enjoyment is wicked, therefore the dispenser of it is evil. Pope John Paul II pontificated that prostitution is "intrinsically evil" and can never be "subjectively good or defensible." On the other hand, Aquinas and Augustine were willing to go beyond that concept and accept prostitution, particularly if it controlled rampant male lust and sexuality for the good of the marriage contract. Even Jesus was tolerant of concubines, harlots and such women. I contend that most hookers are people just like the rest of us with the same problems, goals and aspirations.

Many researchers have attempted to provide psychological motivations for prostitution. I'm sure that some hookers have deep-seated psychological problems. Many have low esteem. Some suffer from bipolar disease or ADD. A few are psychotic. But what profession doesn't have those with a few screws loose? Many of the prostitutes I knew were smart businesswomen, trying to make a buck.

Most prostitutes start their sex life in their middle to early teens. Seventy-five percent of the prostitutes I have known began their careers as sex workers between the ages of sixteen and twenty-five. Only about ten percent started hooking after the age of thirty. The younger ones may have been promiscuous teenagers with long histories of coital activity, while others may have developed expensive drug habits, or had children to support, or both. The girls who entered prostitution in their twenties seemed to do so out of a clear, rational, economic choice. In fact, forty percent of these women professed to have made the choice out of the desire to have a higher paying profession and live a better life.

Often times they started out with a simple goal, such as the desire to raise enough money to go to school, more away or purchase a new car. They soon discovered that hooking is a way to make a lot of money and have time left over to enjoy it. Consider this scenario: a woman is fed up with her working life, her job, the men she works for and the man she sleeps with, for <u>free</u>, and at his convenience. Hence, some take another path.

The hookers I have known saw nothing wrong with getting paid for sex. They soon learned that men were willing to pay handsomely. After a while, they no longer held mature men in awe, like they did their fathers, and had no moral dilemma about sex. In fact, many hookers enjoys sex. But those who do not treat it like any other job -- just satisfy the client as quickly as possible and move on. Prostitution has always been with us, and always will be. It's not local! It's a global reality. We need to not only change our laws governing sexual activity, but to change our attitudes toward it.

SAMMY

It's true some girls become hookers out of desperation. A patient of mine, Sammy, once told me, "I didn't have money, I didn't have a job. I was very depressed with little hope when a friend of mine told me she was doing bondage and discipline." When Sammy asked her friend exactly what that entailed, this was the reply: "I tie guys up, walk around nude in high heels, snapping a whip and threatening them. They masturbate, and then pay two or three times the going rate. Sometimes I have sex, sometimes I use the whip."

When I asked Sammy how she felt about that, she admitted it was exciting to her. She decided to do it, explaining, "That bastard boyfriend of mine, all he wants is to get blow-jobs and fuck me in the ass! It sounded like a lot of fun to put men down for a change."

When I asked if she was still hooking, she nodded. "Yes, I am. I have my own place now and I'm no longer depressed." It's obvious that Sammy had a problem, but she worked it out in her way. Most hookers are pretty straight, and don't do the kinky stuff, but they know who will and refer those clients.

MONICA

Monica had a three-year old son and two apartments. She worked in one and lived in the other with her son. Monica told me, "I pay a babysitter $20 a night to watch my son while I make several hundred." Monica had half a dozen steady clients that she saw on a regular basis. She had regular check-ups and took very good care of herself. I was surprised when she came in one day and announced that she was leaving the business.

When I asked what had convinced her, she replied that she was getting married. But she hadn't exactly met Mr. Right, at least in the traditional sense. "I'm marrying one of my long-time Johns," she said. "He loves me and he loves my son. He wants me to go out of the business. He wants to take care of us."

Several of the nurses I've worked with were hookers on the side, too. For some, it was exciting and the money was fantastic. They also enjoyed the sex. As one nurse put it, "It's just a different kind of care and it's a lot more fun than giving enemas and bed baths."

The private secretary to one of the highest officials in the Los Angeles County Medical Association was a part-time hooker. She sat right up there with her boss in all the meetings, but she had steady clients and made her real money at night. Many businesses hire hookers when out of town clients arrive on buying tours, especially in the import and export business. Many foreign companies expect it.

One of my bright, upwardly mobile young patients called one day to advise me that she had just become a vice-president. She was very proud of her promotion, but she later called me in tears. She had just been informed that buyers were coming to town and as vice-president it was her job to arrange a party for them. She was further advised to get several good-looking hookers to take care of the clients. She was very upset, but I'm sure such services have helped businessmen close many a deal over the years.

I have heard from my patients that the movie and theatrical businesses also hire beautiful young hookers as assistants. Their real jobs are to lure the investors away from the stars they're trying to hit on. It's the same in the clothing industry. The hooker/assistant's job is to charm the buyers away from the models. That's just the way it is for some industries.

LAURA

Laura was a bartender and felt sorry for the lonely men she met in the club where she worked. She enjoyed sexual activity and would sometime have sex with them. Some would offer her money or gratuities out of appreciation. Finally, at the age of thirty-three, Laura became a hooker and made more money and worked fewer hours. Her attitude was, "I'm already doing it. I might as well get paid for it."

One busy afternoon I got a strange phone call. A sexy, young voice started describing her physical attributes and told me that she was new in town and would love to see me. She was sure she could supply whatever I wanted.

I was confused about the call at first, and then I realized that she must have gotten my name from some hooker's "little black book." Prostitutes move around a lot. They get fed up with the local scene and want to move on, so they sell their list of clients to incoming talent. My name was in someone's book because I was her doctor, not a client. The new girl was just confused. When I didn't bite, she got the picture.

SHERI

I will never forget Sheri, a beautiful, young girl with large, dark, exotic eyes and long black hair. She always had a big smile on her face and the courage of a lioness. Sheri was the only daughter of a local doctor. I didn't know her father personally, though I'd seen him around the hospital and at meetings. When I learned that she was an out-call girl, I was shocked. Out-call girls go to the homes of their clients which is the most dangerous form of prostitution. I was more than just shocked. I was frightened to death. It was the time of the Hillside Strangler, a local Los Angeles prostitute killer. Beautiful young girls were brutally murdered and then left nude on the hillsides along the freeways.

I not only felt it was my duty to reform Sheri, but I had to, to save her life. My fear was exaggerated because, at the same time, I had a patient who worked in the coroner's office. She would describe to me in detail how the victims were murdered, and I didn't want that awful fate to befall Sheri. Out of concern for her, I tried to make her realize the risk she was taking. I couldn't understand why she was literally trying to commit suicide. I tried to help her, but I failed. Finally, I begged her to just leave town. "Go to Chicago or New York; just get out of LA until they catch this lunatic." She refused but thank God, a few months later they arrested the Hillside Stranglers, plural, because it turned out to be two guys.

Sherri was not only living the life of a prostitute, but her behavior was dangerous, even masochistic. It's still very hard for me to understand. Sheri had a happy childhood. She went to Beverly Hills High School and was accepted by her peer group, even though she hated those "stuck-up bitches." In spite of her beauty and personality, she had a very low opinion of herself. Why she became a masochistic hooker I'll never know. She had a death wish much like the young men who force the police to shoot them. Many such women are killed every year and we as a society couldn't care less. After all, they're only hookers. She needed psychiatric help, but didn't receive it. What a waste; it all seemed so needless to me. Finally, she did leave town. Like many of my patients, I don't know what happened to her.

There was another doctor in my area whose daughter became a hooker: Dr. Paul Fleiss, a pediatrician who took care of many of the babies that I delivered. I never met his famous (or infamous) daughter Heidi, who became one of Hollywood's most famous madams. Her very successful career in the sex business must have put her father through difficult times. Prostitutes' families don't have very easy lives even if their daughters have enough extra income to shower them with gifts and money.

I had read an article about prostitution in Australia, and I decided I wanted to conduct an informal study of my own. I asked some of my more liberal-minded patients if they had ever considered becoming hookers. Ninety percent said never, ten percent said they had considered it. I then asked them to give me three reasons why they felt young women became prostitutes. Ninety percent listed a drug habit and the same number also listed unemployment. Forty-five percent listed low self-esteem, forty percent listed being talked into prostitution by pimps, thirty percent listed delinquency or nymphomania, and twenty-five percent listed a need to be loved. These straight-arrow patients assumed that, given a choice, no women in her right mind would choose such a despicable profession unless there was some driving force compelling them to do it.

When I asked hookers why they chose to become hookers, half of them said it was in order to have a better life and more money. Some did indeed have drug habits. A few hooked to pay for their education. I went to medical school with a lovely young woman who told me flat out, "I've hooked my way through medical school." Not that I ever would want that, but my wife worked a lot harder as a secretary for a lot less money to help me through medical school.

A world-famous newscaster met a sixteen year old girl in Europe who needed a job, so he and his wife brought her to America to be their children's nanny. She not only learned the American customs, she eventually became an American citizen. However, unknown to the newscaster's wife, the au pair's duties also included late night visits to her bedroom by the newscaster himself. She told me, "The pay was more than enough and he was a gentlemen, so I stayed for years." Eventually, she got married and had a child whom I delivered. She told me she did not have one moment's regret for the time she spent with the newscaster. In fact, she seemed proud of it. He was probably the most famous newscaster at that time.

I admit that my patients do not represent all the different types of hookers. Pimps or brothels control some of them very tightly. Some are literally sex-slaves shipped in from other countries and kept locked up to work here. The pimps or brothels furnish the clients and take most of the money. I have admitted a few of these girls through the emergency room after finding they were suffering from serious pelvic infections. These promoters are not very careful about their selection of clients. They want the money and take all clientele, even the high-risk types.

When a hooker gets sick, the pimp is nowhere to be found and the poor girl has to be admitted to the hospital as a charity case. No doctor is seeing these girls regularly for check-ups even though they could be seen for free through public health services. Pimps usually have several girls. When one can't work the others can, so his income continues. It is probable that these girls do spread disease. In the studies that I have read, the incidence of STD's and HIV is increased in street prostitutes. In my practice, I have treated several patients who were HIV positive, but I have never treated a hooker who was HIV positive or one who had full-blown AIDS. Hookers make a living with their bodies and know that if they don't take care of themselves it will impact their livelihood. Most practice safe sex. They clean and inspect their clients as part of foreplay. In my examining room, hookers are often cleaner than secretaries.

I remember one afternoon I was asked to make a house call. When I approached the patient's apartment door, I found it ajar. I knocked on the door and a voice said, "Come in." Upon entering, I noticed that soft music was playing and incense was burning. A voice from the next room called out, "Just make yourself at home, I'll be right there." I became a little suspicious, but waited. Then an attractive, young blond, fresh from the shower and wearing a sheer black negligee, suddenly appeared. She came straight up to me placing her sensitive anatomy in my face, pulled her panties aside and pointed at her vulva, "What's that?" she demanded.

Astonished, I looked as she asked, however, I saw very little. There was a small irregularity on the vulva. I had seen this patient in my office once before but didn't remember her anymore than that. I left her with instructions to come to my office the next day. When I did an examination, I was surprised to find that she had syphilis. Later, I learned that she was a hooker just promoting business.

Lindsay & Suzy Crosby

22 HOLLYWOOD: THE BIPOLAR CAPITAL OF THE WORLD

My time at that state mental institution in Camarillo as a gynecological resident gave me first-hand experience with mental disorders. I saw lots of schizophrenics but few manic-depressives (bipolars). I wondered about that - why were there less manic-depressives in treatment? When I opened my practice I soon learned that they were all in Hollywood.

I was asked by a successful older gynecologist, Dr. Harry Lusk, to join his office. Many of his patients were artistic, exciting and fun. Some were celebrities like Cher and Angela Lansbury. Some were hookers who claimed to be actresses. Some were actresses who were also hookers. And some were manic-depressives. Some of his patients seemed just a little insane to me, a little like my patients in Camarillo. Some of Harry's patients belonged to religious cults like Scientology. Some were from the drug world of Haight Ashbury and were taking whatever drug was "in vogue" at the time. On the other hand, most of his patients were ordinary young women having the usual female problems, babies, infections, and other common female issues.

Most OB/GYN doctors at that time acted like wise fatherly figures to their young female patients. I wanted to be different than other doctors. Young women were no longer treated like little girls. They were much wiser and far less intimidated than their mothers. Fatherly men were just men to them. They gave little respect to a doctor just because he had gray hair. I wanted to be their friend and colleague with a little more updated savvy about their body. They were knowledgeable, their education was just different than mine.

Due to the personal nature of my specialty their problems were frequently of a private nature. I was about to examine them in a personal way, and wanted them to be as comfortable and trusting with me as they were with their hairdresser. At times I felt like the handmaiden of other men's wives and that was okay. I shared my patients' innermost fears and joys. Over the years we built a deep friendship and a high level of trust. Many times patients ostensibly would come in for a check-up when in reality they were much in need of counseling on their marriage or their latest affair. By my choice I was often exposed to a patient's mental and emotional problems as well as their gynecological needs.

As I developed my own practice, I realized that a lot of my patients, like Harry's, didn't fit into the organized conservative society that I was familiar with back in Idaho. A lot of them were movie people, actresses, and artists that didn't always follow the strict rules we all try to live by. Movie-land quickly forgives their misdeeds. They were fun loving, full of life, and did outlandish things, but meant no harm to anyone. Many were hyper-manic and look at the optimistic side of life with unbound energy, creativity, and amazing intelligence. They were the life of the party. Everyone that met them loved them. They could think fast and stay active all night with little slowing down. They felt they could do anything. Like little children, they frequently ignored reality, responsibility, and were in peril of being unable to organize their daily lives. A few were truly bipolar with extreme highs and lows. During the hyper-phase bipolar sufferers often are indiscriminate and risky in their behavior, thus leading to thoughtless decisions.

Bipolar and Attention Deficit Disorder (ADD) sufferers attract one another. They live off one another's enthusiasm, excitement, and positive attitude. They understand one another and know that they will not always be their normal selves, and are quick to forgive one another's crazy antics. During the hyper-manic phase they are enthusiastic and full of energy, and sexual drive. During the hypo-manic phase they are lethargic, very morose, and just want to be left alone. Some unfortunately are suicidal. Ten percent of type 1 bipolar sufferers kill themselves.

LOUISA

Louisa first arrived in Hollywood when she was just twenty. She was also a Miss America. The year of her reign was almost over and her agent had brought her here in search of an acting career. Her agent was a patient of mine and it was she who brought Louisa into see me, as she did many of her clients.

Fresh from the Midwest with a sparkle in her eyes, Louisa told me that she had been raised on a farm and that life had been rather simple during her childhood. "My parents loved me. They just didn't understand, so I spent most of my early life with my pets. I made friends of all the animals, not only the ones on the farm but, wild ones, too. They don't ask questions they just love you." As I listened, I thought of myself on the farm of my youth, finding comfort in the same sort of friends.

"I had a goose named Harriet," Louisa laughed. "She was something else. She would chase my mother out of the yard, pecking her on the butt, but she followed me around like one of the dogs." Louisa's beautiful face suddenly changed, the laughter now gone. "My mother called me her little dreamer, her faraway girl. It's true. I did dream of being a movie star. I used to make up stories about being a glamorous maiden in a faraway land."

"Well, you did it, didn't you?" I asked. "You became Miss America."

Nodding, she looked out at the kaleidoscopic sunset beyond my window, seeming for a moment to be locked inside her memories. "My uncle was a famous painter, you know, he painted beautiful sunsets. He loved my stories about beautiful places. We would sit together for hours. I would watch him paint and he would listen to my dreams. My uncle was different. No one understood him either. We didn't have to explain anything to each other. We just knew what the other was thinking." Suddenly, tears came to her eyes. "They found my uncle dead in his painting chair when I was away at the state beauty contest."

Louisa wiped the wetness off her eyes with the back of her hand. "I guess it was time, he didn't like this world, but I really miss him and our special time together."

Curious, I asked if she'd had a good relationship with her father.

"My dad really loves me," she answered. "He used to call me his sun-kissed little angel. Dad's in politics and he made the arrangements for me to be in the contest when I was eighteen. He said I was the most beautiful girl in the whole state and believe it or not, I won. But I dropped out when my uncle died. I just couldn't get it all together in time. I missed too many appointments."

"But you became Miss America?"

"That was two years later. My father kept bugging me and this time we made it work."

At the time of her appointment, I knew nothing about ADD. I thought Louisa was just another beautiful, intelligent, young wannabe. I saw her many times through the next few years and she tried very hard to become a star. She got a few acting roles but not much happened. Again, she missed too many opportunities and always seemed to be in the wrong place at the wrong time.

When she put on a few pounds, she asked if I could help her lose the weight. In those early years, doctors gave patients diet pills, sleeping pills, and tranquilizers without too much thought. I was guilty of this myself, but at the time we didn't know any better. I gave Louisa diet and Dexedrine capsules (at the time they were not schedule 2 drugs). Soon she wanted more diet pills. When this went on for some time, I got worried. Was I making a drug addict out of her? Concerned, I asked her to come in for a consultation and she gave me the following report on her progress: "I lost the weight, but I still need the diet pills because they make me feel really good. I'm keeping my appointments and I'm getting more parts."

When I asked if they made her feel good and speedy, and if she was able to sleep, she replied, "No, I feel wonderful. I sleep all night. I've never been able to do that. I've never felt this good in my whole life. I feel normal."

At this point I was really worried. I felt I had, in fact, inadvertently made her an addict. Shortly thereafter, Dexedrine was made a schedule 2 drug. Now I was sure that I had done Louisa a great disservice and I tried to get her off the diet pills. Fortunately, she went to a young informed psychiatrist who diagnosed her with ADD and gave her Clyert (another stimulant), which she is still taking to this day. When I found out about this, I called the psychiatrist, who gave me a quick course in ADD-101. I had unknowingly treated Louisa's ADD correctly by just treating her symptomatically.

If you are unlucky enough to be a women with both ADD and PMS (premenstrual syndrome) you could be in for big trouble. Often times during this part of the menstrual cycle, stimulants don't control the symptoms nearly as well as they had been previously. Another neurotransmitter (serotonin) is involved in the symptoms of PMS. It also seems to disturb the delicate balance that has been established between the other neurotransmitters like dopamine and norepinephrine. When this happens, the ADD that was under control gets out of whack, and the patient feels like she's going insane. This sometimes requires the addition of another medication such as Prozac or Zoloft to continue control. I have learned through the years that birth control pills are very affective at controlling PMS and also seem to help my ADD patients.

Many patients with ADD are diagnosed for the first time with the onset of menopause. They suffer with ADD most of their lives, overwhelmed by the simple requirements of ordinary living. Anxious, depressed and having problems with personal relationships, they struggle valiantly to cope without the help they need. Some obviously impulsive and hyperactive, and prone to say the wrong thing at the wrong time. Sometimes they even become embarrassing public spectacles. Others are shy, withdrawn, and consider themselves to be very dull. Numerous women prefer to stay home and not even go out. Then menopause comes along and the struggle is lost. No matter what plan they've designed for coping, it no longer works. They're forced to seek help, usually from their gynecologist who probably places them on hormone replacement therapy. They improve, but they still have troubling mood swings, hot flashes, extreme fatigue, memory loss and fear that they are losing their minds.

Hopefully, a modern gynecologist with a patient of this type will send her to an informed psychiatrist who will recognize her ADD, and put her on the appropriate medication. I frequently added Prozac or Zoloft to my menopausal therapeutic regimen and found that it helped, without even diagnosing ADD. In defense of my inability to diagnose ADD, I have to say it is only recently known that adults can also have this disorder. Also, because women tend to be hypo-active (as opposed to hyper) and withdrawn, ADD was thought to be rare in women until further research. It is painful for me to think about the women who have suffered with this disorder, many victims of unnecessary hysterectomies. That's how the procedure was named in the first place. The Greeks taught that the uterus was the seat of hysteria in women. Most men agreed that all of a woman's problems stemmed from her reproductive organs when in truth the real trouble was emanating from the other end.

After ADD is diagnosed and treated successfully it is still not over. Treatment helps keep in check the symptoms, for some it cures, for most the ADD continues at a controllable level. As with diabetes or heart disease, this is a lifelong prospect. However, it never goes away. No one can surgically remove it, or make it vanish with magic potions. The struggle with low self-esteem, impulsive behavior, depression, self-mistrust and anger over past abuses will continue. The wounds of ADD never completely heal. But the proper treatment (and it can be different for each individual) can salve their problems, and make the pain manageable. But is this all that any of us with or without ADD can hope for?

ANNA

Anna was a love. She was only twenty-one years of age when I first met her. She was very voluptuous and stunningly beautiful with big dark eyes and long black hair. In addition to her beauty, Anna was incredibly smart. I fell in love with her on that first visit. The firm she worked for employed seventy-five mathematicians, and she was not only the youngest in the firm, but also the only woman. Even as a math major in high school and a keen interest in physics, I had never met a female mathematician. Over the next few years we became good friends, sharing information on astrophysics, sub-atomic particle physics, and stem cell research. I have yet to meet another human being with so much knowledge, enthusiasm, and energy.

She loved animals, and had all kinds of wild animals as pets. Some how she found the time to compete in the greater equestrian shows throughout the state and won many awards. She knew everything about everything and everyone that knew her loved her.

Shortly after our first encounter, she married an astrophysicist at Cal-Tech. He was working on the Pioneer Space Program (one of the probes is still in outer-space.) Within a year I delivered their first son. They were very happy. One morning when the baby was about two weeks old I got a call from Anna. "Doctor, I'm sitting here looking at my babies fingers. I think I should cut them off. So, I got the scissors to do that. What do you think?"

I was shocked beyond belief. But I managed to calm myself down and say, "What would you want to do that for?"

"I don't know, they don't look right, and I need to cut them off."

I knew her sister lived just down the street on the same block. I asked Karen, my office manager, to call her sister and have her get over to Anna's house while I kept her on the phone. It worked and we were able to stop Anna before she injured her baby. Anna had postpartum psychosis and had no idea of what she was doing. We hospitalized Anna for two weeks and within a couple of months she returned to normal. Within a few months Anna was pregnant again, and was absolutely thrilled with the new pregnancy. She wanted a little girl and when the ultra-sound indicated that it was a girl Anna was utterly ecstatic.

In spite of being pregnant Anna worked to carry on with all her outside activity. I remember that I eventually had to stop her from riding horseback competitively when she was seven months pregnant. She was a good horsewoman, but I was afraid that if she fell off the horse at seven months pregnant, her uterus would burst like a dropped watermelon.

Her prenatal care went perfectly. She did all the right things. Her psychological behavior was normal and she was very enthusiastic about her new girl. She went a bit over the top in decorating the little girl's room and spent more money than they could afford decorating it. We doctors didn't know that much about postpartum psychosis at that time, but I was concerned about Anna. I didn't know what she would do after her second baby was delivered. Would she repeat her previous performance? Just in case, I made arrangements for Anna's mother to stay with her for a few weeks after the baby was delivered. Everything went well. Anna's behavior remained absolutely normal.

It was at about that time that I learned that postpartum psychosis frequently does repeat and could even become more severe with subsequent pregnancies. I was thrilled that it didn't seem to be happening with Anna. Then about one month later I got a chilling call from the emergency room. Anna was there in a deep coma from an overdose of sleeping pills. Her coma was very deep and she was on life support for two days. It was touch and go, and we didn't know whether she was going to make it or not. We were confused about Anna, including her psychiatrist. He said, "This is not postpartum psychosis. She has some other deeper emotional problem. When she's discharged, I'll follow her in my office and see what we can do for her."

While she was still in the hospital I asked Anna, "What happened?" I didn't expect an answer but she responded.

"My husband was out of town and I was home alone with the babies." She did not continue for some time. I waited. "I'm not a good mother. I wanted to get away from myself. I didn't want to be where I was. I wanted to get away from my pain."

"So, what happened?"

"I took a swig of vodka and went back to bed. It didn't help. I wanted to feel normal, so I took another drink of vodka. It didn't take away the pain." There was a very long pause, and then she continued, "I'm no good for my two babies." She looked up at me with a very sorrowful expression and then said, "The children would be better off without me. I had to get away. I didn't care if I died doing it. I got out of bed went to the medicine cabinet and what ever was there I took."

A few months later her psychiatrist told me that Anna was a manic-depressive and doing quite well from being on lithium. It wasn't until about a year later when I next saw Anna. She was still beautiful but different. She was acting sexy, dressed provocatively, and was coming on to me. I was confused. She was brilliant, loquacious and tempting.

"What's going on?" I asked.

She answered with a provocative smile, "I'm pregnant again."

"That's great," I said. All the time thinking, here we go again. I asked, "Are you still taking your lithium?"

"No, lithium makes me sick and I don't need it. I'm fine. I got rid of my husband and that psychiatrist you sent me to."

"Are the children alright?"

"They're with my husband."

"How does your husband feel about the new baby?" I changed the subject.

"I don't know. I haven't told him. Why should I tell him?"

"Is your husband the father of this baby?"

"Hell, how should I know? I have lots of lovers."

At first I couldn't believe the whole scenario. Anna was one of the most inspiring women I had ever met. I realized that Anna must be in a hyper-manic state. This was not the Anna that I had known. I asked, "What are you going to do about your pregnancy?" She didn't answer for a long time. "Are you going to get an abortion?"

"No. I love children. I'm going to have him and keep him. I love him."

"You know it's a boy already? Did you have an ultrasound?"

"No, I just know." At this point I knew that I was in for a very long and arduous journey. Somehow we all survived the pregnancy and she did have a little boy. As the months went by Anna calmed down, got back with her husband and found a new psychiatrist. She went back on lithium.

Over the next few years Anna returned to the old Anna that I had known years before. I delivered two more babies. She stayed on her lithium most of the time. Oh, she did go off her medication a few times. She had other suicidal attempts, but we were able to save her every time. The white knight happened to always be there for Anna.

Anna was now in her mid-thirties. She and her husband were happy with their five children. She was staying on her lithium. Then one day I got the phone call that I feared the most. It was Anna's distraught husband. She had taken yet another overdose of sleeping pills. Only this time she had a successful suicide. She was dead, and he was left to take care of five disturbed children.

If Anna were here today and I asked her if she had the choice of being bipolar or "normal" would she choose to be bipolar? I'm sure she would say yes. We discussed it many times. Her depression was painful beyond our understanding, the night terrors, and the total exhaustion, the powerlessness to the point of not being able to move or think. When down she had no capacity to enjoy life. If this was her total life, I'm sure she would rather be dead. Manic Anna loved life, sex and had the energy to live it fully. All her senses were enhanced. She felt deeper and stronger and thought faster than I can imagine. Her brilliant mind was incredible, a beautiful thing to behold. On lithium Anna did well, but when she was on lithium she wasn't the Anna she wanted to be either.

I was left devastated and wracked with guilt. Had I done Anna and her family a disservice by saving her life many times when all she wanted was to die and get out of her pain? Did I do her children a disservice? How will they cope? I had no answers.

LINDSAY

Bing Crosby's four sons from his first wife, Dixie Lee, were said to be manic-depressives. I knew all four of them and most of their wives. My dearest friends of the bunch were Susan and Lindsay Crosby. I delivered their two sons, Chip and Kevin. I first met Susan Crosby shortly after she moved to Hollywood during her reign as Miss Alaska. She was twenty and obviously beautiful, but she was also much more. She was fresh, radiant, and a free spirited country girl.

The first twelve years of her life were spent in Easter Creek, a small gold mining town near Fairbanks, Alaska. There, Susan was raised in the open, primal territory of our largest, and northern most state. Her best friend was a wolf, but there were countless others, such as horses, dogs, cats, and many more small animals of the wild. Suzy was raised as a real tomboy, but as a young beautiful woman she found Hollywood to be different, and was soon embroiled in the show business party scene. She loved sports and outdoor activities, playing baseball with the gang (a group of actors and other movie brats). That's where she got to know Lindsay Crosby.

Lindsay was the youngest and the favorite of Bing Crosby's four sons. He could sing just like Bing, but was also the outdoor type. He loved playing golf and was good at it. He spent much of his time at the Crosby ranch in Elko, Nevada enjoying the animals and ranch life. Suzy said, "I was born in a small cottage in the woods and dreamed of living in a mansion. Lindsay was born in a mansion and dreamed of living in a small cottage."

After their marriage, Suzy and Lindsay lived in a house with a white picket fence with their two boys, their horses and dogs in Calabasas, California. It was a simple ordinary life until one day things began to change. Susan noticed that once a year, around the time of his birthday, Lindsay would go into a manic phase. He would start acting and sounding like a cowboy. He'd get in his car and take off for the northwest and be gone for a week or two. One January he went into his closet took out his cowboy hat, boots and spurs, got dressed totally in black and took off for Colorado. During these escapades he would go into a small town western bar, throw money around, buying everyone drinks. He had money, the Crosby name, and was out of control. Men and women flocked around him. There were plenty of creeps out there to take advantage of him and they did.

As the years passed his manic episodes got more and more severe. One year he bought a Mustang convertible with flames painted on the side and took off for a small town bar. While there he bought a ranch and a head of cattle. Suzy had no idea where he was or what he was doing. She hired some men to find him and bring him home. When the men brought him back one of them said, "Your husband's real nice Mrs. Crosby. I had no idea that he was a rodeo rider."

"That's the problem he's not," she said.

In the beginning, Suzy thought that his actions were a little peculiar, but he was a Crosby and had plenty of money. When he came out of his manic phase he had no memory of his reckless pranks, was embarrassed, and full of guilt. For the rest of the year he would be a perfect husband. In the meantime Suzy was left to pick up the pieces of Lindsay's manic behavior. Debts were incurred. Hangers-on had to be dispensed with and pregnant girls taken care of. Suzy had a minefield to clean up. Yet she always forgave him. I too enjoyed spending time with him.

One sunny morning Susan took Chippers with her to Palm Springs for a visit with her parents. Lindsay stayed behind. When she returned home there was a huge party in progress. There were girls, girls, girls and all kinds of weird looking men that Lindsay would normally not associate with. The house was a mess. The girls had taken Susan's clothes out of her closet, and were wearing them. Lindsay was dressed in his black cowboy outfit. Seeing Susan he took off his hat, bowed, looked at her and said in a loud voice, "Come on in Suzy. Join the party."

Susan hardly recognized her own husband. He looked completely different. His voice, facial expression, and exuberance did not belong to her husband. He was normally a quiet, relaxed guy. Before her that day stood a macho-man that was bigger than life. Lindsay was only five foot seven, but it took five men to hold him down when he was manic.

She blew her stack and threw everybody out. She was so pissed-off at the girls that she took their cloths and threw them in the horse shit in the back yard. One of her friends said, "Calm down; take a Valium; guys are like that." But Susan knew that this was a problem that Valium couldn't cure. Her husband was in serious trouble.

They took Lindsay to the hospital where he stayed for the next few weeks. When he came home he had no memory of the whole affair, but I've been told that he had spent a lot of money and screwed a lot of loose women. Lindsay was ashamed and embarrassed. He didn't want to face anyone. Susan was hurt and didn't understand what was happening to her husband, and her life. She'd painfully learned that the manic Lindsay was not the man she knew and loved.

After that, Lindsay decided to check himself into the hospital every year in January and start taking lithium. He did well on lithium but experienced severe side effects. Unfortunately, he felt so normal he'd go off his lithium and without warning fly into a manic phase. One day he took Chippers and disappeared. He returned twenty-four hours later without the baby. Susan was hysterical. Lindsay had no idea where he left their son. Susan was frightened to death and frantic until she found her baby.

Susan deeply loved Lindsay and knew he needed her, but she had to protect her children. Finally, as a last resort, Susan divorced Lindsay and forced him to move out into an apartment to protect her two boys. He still spent much of his time with Susan at her house.

The following spring Lindsey checked himself into the hospital. A few days later he called a "friend" who checked him out of the hospital while he was still confused. Lindsay returned to his apartment and called Susan. She immediately knew that he was very depressed and called his psychiatrist. They were unable to see him right away so she rushed over to Lindsay's apartment herself. By the time she was able to get to him, it was too late. Lindsay blew his head off with a shotgun.

For twenty-five years Suzy tried to control her husband's manic-depression (now known as bipolar disorder) medically and legally through the courts. In the end, she had a dead ex-husband and two severely traumatized boys. She tried to protect their estate from Lindsay's wild, hysterical spending when he was manic. I asked Suzy, "After all you've been through was it worth it? Would you do it again?"

"Oh, yes. I loved Lindsay; he was my soul mate. We were buddies before we were lovers. I'll never love another man. I loved my husband. We went to church together and we will meet again. I just wish someone could have helped us. I cried out for help, but no one heard me." She remains single to this day.

In the way that truth is stranger than fiction, seventeen months later Dennis Crosby (Lindsay's older brother) killed himself in the exact same way. Susan's son Kevin was devastated. He thought, "First my father, now Uncle Dennis. Is this the Crosby way? Is this going to happen to me?"

Both Susan and Arlene (Dennis's wife and my patient) screamed for help for their husbands for years but help did not come. Today they worry about their own children and all the Crosby cousins. If one parent is bipolar, ten percent of the children will be affected. If both parents are bipolar seventy-five to eight percent of their children will be affected.

Dennis was probably unipolar. Unipolar depression is similar with bipolarism except they are clinically depressed most of the time. They spend most of their time in severe emotional pain. His twin brother, Phillip (also unipolar) remained alive much longer, but spent much of his time heavily self-medicated in deep depression. He lived in a mansion in Woodland Hills with the grass knee-high in his front yard. The windows were blackened out to accommodate his lifestyle. He slept all day and watched old movies all night. He had a rough life and now he is dead, too. It is said he died of natural causes. His wife Peggy (one of four) was also my patient. She divorced Phillip years ago after having a son with him. I've been told that Peggy was very happy and with the actor Jack Klugman until he died.

Bing Crosby's oldest son, Gary, died of lung cancer. I did not know him well. He was a successful television actor, had a successful marriage, and lived a reasonably happy life, I'm told. He probably was mildly bipolar. He had a drinking problem and wrote a pessimistic negative book about his father. It is safe to say all four Crosby boys lived a mentally difficult life.

Bipolar brains are wired differently. They respond unexpectedly, excitingly and are sometimes frightening to us. They have difficulty functioning in a tightly structured society. Often they just give up. They are told, "Here are the rules, and if you obey them, all will be well." Many creative people cannot follow the rules, certainly not all of them all the time. We do not give one another an opportunity to respond unexpectedly or in our own distinctive way. One size fits all, and if you are the wrong size then that's too bad.

Recent advances in brain neuro-chemical functional studies have made it possible to have a better understanding of brain function. Not all of our brains function in the same manner or respond to stimulation in the same way. Creative people are more aware of their environment than the other members of humanity. Even in ordinary surroundings they are frequently over stimulated. They find the customary unusual and fascinating. It is this quality that makes us love and admire them. They are much more sensitive to the world around them and are able to express that sensitivity in a way that most people cannot. Simply -- they see the world different. Their moods may swing from ecstasy to deep sorrow and from being energetic to being exhausted, but they are rarely boring.

Society needs these unique unbelievable minds. Medicine just needs to learn better ways of treating their illnesses. Many of the most talented and creative members of our society are bipolar or somewhere on that spectrum. Out of sight, many of them are also alcoholics, drug abusers and dangerous risk takers. They try every way conceivable to escape the pain of their depression. The celebrity that you see on the public stage is not the person that I often see in my office.

Everyone tells bipolar people that they are wonderful, brilliant, talented and good-looking, but they rarely believe it. The public wants to share their lives, be as close as possible to them. We seek their autograph, steal a piece of their clothing, or pay them large sums of money to have them make appearances and give speeches. We really don't care what they say, we just want to feel special and share a few minutes with them.

There is a long list of people who achieved greatness who also had difficulty learning in a highly structured classroom. One has to wonder why Albert Einstein, Edgar Allan Poe, George Bernard Shaw, Salvador Dali, and many other great talents were expelled from school. Maybe they were bad boys, or maybe they had ADD. I am very proud to say that I actually attended one of Albert Einstein's lectures while in college. I sat in the front row, but couldn't understand a word he said. Even if he had spoke in perfect English, I probably wouldn't have understood his complex mind, yet I am very proud to have been in his presence.

Michael Faraday, Buckminster Fuller, Howard Hughes and many others were probably bipolar. Where would physics and mathematics be today without these great minds? We love and admire these, brilliant electrifying humans. The same can be said for many of history's most memorable leaders like Winston Churchill, Abraham Lincoln, Napoleon Bonaparte, Theodore Roosevelt, Adolph Hitler, Joseph Stalin and others. These brilliant minds radically changed and shaped the world in which we live.

What would literature and art be without the likes of Ernest Hemmingway, F. Scott Fitzgerald, his wife Zelda, Dylan Thomas, Amadeus Mozart, Van Gogh, Gaugin? I could go on forever. How about our entertainers? Woody Allen, Charlie Chaplin, Judy Garland, Mike Wallace, Jonathan Winters, Jim Carey, Robin Williams, Dick Clark, Anthony Hopkins, Art Buchwald, Rod Steiger and countless others, what would our lives be like without them?

The Hollywood I know is a relatively nonjudgmental place. If you can perform or produce -- no one cares how you do it. Few in our town truly judge your private life. Gossip runs rampant, but no one really cares. We routinely forgive celebrity drug users and give them another chance, again and again and again. I ask myself, what is unique about Hollywood? Why are these novel but exhilarating people here? Is there something about Hollywood that attracts them? Some make it, most do not, but they all try. In Hollywood, each feels the full freedom of choice, to live outside the rules. Hollywood is a crazy place, but it is one of the freest places on earth.

Modern mankind has designed a uniform, computerized, and ultimately dehumanized world. We no longer have to talk to one another. We text. Work hard, save money and get ahead. However, human beings are better equipped for a more primitive world. Our genetics have not kept up with our civilization. The chimpanzee learns by watching other chimpanzees performing tasks. At the turn of the century many human tasks were taught through apprenticeships. Like the chimpanzee we first learned by watching others. We did not judge one another by how fast or by what means we got there, as long as we got there. Today we think we have a better way. We have cell phones, computers, and the Internet to assist us -- and for most of us, modern teaching methods work just fine. For others it just doesn't work at all. Some of the most brilliant minds would flunk George W. Bush's "leave no child behind".

In the past thirty or forty years we have made slow progress in the treatment of mental illnesses including bipolar disorder. This is primarily because we have treated the brain like it's a sacred organ. Today's young doctors have grown to accept the idea that mental illness is a brain disorder just like diabetes and heart disease. The brain isn't much different it's just another organ. Doctors are slowly learning that brain disorders can be treated like all other diseases.

In recent years some progress has been made in the treatment of bipolar disorder especially with the development of effective new drugs. Drugs don't always work for all the people all the time. Some patients develop severe side affects with certain drugs and they must try others. It's important to do just that, and keep on trying. New drugs and new methods are being developed every day.

Without bipolar minds we'd have a dull, homogeneous, flat, boring world and scientific progress would be much slower. These human beings represent about one percent of us, but they also represent the best and worst of us.

The chemical structure of estradiol, the major estrogen
sex hormone and a widely used medication

23 THE ESTROGEN CONTROVERSY

Menopause is the end of the reproductive part of a woman's life. The ovaries are slowly dying and eventually stop producing eggs, and her hormones are suddenly reduced until they are no longer available. Life that some women have known for the last fifty or so years will never be the same. For some it will be better, but for far too many it will mean a heightening of already existing problems. More intense mood swings, emotions out of control, loss of interest in sex, no passion for life, loss of goals and interests. A few will develop dry thinning skin, especially within the vagina and urethra, which results in the need for Depends and strong perfume. Oh, and don't forget the fatigue, insomnia, backache and loss of memory. That's what menopause can be, but it's unnecessary.

Some women feel old. Their childbearing years are over. They are "over the hill", no longer desirable. This is easy to understand since they have been bombarded their whole life with the importance of youth and beauty. Happily, for about one third of women there is basically no change. Life goes on as before only now with a bit more freedom. Pregnancy is no longer an issue and many women have well-established lives and careers.

In the distant past, women approached menopause with little choice but to endure the hot flashes, night sweats and radical emotional roller coaster rides. In the 1930s, when estrogen was first made available, menopause became less of a problem. For many years, women didn't have to suffer the "change of life" blues. Doctors advised, "Just take your Premarin and it'll all go away." And they weren't far off. Treated properly, ninety percent of menopausal women make a smooth transition, just another passage in life. Then a new monster raised its ugly head: <u>increased risk of cancer</u>.

But what exactly does increased risk mean and increased by how much? I know it sounds frightening! Cancer is frightening. But the numbers, the statistics, can be very misleading. Almost from the beginning of the introduction of estrogen into our armamentarium, there were those doctors who said, "Estrogen increases the risk of developing uterine cancer." It took almost fifty years to prove it. They first had to invent the computer to establish the proof.

Of course an increased risk of cancer can be devastating, but I don't think the human mind can truly comprehend what increased risk really means. What is the difference between one in a hundred, one in ten thousand or one in a million? All three are "increased risks". When the front-page headline reads HORMONES INCREASE RISK OF CANCER, what does that really mean to you personally? Do you stop taking hormones even if it is one chance in a million? For some, their fear of cancer is so great, their answer would be yes. To them, increased risk means that they are going to get cancer.

However, we take increased risks every day of our lives, sometimes every hour. We drive on the freeway, we fly in airplanes, and we even go so far as to jump out of them. Regardless, if you're a doctor, you may end up being taken to court because you've given a patient a medication with an increased risk of cancer.

Cancer is the number three cause of death in the United States, and that is terrifying -- but these statistics are also true for those who don't take hormones. True also for men. Talk about increased risk, fifty percent of today's cancers are directly linked to smoking or inhaling secondhand smoke. Some women smoke while nursing their babies. Now that's increased risk. Lung cancer is the number one cancer killer of women -- not breast or uterine.

During the nearly fifty years that I have been a physician, life expectancy has increased almost a decade. We are not only living longer but also much better. For women in their senior years, some of that "better living" can be credited to taking hormones. From the moment I started practicing medicine until the day I stopped, I prescribed estrogen for the patients that needed it. I did this after thoughtful study of the information as it became available, and made my patients aware of the changing risks. At that time it was standard advice from almost every medical university in the world to prescribe estrogen for menopausal symptoms and this was obviously based on many studies done around the globe. Cardiologists and dermatologists even prescribed it. Orthopedic surgeons insisted that women take it to protect their bones. Gynecologists loved it. Estrogen was truly a panacea. It made many women feel "normal" again.

I also gave birth control pills to my patients from the very moment they were available. Birth control pills contain estrogen. Millions of women from all around the world now take birth control pills. Oh, there were always a few researchers who continued to insist that estrogen caused an increased risk of uterine cancer, and yes, that is true. Later it was proven that unopposed estrogen also increased the risk of cervical cancer. Unopposed because ovulating woman produce progesterone as well. Thus, progestin was added to the mix, which decreased the risk of cervical cancer. Unfortunately, we soon learned that the addition of progestin increased the risk of breast cancer. It all became very confusing, so a comprehensive study was done to solve the mystery once and for all.

There were well over sixteen thousand women in a study that was done in fifty different locations and conducted by The Woman's Health Initiative. In 2002, the results of this brilliant and comprehensive effort were published in the Journal of the American Medical Association stating overall health risks exceeded benefits from use of combined estrogen plus progestin for healthy postmenopausal US women.

This prompted many doctors to take their patients off estrogen entirely, returning them to the miseries of the 1930s. They were unwilling to take the malpractice risk. These trials did not distinguish the individual effects of estrogen from those of the combination of estrogen and progestin. I personally feel the effect on both breast cancer and heart diseases were probably more due to the progestin. There are many studies of low dosage estrogen that do not show this increased risk of cancer. In any event, I ask you, was it really necessary to stop taking estrogen? Or did doctors stop giving it to patients because of increased risk of malpractice? It's very easy for doctors to tell their patients to not take a drug just to feel good, especially when it is at the doctor's increased risk of litigation. Men don't become menopausal, so they have no genuine understanding of the havoc that some women suffer.

For many years, doctors were also told that taking estrogen was good for the heart and in turn we informed our patients. This recent study demonstrated that estrogen plus progestin are of no benefit to the heart and may actually be harmful, especially in the beginning. Other studies using estrogen alone, in low dosage, show that it apparently has no ill-effect on the heart. It may even have a good effect. Who knows? The jury is still out. In the meantime, we know the risk of taking low-dosage estrogen is minimal. For the curious, a low dose goes from .3 milligrams, the lowest possible dose, to the once-popular purple pill at .625mg). In women who have had hysterectomies, I would say that risk is non-existent.

Estrogen plus progestin does increase the risk of developing breast cancer, but consider these numbers. If ten thousand women took these drugs for one year, eight more would get breast cancer than if they hadn't taken hormones. That's eight in ten thousand. But in the same study, there was no increase in the death rate from breast cancer. Part of the doctor's job is to help the patient understand the risk benefit ratio of taking or not taking a drug. The final decision is up to the individual, or should be, but it often is not. A doctor may have decided this for you when he should have given you the choice. Sometimes, too many times, this decision is made on the basis of the doctor's fears for themselves and not for their patients' good. And can we really blame the physician in a system where patients decide routinely sue doctors for prescribing a drug with a stated increased-risk factor? Bad things happen, and money is money, and some don't care where it came from.

MAGGIE

Menopause can be absolutely devastating for some women. Maggie, a sixty-seven year old patient, came in with a severe vaginal infection. She was so estrogen deficient just touching her vaginal mucosa with a gloved finger provoked bleeding. The vaginal lining was as thin as tissue paper where it should be as thick and tough as the skin on the palm of your hand. The only way to cure this infection was to first strengthen and thicken the vaginal lining and that can only be done with hormones. Maggie also complained that she was unable to control her urine and in spite of her pads and perfumes, she smelled like a ladies room all the time. When I asked her about sex she just laughed, "I haven't had sex in over two years. It's too painful. Besides, with my odor problem, I don't want to go near my husband."

I put Maggie on estrogen and treated her infection. Within six weeks, her vaginal infection was cleared up and her lining was thickening nicely. Six months later when Maggie came in for a routine check-up, everything was fine. After the exam she said, "I have a question. Can a woman my age have too much sex?" I couldn't help smiling a little, but I reassured her that there was no such a thing as too much sex at any age.

She smiled back. "I have another question, but it's very embarrassing." I encouraged her to speak freely so she went on. "How about oral sex? My husband wants to do that for me."

That may seem like a naïve question for a woman of Maggie's age, but at that time, it was possible for a woman of sixty-seven to believe she was too old for sex let alone oral sex. Many then thought oral sex was a form of perversion, and not an accepted part of lovemaking. In return I asked her probably the most important question regarding any type of sexual activity, "Do you want him to?"

"I love it, "she admitted shyly. "Especially now that my urinary problem is gone, I hope forever."

I responded with a wholehearted, "Terrific!" And this was hardly a surprise. Estrogen thickens the lining of not only the vagina but also the lining of the urethra. When young, the lining of the urethra is fluffy like a sponge, and when the muscles are tightened around the urethra, it creates a watertight seal. The post-menopausal woman's urethra looses its fluffiness, becoming stiff and slick like leather so the muscle is unable to hold tight enough to effect a perfect seal. Life is better with thicker vaginal lining, believe me, and much less messy. Estrogen does not prevent all cases of urinary incontinence. Sometimes the problem is due to a gradual dissension of the bladder and urethra. As we get older everything falls down. With the passage of time gravity always wins. Kegel Exercises help, but sometimes surgery is necessary. A post-menopausal woman should enjoy a satisfying sex life as long as she has a willing partner!

SALLY AND CHRISTINA

Sally and her daughter Christina were both patients for many years. I first met Sally through Christina who was working on a movie with Clint

Eastwood. Sally was an attractive, intelligent, retired nurse. She had given up nursing to spend full time at motherhood. After her two children grew up, graduated from university and made successful careers, Sally began suffering from the proverbial empty nest syndrome. Her husband's job forced him to be out of the home at odd hours, leaving Sally home alone much of the time. Sally didn't want to go back into nursing. She said, "With all the new drugs and new procedures, I can't do that anymore."

Sally's family was living their own lives, and she had gone from a busy work schedule to a life of solitude. Then without warning, menopause hit. From her twenties through her forties, Sally had been an outgoing, friendly, social person. Being a retired nurse, she was always there for everyone. In Christina's words, "My mother was such a joy to be around, but when she hit fifty, everything changed. Her hormones went crazy. She had hot flashes and night sweats that were driving her crazy."

I tried to prescribe estrogen to replace the hormones that her ovaries were no longer producing but she absolutely refused. "I'm a nurse and I'm not going to put a pill made from horse urine in my body! No, I'll use herbs." Any doctor or chemist knows there is no actual horse piss in the pill, the hormones are simply extracted from a pregnant mare's urine, but she had already made her mind up.

It wasn't long until she came in with a cast on her arm. Becoming dizzy on the stairs at home, she had fallen and broken her arm. I put her on calcium and advised her that she needed estrogen to force her body to absorb the calcium into her bones. She refused to take it, leaving her family and me helpless. Slowly things became much worse. Sally developed radical mood swings, where one minute she'd be very happy and the next she'd be very angry. Sometimes when I talked to her on the phone she would slur her speech. I was worried that she must be drinking alcohol, sitting there alone all day and sometimes all night. One night she was so angry with her husband she chased him around the house with a butcher knife! Life became almost unbearable for her husband and daughter.

Over the next few years, I saw Sally off and on. Sometimes she was happy sometimes she was sad and depressed. The menopause changed Sally from an outgoing, vivacious, sexually active woman to an angry, rebellious human being. She was mentally troubled, refused to have sex for the last twelve years of her life, and suffered from severe osteoporosis. Her bones had become thin as an eggshell and would fracture at the slightest provocation. There were a number of falls resulting in broken bones. She was seeing several doctors, but still refused to take estrogen. Sally had a stroke and died at the age of sixty-two while sitting in the waiting room of her cardiologist.

Estrogen is known to help osteoporosis and many other problems, including mental difficulties. There are recent studies indicating that estrogen may retard the onset of Alzheimer's disease in those destined to develop it, but that is still unproven. Replacing the estrogen that the ovaries are no longer producing would help many women. All women should have the advice and opportunity to choose to take on the increased risk. Naturally some would refuse like Sally did and that's okay. Some others will seek alternative measures, but what about those? Do they work? Are they safe? There are many choices: herbal medicine, Traditional Chinese Medicine, Ayurveda, naturopathy, chiropractic, osteopathy, massage, yoga, relaxation therapy, homeopathy, aromatherapy, and therapeutic touch.

After my extensive review of the medical literature, I found these alternatives very disappointing. Of the herbal remedies, only black cohosh was effective at relieving hot flashes in three out of four studies. Chaste tree berry, dong quai, ginseng, evening primrose oil, motherwort, red clover, and licorice showed no significant change in symptoms in double blind studies. Black cohosh has not been studied on a long-term basis, therefore the safety of long-term usage has not been established. Questions remain about the safety of long-term usage of most herbs. Anecdotal experience is not a study. *The studies just haven't been done. The risk has not been established.*

Many food plants contain phytoestrogens. Phytoestrogens are different from estrogens in that they are phenols not steroids, so they modulate endocrine activity in the body while acting like estrogens in many ways. Phytoestrogens are found in soy, other beans, clover, and alfalfa and to a lesser degree in many other foods. Soy foods are very popular for the treatment of hot flashes despite no supporting studies.

Many recommend Vitamin E for hot flashes but again in double-blind studies there was no statistical benefit in taking Vitamin E for these symptoms. Acupuncture, behavioral therapies, wild yams and natural progesterone creams have shown no proven beneficial effect. Snake-oil salesmen sold lots of snake-oil years ago. It was said to cure everything. About one-third of patients feel they are helped no matter what they take and that's good, but the other two-thirds keep on searching. We have studied drugs extensively and we know and can catalogue their increased risk, but no drug, food additive or herb is without the *possibility* of increased risk. Those substances that are not subject to review by the Federal Drug Administration and their safety has not been proven. Yet as should be the case with all matters of being a woman -- it is her body, her choice, and her life. I retired from the medical field many years ago, but I still feel the same about estrogen.

Warm Welcome From a Waiting World

Alternative Birth Center: How It All Began

"Someone said pregnancy is a disease of nine months' duration with a surgical solution," says Dr. Boyd Cooper. Unfortunately, he adds, there's some truth in that. "That is a natural process. We doctors have made it almost a pathological process—and for a very good reason. In obstetrics, when a disaster happens, it is a catastrophe."

He has just arrived late for a luncheon interview, explaining, "We just doubled the census" at Hollywood Presbyterian's new Alternative Birth Center. (That was June 15 and the census was then two; at press time, there had been eight ABC births.)

The ABC is his pet project, he is saying, and the majority of women scheduled into it are his patients. Other doctors on the hospital staff had started to express interest but, he says, others resist change. "They've learned what they do works and they're very reluctant to give up what works for something that works better."

Forced by His Patients

He makes no claim of having awakened one night with a grand inspiration, an ABC finisher, he is quick to say he was "forced into it" by his patients during an era when he, and other obstetricians, were almost routinely giving caudals (a regional anesthetic, that is injected adjacent to the spinal canal).

When women started asking for birth without ...

An 'At-Home' Birth With Hospital Backup

BY BEVERLY BEYETTE
Times Staff Writer

Dr. Boyd Cooper, a hulk of a man in a fluorescently slitting green scrub suit, plopped on the foot of the double bed and, somewhat in the manner of a cheerleader for the home team, urged Christine Meyer, "C'mon, honey! Push the kid out! Push, push, push, push, push . . ."

Propped against her husband, Carl, Christine closed her eyes, clenched her teeth and bore down again. Her head was against his chest, with all his strength her held her trembling legs. As she pushed, he softly counted backwards from 30, hoping she would make it all the way to zero.

She had had no anesthesia, she had asked for none. But, now, late on a Wednesday afternoon, after two days of labor, she was flushed and exhausted. Carl stroked her damp hair and whispered words of encouragement.

The Baby's Just Late

"I wish the baby would come out," she said, it was almost a plea. Carl's mother, standing near the foot of the bed, told her she was doing great, then added, "The baby's just late, that's all. You two are always late." Christine managed a little smile.

DR. BOYD COOPER
". . . fear is a big component of pain."

Los Angeles Times | 1970's

24 OBSTETRICIANS: A VANISHING SPECIES

It was April 2002, and by now I was practicing medicine three days a week. I was referring all the difficult cases to younger men and I assisted them rather than being the primary surgeon. One Monday morning I came to the office and Karen, my office manager, greeted me with a note from my malpractice insurance company. They were no longer going to write insurance for the state of California, but that it would be no problem as my current policy would be transferred to another company. But there was a problem -- the unbelievable new price. I would have to pay $78,000 per year. OB/GYN doctors are sued the most and pay the most. Currently a little over seventy-seven percent of the American Congress of Obstetricians & Gynocologists' fellows have been sued. Even the $40,000 I had been paying was excessive. Now they were nearly doubling it? My first question was *WHY?* I had a good record with the insurance company and I had no cases pending. Nonetheless, they wanted the $78,000 and they wanted it in ten days.

I stared hard at the figures on the paper in front of me -- 7-8-0-0-0. That's what the bastards wanted from me so that I could continue to open my doors. I jotted some numbers down on a pad. If I worked my ass off all year, I might be able to just break even. What a concept! After delivering thousands of babies with no serious problems for over forty-five years they want $78,000. I felt like a shopkeeper in Chicago who had just been paid a visit by Al Capone's goons. But this was even worse; it was legal. It took me but a minute to decide. Right there and then I told Karen, "I'm through." In that moment, I felt like I was being kicked out of the profession I love so profoundly. What a problem though - I still had a household to maintain and a twelve-year-old to send to university. How was I going to pay the bills? What was I going to do with my time if I retired? I don't play golf. I hate traveling. I'm already listening to all the classical music I want to hear. Delivering babies, doing surgery and consoling patients had been my whole life.

I sat there thinking about my patients that I would no longer be able to see. I would really miss them. I was almost 80. Most of my celebrities were also much older and had moved on to internists or other specialists. Most of my work now was for the young and poor patients on welfare. For a moment I thought, maybe this is a signal for me. Yet, I didn't feel old, and was as good a surgeon as I'd ever been. Maybe I was just feeling sorry for myself. I talked to an obstetrical friend in Las Vegas. He said, "Why are you complaining? My bill was $120,000." That made me less personally concerned, but troubled all the same. What was happening to American medicine? The best medical care in the world is being destroyed by frivolous lawsuits? That Monday morning, which promised to be routine, like any other day -- wasn't. Instead it changed my life.

For those less legally inclined, tort is a wrongful act leading to legal liability. If there was any amount of tort reform, there would be a cap on the dollar amount a patient could receive from a malpractice suit. This would also limit the amount of punitive damages a judge can order a physician to pay. That being said, tort reform has little chance of ever occurring. Tort reform wouldn't change the cost of medical care dramatically. However, because of lawsuits, obstetrical services are not available in some states. There has to be a better way. When a doctor receives a letter from a lawyer's office it's as if a knife had been plunged into his heart, and he asks himself, "What did I do wrong?" There is a solid implication that a mistake was made and a patient was suffering because of his misdeed. It brings many sleepless nights. Doctors are sensitive people who go into medicine to help people. When they are accused of harming the very patient they set out to help, it can be devastating. The last thing a good doctor wants to do is harm his patient.

Much of the time doctors don't recall the patient. Recently I received notice from an attorney of his intent to claim damages against me because I allowed my patient to develop cancer. I didn't remember the patient in question, so a quick check of my records indicated that in fact I had no such patient. After an investigation and legal expense it was determined that she had come into my office under another name. I had seen her once and her cancer smear and exam were negative. During my entire career I've never been in court on a malpractice case. I've received letters of intent to sue, and have given a few depositions, but otherwise I learned to live with the constant fear of sitting next to the bench.

When malpractice claims are real they have less to do with malpractice than with a choice that didn't work as expected. Methods of treatment are made in good faith and performed with high hopes, but they are not always successful -- even in Ivy League Medical Schools. They get sued the most. Medicine is educated guessing. The best choice is not always obvious even in our universities, but the doctor must choose. If he operates on his patient they may live or die, if he doesn't operate, the risk is the same. Doctors are just like the rest of the world: human beings, but they are not allowed the luxury of being less than perfect.

The unprincipled lawyers are out to save the world from doctors that make mistakes, and the lawyers get rich doing it. Most people, even lawyers are decent honorable people, but some are greedy looking for a fast buck, and feel doctors must be punished for their grievous ways. The smarter the lawyer, the more cases they win and the more they can charge. It's all about winning not justice. And once again, it frequently can have little to do with true malpractice. I should note though, corrupt people exist in all professions.

I recall a doctor-lawyer conference that was held to determine how a certain case should be handled. A group of doctors and lawyers sat around a conference table and after a discussion of the pros and cons of the case, it was determined to go forward. The lead defense attorney disagreed, "I think we should try to settle this case. Their expert witness is cunning and vicious. I've been up against him in other cases and lost." So after further discussion, it was decided to settle the case on the quality of the expert witness not on the merits of the case.

If a doctor commits malpractice and the patient is seriously injured, the patient should be compensated and adequately. The lawyer's fee is based on the meaning of the word <u>adequately</u> and there's no dollar amount too high. In the end many lawyers take the lion's share of the money. By the time they take out their questionable expenses and their percentage cut, there can be little left for the patient.

There are, unfortunately, doctors that are just as predatory and unethical. Some doctors are willing to say or do anything if the price is right. I hope there are few of them. Sadly, higher education does not create morality. Educated people are no more moral than the unschooled. Morality should be taught in the home and emphasized during those long impressionable school days. This idea seems to be ignored in our present society.

There is no more malpractice today than when I first started practicing medicine in 1960. In fact I'm sure there is far less malpractice today given medical advancement. I hope we have more transparency. Medical care has improved over the last forty odd years. I can hear the swelling voices of trial lawyers screaming their disagreement. They think it's their duty to protect people from bad doctors. It takes a dozen years of higher education to become an obstetrician. There are very few truly bad doctors, just good doctors that occasionally make a bad choice. One of the greatest joys of being a doctor is the opportunity to accept responsibility for the choices we make. What we don't expect is to be wiped out by a wrong choice. In the end it's frequently an educated guess.

We obstetricians don't act alone either, most of the time we work in groups of doctors and nurses with many eyes watching. When something goes wrong, everybody is responsible and everyone gets sued. The obstetrician is the first one sued because he has the primary responsibility, but problems are usually discussed before a decision is made. It's almost impossible for a doctor to commit true malpractice under these circumstances. The other doctors would immediately purge themselves of such a doctor in their ranks. They become a liability.

An obstetrician's malpractice fee is ten times that of a pediatrician's. Does that mean that the pediatrician is ten times better than the obstetrician? We both take care of babies - they after delivery, we before. Most of the malpractice against obstetricians is because of problems with the baby at birth. Outcome of childbirth has always been problematic because the final result and health of the baby is unknown until after delivery. Most babies are normal and beautiful and everyone is very happy. No obstetrician wants a defective baby, but we all get them even though we do our damnedest. Statistically it is impossible for every delivery to produce a beautiful baby that will one day graduate from Harvard. When this doesn't happen it is not malpractice. By the time the lawyers get through with the obstetrician you'd think the doctor should have his license taken away and he put in jail.

We can't blame the lawyers either. They are just doing what they are trained to do and what is legal in our system. The more they mangle the doctor the more money they make. Yet there's got to be a better way to compensate those that are injured and get rid of the few bad doctors. This litigious society we live in is totally destroying the best medical care the world has ever known. With all our technical knowledge and scientific skills medicine is still less than perfect. Perfect or not, decisions still have to be made. We are a nation of laws and the law has helped us be the greatest nation on earth.

The law tries to be very precise, the more details the clearer the guidelines. That way we will know precisely what is required. At least that's the way it's supposed to work. Medicine is not precise. It's an art as well as a science. It requires not only knowledge but also judgment based on common sense. However, the drive toward certainty has annihilated common sense. Modern law has become so complex that the simplest event has to be interpreted by two legal teams.

Towards the end of my career, for example, during the delivery of a baby I inadvertently left a sponge in the mother's vagina. Later that night the resident was called to see the patient because of bleeding. The bleeding was minimal and quite normal following a delivery. He found the sponge I'd left in her vagina and removed it. There was no further problem. Later the baby developed a skin rash over his face and again, no serious problem. However, the mother sued and two teams of lawyers were called in to sort out the case. The case was absolutely silly. The baby traversed the vagina before the sponge was left behind so in no way could it have anything to do with the baby's skin rash. The mother alleged that she got an infection from the sponge, which was then passed through her milk to the baby. She had no fever in the hospital, nor did the baby. It may be worth noting, another type of sponge left in the vagina is called a tampon and I have removed them after being inadvertently left there by the patient for weeks.

This case thankfully never went to trial and was eventually dismissed, but not before those two sets of lawyer's fees were generated. It's not the malpractice lawyer's duty to search for the truth. His duty is to advance his client's cause by any legal means available - by delay, confusion or redundancy. Forget the facts -- if you talk long enough and throw out enough meaningless material the jury may forget the facts.

The American Medical Association said medical malpractice fees for obstetricians across the nation could reach $200,000 annually for some physicians. The AMA surveyed doctors in all fifty states and came to the conclusion that more than thirty of these states were in a medical malpractice crisis. These states will not have obstetricians at all unless something is done quickly. While I was practicing in California, we managed to escape that crisis. Laws in California limit the amount that can be paid for pain and suffering and limit the amount lawyers can charge for contingency fees. Unfortunately, today - doctors in California are experiencing a much different malpractice landscape.

I remember my malpractice insurance bill for my first year in private practice, in 1960. It was three hundred and fifty dollars. For the first twenty-five years I was in practice, malpractice went up slowly but the change was minimal. In the beginning I paid the insurance fee with very little concern. It was just the price of doing business. Then it began doubling every year to the point where it finally knocked me out of commission. Who can blame the insurance companies for wanting to get out of the medical malpractice business? St. Paul Companies (at one point, the nations largest provider of malpractice insurance) claimed that they paid out $1.75 for every dollar collected from doctors in Georgia in malpractice claims. They eventually left the medical malpractice insurance business -- they started out to make money not lose it. Even President George W. Bush was concerned about the devastating rise in the cost of malpractice insurance, and recommended tort reform. It didn't seem to change anything, as we are still in one hell of a mess.

We can no longer do medical research without the benefit of reams of legal documents and markedly increased malpractice fees. Every conceivable test must be ordered and documented. Research is at high risk, because its results are unknown. That's the reason we do research, and try to advance our medical knowledge. Even an aspirin or simple lab test requires that a form be filled out carefully. They say this is to assure that everything is in order. When I first started practicing medicine, the patient's hospital chart for delivering a baby was five or six pages, now it's twenty-five or more. I don't think all that paper improved patient care. They say that all that charting is to make sure the care is well documented. I think it's in part to create a paper trail for the trial lawyers. Hospitals spend more than twenty-five percent of their budget on administration; most of this is to comply with the paper requirement. It's amazing how much time most of us - doctors, nurses and staff now spend on paperwork.

I participated in the clinical trials of the CU7 IUD (an intra-uterine contraceptive), commonly known as the Copper Seven. When Lederle Laboratories (now Pfizer), the drug manufacture of the CU7 IUD, stopped producing the IUD years ago, I called to ask why. They answered, "When our legal staff got larger than our medical staff we decided it was time to get out of the IUD business. We're in the medical business not the legal business." At the time they stopped manufacturing the CU7 IUD, they had ninety percent of the market share. I personally inserted thousands of these IUD's and they were effective and safe, but they are no longer available because of litigation.

Vaccinations have become almost prohibitive in cost because of litigation. Many are dubious because of false claims that associate vaccines with autism. Recently there has been a lot of press on the consideration of small pox vaccinations and we have been repeatedly advised that one or two per million may die from the vaccination. Do we really need to know that, one or two per million? The law says yes, we need to be fully informed! Do we really understand what one or two per million means? I doubt it. But to protect against that probability the cost will surely go up.

Litigation has taken all the joy out of being a doctor. Sadly, forty percent of all doctors say they would not choose their profession again. I personally would not recommend that my son or daughter go into medicine, as much as I love it. It's not only the actual malpractice, but also the constant tension and harassment that goes along with it. A doctor cannot concentrate on what is best for the patient when he's forced to think, "What is safest for me?" We are paralyzed with the cost and fear of malpractice, so we do unnecessary tests. It's always lingering in the back of our minds. What doctor can fully concentrate on what is best for a patient when he or she is forced to think, "What's their lawyer going to do if I'm wrong?"

Barry White & daughter, Shaherah   Boyd with Angela Lansbury

25 STARDUST MEMORIES

Tourists come from all around the world to visit the land of stardom. The boulevard outside my old office is paved with glittering stars honoring celebrities from the world of movies, television and music. It was my great fortune to have many of these artists and their loved ones come through my door and treat me as an equal. It's unfortunate that many are not still with me today.

One such artist and friend was Sam Fuller, a maverick film director, who to this day is respected by the likes of Spielberg and Tarantino. Sam did things his way. Instead of yelling "Action!" at the beginning of a shot, he would literally fire a pistol into the air. He brought issues like racism and women's sexuality into Hollywood films way before they were acceptable topics.

About the time he was making the brilliant film about his experiences in WWII (*The Big Red One*), I delivered his only child, Samantha. Sam had filmed many hours of his wife's delivery and this gave him an idea. He decided that I was going to play a sergeant in the film and actually deliver a baby in a bombed out tank. He battled with Paramount and with me and finally we talked him out of it, so my movie career was over before it got started. I was too old to be a dogface and I couldn't leave my practice to shoot a film in Europe. However, I was thrilled that he asked and I would always remind Sam that I was the star of his best production, his daughter's delivery.

Sam was married to a lovely, incredibly smart German actress, Christa. Dinners were always interesting at their house. At the end of the evening, we'd end up in the library, actually it was a huge garage crammed with thousands of books and scripts. Sam would regale us with amazing stories, climbing on chairs to act out scenes from his latest script. He was such a raconteur, and so passionate about films. He would describe every detail of each and every scene of an upcoming movie to anyone who would listen. It wasn't hard to listen to Sam, and we all miss him to this day.

My wife loved the way Sam and Christa brought up their daughter Samantha. She was exposed to all the inspiring conversations that took place at their home and she was taken everywhere with them. We named our first daughter after little Samantha and tried to introduce her to a similar world. It worked so well we did the same for our second daughter, Alexandra. They will became better little girls because of Sam Fuller.

When my patient Robyn Smith, a well-known jockey, told me she was marrying Fred Astaire, she was so happy it was almost contagious. But I still had my concerns for her. Astaire was more than thirty years her senior. I had to ask, "Are you sure? You won't find it a little dull?"

"No, I won't," Robyn, said with strong conviction. "Fred Astaire is not an old man. He is exciting and vibrant. Every night with him is an adventure as we dance the tango together after dinner. And the people in our lives, oh my God! Can you imagine? I get to dine with Kirk Douglas, with Gene Kelly and Gregory Peck. Definitely not dull!"

Robyn shared with me how they had met when she was riding horses for Alfred Vanderbilt and Fred Astaire was his friend. She warned Astaire not to bet on her horse *Exciting Divorcee* as her horse was a long shot. Miraculously the horse won. Everyone was thrilled including Astaire who had ignored Robyn's warning and betted on her horse anyway. Astaire did not heed Robyn's warning and Robyn didn't heed mine. They married and spent many happy years together dancing up until his death.

When my patient and friend Ellen Siano started dating Mickey Hargitay (Mr. Universe) I was happy for her. Then one awful day Mickey's ex-wife (Jayne Mansfield) was killed in an auto accident. Mickey had three children with Jayne including her super star daughter

Mariska Hargitay. Ellen was such a love. She raised all the children as her own with generosity and care. Mickey and Ellen never did have children of their own. Through Ellen I met Mickey and we became very good friends. He was the most famous bodybuilder until Arnold Schwarzenegger came around. Outspoken journalist and broadcaster, Walter Winchell, once said "that what [President] Eisenhower did for golf, Mickey Hargitay did for bodybuilding." I would go to their lavish house high up above Beverly Hills for dinner. Mickey sat at the head of the table. Though he was buff and strong he was dwarfed by a massive self portrait in a grand ornate frame on the wall behind him.

My dear friend Barry White was one of my favorite people for twenty-five years. Barry married Glodean, who was the lead singer of Love Unlimited. Glodean, known as Glow to her friends, was aptly named. She sparkles! Beautiful inside and out, she has huge brown eyes, a mass of luscious hair and the longest fingernails I have ever seen. Between Glodean and Barry, they had their own "Brady Bunch"— six kids, three apiece. Then I delivered their daughter Shay-Shay, making it seven. I went on to deliver Shay-Shay's daughter who is now eighteen and blossoming into a talented filmmaker.

Barry and Glodean built a compound in the San Fernando Valley (a Los Angeles suburb). It was a cul-de-sac with several homes (they owned them all) and security guards at the entrance. Barry had his office and recording studio in one of the homes and they lived in the main house. Their home was impressive, each room decorated mono-chromatically. They had the gold room, the blue room and a den in yellow tones. The living room was in green marble. The theater, where we watched the latest movies (often before they were released) was decorated like an opera house with gilded seats and red velvet upholstery.

When it came to giving a party, the White's were untouchable. They had the place and the friends. They knew everyone in the music business, and I met many of them, including the Jackson Five. Glodean was best friends with Germaine Jackson's wife, who was Mr. Motown's (Berry Gordy) daughter. Both of Barry Gordy's two daughters were my patients. I remember one birthday party Barry gave for his little daughter, Shay Shay. I took my daughter Samantha, who was one year younger, and she was thrilled. Barry had a camel and an elephant for rides, plus many different baby animals for the children to pet and cuddle. They invited mega-celebrities and their children. I'd never been to a birthday party quite like that before.

My wife and I spent lovely evenings with the Whites, in their garden with its wondrous waterfall. Beautiful music was piped throughout the garden and sometimes live bands were jamming. A ticket to those evening performances would have cost a fortune! At the height of their fame, Barry and Glodean arrived at one of our traditional Christmas parties. Although there were many other celebrities there, the Whites outshone everyone. Glodean was dressed from head to toe in shimmering gold; her hair like Bo Derek's, braided with ornate gold beads. Barry, a very large man, was dressed in a floor-length white mink coat. They were something to see and the stars of the party, mingling with everyone, chatting away so naturally. They were always themselves, no star egos. Fame and fortune never did change those two people. In fact, on his last CD, Barry put my name, (his "gynecologist") on the people-to-thank list. Now I have the opportunity to publicly thank Barry White, for it is he who enriched my life and the lives of millions with his deep masculine voice and his inventive romantic music. As a friend from Capitol Records once said to me, "Between you and Barry White's music, you're probably responsible for most of the births in Hollywood." Though it's not really true, I think that's a very nice way for both of us to be remembered. Thankfully Glodean and I still see one another frequently. Between Glodean, their daughters and grandchildren -- I only wish Barry could see the legacy of his artistic genes and caring nature.

About fifteen years ago, Johnny Cash, one of the greatest western singers, died. I didn't know him personally, but the early part of my life was spent in Idaho where western singers like Johnny Cash were about all we ever heard. I loved his music; there is something very real about western singers. They make you feel like you're part of the family. I was thrilled when I was able to deliver one of his grandkids. I delivered Roseanne Cash's first born. Roseanne, a singing star in her own right, recorded a duet years ago with her father "September When It Comes". It was a song about an adult child and their parents as they approach their later years. That song is even more touching now after Johnny's passing and as I grow older myself.

Unfortunately Glen Campbell just died at the age of 81. Another great mellow voice and guitarist is gone from us forever. I wish I could have gotten to really know him. Still, I'll never forget that party at Jimmy Webb's Encino Estate where I was lucky enough to attend and meet Glen. A group of us were fooling around telling jokes. Glen Campbell told a golf joke, Cher told a funny one, and I told one about a gynecologist. Michael Douglas seemed to be bored with us, so I turned to Michael and said, "Okay Michael its your turn." Without missing a beat he said, "I'm not paid to entertain you."

Over twenty years ago my dear friend Barry Sullivan died. I was at his home just the day before he died. Even though his daughters Jenny and Patsy were there for him, it was sad to see a big star like Barry, who was in over eighty films, living those last few months in the twilight of his life, removed from the limelight. It's sad for all of us when we live beyond our important years.

As a doctor I was always there for my patients. I would spend forty-eight hours straight at the hospital, waiting for a patient to deliver naturally because that was her wish. I believe I was a dedicated doctor. I regret nothing of all those hours wasted in the doctor's lounge when I could have been out at a picnic or swimming at the beach. What I do regret is that I missed so much of my children's growing up. It's sad but true; you cant be in two places at the same time. I wish I'd been there especially for Doug. Irene had been there for Lonny and for especially for Lynne in my absence, but a young son needs a dad. Lynne threw me a spectacular party for my ninetieth birthday, and had made a lovely video of my early life. Alex, Samantha and Susan made a funny video where they had convinced all the characters on Hollywood Boulevard to appear on film reading my book Sex Without Tears. Tuesday had the Mayor of Las Vegas declare November 21st officially Boyd Cooper Day. Lonny sang a special song he'd written for me. Then Doug got up and softly read a poem he'd written for me. It blew everyone away. It was so poignant and so profound. My loving, shy Doug has a lot of talent buried deep inside.

I'm now ninety-four years old and have been retired for about fifteen years. I was a poor, ill-informed boy who magically found my way to starry Hollywood. As I look back, I realize that I was fortunate to arrive in Hollywood at the height of its glamour. My office at the entrance to the world famous Hollywood Boulevard has seen its share of movie stars, but over the nearly fifty years I practiced, I saw my fair share of everyday women with everyday problems, too. It should be noted whether the next big star or an ordinary woman came seeking my help - they were all the same under my care and experienced the same joys and problems of pregnancy.

I've spent my life learning about women. How life has changed for them through the years. Not only finding their voice, but becoming truly empowered. For that I am truly grateful. Their deepest secrets, told to me in the privacy of my Hollywood office, I will carry to my grave. I was motivated to write this book to share my thoughts and experiences from a different point of view of Hollywood. Practicing medicine in Hollywood, as you can tell, was not all glitz and glamour. Hollywood encompasses all kinds, and when a woman is at her most vulnerable, nervous of a prognosis, with her legs open for examination, you learn quickly that we are all looking to be taken care of. I wanted others to know the thousands of fascinating women who have crossed my path in Hollywood. Blessed are they, my two wives and my three daughters for teaching me the most important lesson of all - how to love and be loved.

Boyd Cooper M.D. with Glodean White

ABOUT THE AUTHOR

Boyd Cooper M.D. grew up in a simple country home in Idaho. He was a highly decorated navigator in World War II. He became a gynecologist to the stars in Hollywood for nearly fifty years. His book, *Sex Without Tears*, received rave reviews from the New York Times and was published in two languages. In 2003, he published his first fiction, *Unlikely Hero*. Boyd Cooper is ninety-four years of age and lives with his family in Hollywood. He continues to write every day.

Photo Credits

Marlon Brando (page 64) - CC BY - SA 2.0

Madame Claude (page 163) - Photo Archives du musée de la police.

Special thanks to Lynne Herrera for locating and providing family photos.